Accountancy in Transition

Edited by Richard P. Brief, NEW YORK UNIVERSITY

A GARLAND SERIES

The American Accomptant

Chauncey Lee

Garland Publishing, Inc.
New York & London 1982

This facsimile has been made from a copy in the New York University Library.

Library of Congress Cataloging in Publication Data

Lee, Chauncey, 1763–1842.
The American accomptant.

(Accountancy in transition)
Reprint. Originally published: Lansingburgh : Printed by W. W. Wands, 1797.
1. Accounting—Early works to 1800.
2. Arithmetic—To 1846. I. Title. II. Series.
HF5611.L43 1982 657 82-48375
ISBN 0-8240-5324-9

The volumes in this series are printed on acid-free, 250-year-life paper.

Printed in the United States of America

AMERICAN EAGLET.
CAROL·III·D·G HISP·ET IND·R· 1780
AUSPICE·DEO·IN·UTROQ·FELIX M·PI
Sp. Pistole.
LIBERTY 1795
UNITED STATES OF AMERICA
IOANNES·V·D·G·PORT·ET·ALG·REX 2000
IN HOC SIGNO VINCES 1715
½ Moidore, Port.l
LUD·XVI·D·G·FR·ET NAV·REX
CHRS REGN VINC IMPER 1786
Fr. Guinea.
Johannes Port.l
JOSEPHUS·I·D·G PORT·ET·ALG·REX 1766
GEORGIUS III DEI GRATIA
M·B·F·ET·H·REX·F·D·B·ET·L·D·S·R·I·A·T·ET·E 1787
Br. Guinea.
Eng.d by A. Reed.

THE

American Accomptant;

BEING

A PLAIN, PRACTICAL AND SYSTEMATIC

COMPENDIUM

OF

FEDERAL ARITHMETIC;

IN THREE PARTS:

DESIGNED FOR THE USE OF SCHOOLS,

AND SPECIALLY CALCULATED FOR THE

COMMERCIAL MERIDIAN

OF

THE UNITED STATES OF AMERICA.

BY *CHAUNCEY LEE*, A. M.

LANSINGBURGH:

PRINTED BY WILLIAM W. WANDS.
M,DCC,XCVII.

[*Published according to Act of Congress.*]

RECOMMENDATIONS.

Rutland, (Vermont) February 7, 1797.

WE have perused and examined the following work, entitled "The American Accomptant, &c." by Chauncey Lee, A. M. and are of opinion it is calculated very greatly to facilitate the learning of Arithmetic, in its various branches;—that, in many of the branches, it proposes a more simple, as well as more compendious method, than has yet been adopted;—that it will be extensively useful to men of business, and is particularly calculated for usefulness in the United States.

NATHANIEL CHIPMAN,
ENOCH WOODBRIDGE,
LOT HALL, } *Judges of the Superior Court.*

Williams College, (Mass.) March 9, 1797.

HAVING examined, with some attention, the following work, entitled "The American Accomptant," by the Rev. Chauncey Lee, A. M. I am pleased both with the plan and the execution of it; and think it calculated to promote the knowledge of Arithmetic among the Youth in our common schools, in a more easy and expeditious manner than any work of the kind now in use. In some branches it proposes new rules, which are highly recommended by their sinplicity and conciseness; and, on many accounts, appears calculated for extensive usefulness among men of business in the United States.

EBENEZER FITCH, *President of Williams College.*

HAVING perused, in manuscript, the American Accomptant, by the Rev. Chauncey Lee, I find many things therein attended to of much consequence, and a number of judicious remarks on long established customs, with alterations proposed; which, should they obtain in common practice, according to the eventual probability, would very much ſimplify many of our computations, by making all leſs denominations of integral parts more generally deſcend upon a decimal ſcale, agreeably to the author's plan.

Conceiving it to be a work of merit, I am therefore of opinion, the general plan will meet with the approbation of the public—it being ſo happily adapted to the capacities of young ſtudents, and firſt beginners in *Arithmetic*, that it cannot fail in communicating to them juſt ideas, and a due comprehenſion of the foundation principles of that firſt branch of the *Mathematics.*

SAMUEL MOORE, *County Surveyor.*
Saliſbury, (Connecticut) March 3, 1797.

Copy of a letter from the Reverend JOB SWIFT, *to the Author.*

Bennington, March 21, 1797.

Dear Sir,

THE manuſcript copy of your "Compendium of Federal Arithmetic," with which you favored me, I have examined with attention; and, as you requeſted my obſervations upon it, I cheerfully expreſs my warmeſt approbation of the work, both with reſpect to its general plan, and alſo the ſeveral novel rules and arrangements introduced as improvements in its various branches.—In a word, I conceive it to be judiciouſly calculated to anſwer the valuable purpoſes mentioned in your propoſals, "the more eaſy inſtruction of Schools, and the benefit of young gentlemen in all occupations."

Accept, Sir, my beſt wiſhes for the ſucceſs of your undertaking; and, ſhould my name be thought of any conſideration in the premiſes, it is freely at your ſervice.

Yours, &c.
JOB SWIFT.

Rev. Mr. Lee.

INTRODUCTION.

THE work contained in the following sheets, was originally begun with no further design than as a short catechism upon the first rules of Arithmetic, for the instruction of a particular school; but finding it open an extensive field of practical Arithmetic, and a door for many *apparent* improvements, so necessary to meet the exigencies of school education in general, which arise from the present peculiar commercial circumstances of our Country; I was induced to extend my plan, and continue the work to that serious length which is now presented to the public eye in the size of a volume.

I shall not affect to entertain my readers, with all the customary apologies for a new publication. The work will speak for itself. That it has its full share of imperfections I have not a doubt. If it possess any merit, the candid Instructor, and the intelligent MAN of BUSINESS, will readily discern it—if it be undeserving of attention, the consequences are as obvious; and in either case apologies would be impertinent. In this view of it, I have only to say, that I have spared no application nor pains in my power to insure the highest object of publication, *the benefit of my country*. How far I have succeeded, is humbly submitted, with the assurance that I shall not only receive the criticiſms of candor without a wound, but feel indebted to the friendly hand that ſhall point me to its defects.

Leſt any one ſhould entertain a miſtaken idea of the *deſign* of this compendium, and hence be lead to expect many things in it which he will not find; I would here appriſe him, that I have attempted in it to treat of and ſimplify the ſyſtem of *commercial* arithmetic only—to render many of its rules more eaſy and conciſe, and better adapted to the inſtruction of young minds in the method and progreſs of common ſchool education. With this view, I have omitted ſeveral rules contained in former Arithmetical treatiſes, that are perhaps more calculated either to amuſe or puzzle, than to profit the common ſchool ſtudent, or at leaſt are inapplicable or unneceſſary to trade and buſineſs, and the common affairs of human life; and added others in their ſtead deſigned to facilitate and promote theſe important, practical objects. In a word, without aſpiring to the higher branches, and more intricate rules and reſearches of the art, which indeed are rendered unneceſſary, by the labors and publications of abler hands, this compendium is deſigned as an eaſy guide to the young ſtudent—an uſeful Aſſiſtant to the common ſchool Inſtructor, and to the man of buſineſs in all the variety of commercial tranſactions.

Senſible, however, that all innovations upon old rules and long eſtabliſhed modes of inſtruction or practice have to combat the united force of prejudice and habit; are viewed with a ſuſpicious eye, and received with a cautious hand, I conceive it a duty, I owe both to the public and myſelf, to exhibit the reaſons and grounds upon which I have ventured to project ſuch a variety of alterations as appear in the following work. Whilſt thus aſſuming the burden of proof, I have only to requeſt the reader's patient attention, and that he would not uncandidly paſs ſentence before trial, but firſt examine and then judge.

There is, I conceive, this imperfection in the mode of moſt Arithmetical authors who have publiſhed, that is, not to have treated with ſufficient explicitneſs and perſpicuity upon the firſt principles and fundamental rules, ſo as to render them palpable to the underſtanding of the new beginner—but taking many things for granted, as already well known and underſtood, tho' needing at the ſame time as particular explanation as the more abſtruſe and complicated parts, the ſtudent, as he proceeds, is ſubjected to the arduous taſk of erecting a ſuperſtructure without a foundation.

Hence too originates a ſimilar error, I mean, a ſuperficial mode of inſtruction in many of the common ſchools. The boy, advanced perhaps ſome way in his *teens*, is ſent to a winter ſchool for two or three months to complete his education; for he cannot attend in any other ſeaſon, nor then indeed but quite unſteadily. But as he is almoſt a man he muſt go to ſchool to *cypher* ; and as he has but a ſhort time for the buſineſs he muſt *cypher* faſt. He goes to ſchool, vulgarly ſpeaking *raw*, perhaps ſcarcely able to form an arithmetical figure. His maſter *ſets him a ſum* in addition, and it may be tells him he muſt *carry one for every ten* ; but why, is a myſtery which neither maſter nor ſcholar gives himſelf any trouble about ; however, with a deal of pains, he at length *gets his ſum done*, without ever being aſked, or knowing how to read the ſum total, or any number expreſſed in the ſtatement. * But it is *cyphering*, and that is ſufficient. If he is taught to commit any of the rules to memory, he learns them like a parrot, without any knowledge of their reaſon, or application. After this manner he gropes along from rule to rule, till he ends his blind career with the *Rule of Three* ; and in the end, the only and the trueſt account he can give of the whole is, that he has been *over it*. But he has completed his ſchool education, and is well qualified to teach a ſchool himſelf, the next winter after.

---

* *As a ſtriking example of this method of inſtruction, I have actually known a lad of eighteen, who, after having, in this way, gone over all the firſt rules of Arithmetic, at a common ſchool, was utterly unable to read or enumerate any number conſiſting of four places of figures.*

This repreſentation however is not meant to be generally applied. On the contrary I have the pleaſing ſatisfaction to believe that the mode of common ſchool education in this country has of late years been much improved and is ſtill improving; and it is the deſign and wiſh of the author to contribute his mite for the furtherance of ſo deſirable an object.

To remedy the aforementioned defects, it appears highly neceſſary that the elementary parts of Arithmetic ſhould be accurately explained and clearly diſtinguiſhed—their various combinations pointed out—the reaſon of every rule explained to the underſtanding of the ſtudent, and the whole ſyſtem analyſed with exactneſs and preciſion. Our knowledge of any art or ſcience is not born with us, but acquired—the acquiſition is progreſſive and not immediate—we proceed ſtep by ſtep—from ſmall to greater, from ſimple to complex. The foundation muſt be laid, before the ſuperſtructure can be raiſed. The child muſt firſt learn the alphabet before he can read or ſpell; and that mode of ſtudy and inſtruction is confeſſedly the moſt judicious, which places each ſtep in its natural and juſt order, and caſts the ſtrongeſt light upon the intimate connexion and mutual ſubſerviency of the ſeveral parts.

Theſe were my reaſons for adopting ſundry alterations of method to ſimplify the firſt rules, and claſſing each part in ſhort and eaſy leſſons, which, expreſſed in queſtions and anſwers, may be thoroughly ſtudi-ed, regularly recited and eaſily retained.

NOTATION is the firſt ſtep. This is as it were the A, B, C of Arithmetic, and bears the ſame important relation to all the following rules, which the Alphabet does to the art of reading. Let the learner therefore, after writing figures enough to be able to form them handſomly and place them orderly, acquaint himſelf well with this rule, by attending to the Numeration Table—the names and order of the ſeveral denominations of whole numbers—their mode or ratio of increaſe in value as he names the figures either from right hand to left, or from left hand to right—the uſe and effect of cyphers interjected between ſignificant figures, or digits, &c. and alſo by the exerciſe of expreſſing written numbers in figures and the reverſe; paying the like attention as he proceeds, to the notation of mixed quantities.

ADDITION is the next in order. In this the learner begins to calculate the operation and power of numbers expreſſed by figures in Notation. Let him begin with the eaſieſt and plaineſt examples; with numbers whoſe aggregate ſhall not exceed *ten*—then let him proceed to larger ſums of two or more figures, and nextly to the addition of the mixed quantities of money, weight, meaſure, &c. learning each table well by heart as he proceeds, together with their reſpective uſes.—In the addition of whole numbers, let him clearly ſee the reaſon and propriety of adding *one* to the left hand column, for every *ten* contained in its right hand one, ſetting down only the overplus of the tens. And alſo in the mixed quantities *one* for the *terminus* of each denomination to the next higher denomination, according to its table.

SUBTRACTION. Let the learner, in this alſo, begin with the ſimpleſt and eaſieſt examples, where every lower figure expreſſes a ſmaller number than the one directly above it. When the lower figure is the larger, for inſtance, as in ſubtracting *nine* from *fifty-ſix*, placed 56 over 9, inſtead of going the circuitous route of ſaving 9 from 6 I cannot, but 9 from 10 leaves 1, and 6 is 7; and then 1 that I carry to 0 is 1, which from 5 leaves 4; let him, by a mere mental operation, ſubtract 1 from the left hand figure 5, and annexing the right hand one to it for 16, ſay at once, 9 from 16 leaves 7, and then the left hand figure in the remainder is 4, without any ſubtracting, borrowing or paying, ſtanding 47. This I conceive to be a more ſimple, natural and eaſy mode, eſpecially in whole numbers, than the former which is uſually taught and practiſed. *This* is purely Subtraction, whilſt *that* is Subtraction and Addition blended together.

Theſe two laſt rules, both in integral and fractional quantities, are purely ſimple. In this I ſpeak only of their mode of operation; and by this alone I diſtinguiſh between *ſimple* and *compound* rules. The addition of *money*, *weight*, *meaſure*, &c. is performed by the operation of Addition *merely*, and is therefore as *ſimple* Addition as that of whole numbers. It is ſimple Addition of compound or mixed quantities. And on the other hand, there is compound Addition of ſimple as well as mixed quantities. The ſame alſo applies to ſubtraction. Theſe diſtinctions, appearing to me juſt and forming a more accurate analyſis of the firſt principles of the Art, I have ventured to make in the following work.

MULTIPLICATION, all excepting the Multiplication Table, ſo called, and in caſes where the multiplier conſiſts of a ſingle figure whoſe ſquare or product with each figure in the multiplicand does not exceed *nine*, is a compound of Multiplication and Addition. The new propoſed method of *Croſs Multiplication* is conſidered as an improvement in the art; and after the learner is firſt well verſed in the common method, may, by a little practice, become equally familiar and eaſy. It is a general rule wherever the multiplier conſiſts of a plurality of ſignificant figures, and in every ſuch caſe will be found of ſpecial utility in practice. There are ſeveral other curious methods of contracting Multiplication in certain caſes, which, as they apply but to a few particular multipliers only, whoſe operation can but very ſeldom occur in practice, I have deſignedly omitted—judging thoſe rules to be the moſt uſeful, and the beſt adapted for the inftruction of the learner, which are the moft general in their application.

DIVISION, whether fhort or long, of fimple or mixed quantities, in its mode of operation, is never fimple, but is a compofition of Divifion, Multiplication, Subtraction and Addition—unlefs we except merely the reverfe of the Multiplication Table, where neither the divifor nor quotient exceed 12. And yet this becomes compounded as before whenever there is any remainder. The divifor is alfo a multiplicand, the quotient a multiplier, their product a fubtrahend, and the dividend a fubftratum. In the proof by Multiplication, the quotient becomes the multiplicand, the divifor the multiplier, the laft remainder, a fum to be added to their product; and the dividend the fum total.—The method of contracting long divifion by fetting down only the remainders, may be eafily attained and familiarized by practice, after the ftudent has become well verfed in the common method; accordingly I have ufed only thefe contracted modes of Multiplication and Divifion, in all the examples of the Second and Third Parts, where the operations are fet down. The propofed method of proving Divifion as well as Multiplication by the *Ecks*, is calculated greatly to leffen the labor both of the Scholar and Inftructor. Rules of proof in all cafes, fhould be as concife as poffible, confiftently with rectitude, and general application. Otherwise, if the operation of the proof be as lengthy and laborious as the work which it is designed to prove, it will not only form a heavy tax upon the students' time and patience, but oftentimes the testimony of the witness may be called in question and the proof itself equally want proof.

Our tables of weight and measure, (as all the parts, both of the ultimate and *mesne* integers, are in the ratio of vulgar fractions) are as illy contrived for ease of calculation and practical convenience as can well be imagined. Indeed, in my humble opinion, vulgar fractions are a very unimportant, if not useless part of Arithmetic, and decimals only of any considerable practical consequence.—All mixed quantities become obscure and intricate in calculation in the same proportion as they deviate from a decimal standard.—Their processes are indirect and in a greater or less degree difficult and uncertain. In this consists the wisdom and excellency of our Federal money currency, which, I am bold to say, is the highest pitch of improvement, to which money calculations can or will ever be brought. But, at the same time, it increases the above-mentioned inconveniency of mixed quantities, whilst continuing upon their present standard, through the want of an uniformity ; and I am pursuaded that experience will soon evince the expediency, if not the absolute necessity of federalizing all the tables of weights and meaſures, and other mixed quantities, which have an immediate relation to commerce, upon a decimal ſcale. There is no man, who has any knowledge of figures, but who will, by a minute's attention, perceive the inconveniency and difficulty of multiplying a vulgar and decimal fraction together, or of dividing the one by the other, without firſt expreſſing them both in vulgars, or both in decimals. This difficulty will be ſtill increaſed, where the vulgar fraction is a compound fraction, or a fraction of a fraction, which is always the caſe where there is a plurality of denominations below the integer expreſſed in the given quantity. For inſtance, £1 : 13 : $7\frac{3}{4}$ is £1 and $\frac{13}{20}$ and $\frac{7}{240}$ and $\frac{3}{960}$ of a pound—theſe fractional parts of a pound, are alſo fractional parts of each other, each denomination of all its higher denominations. After the ſame manner alſo 1 *ton*, 9 *hundreds*, 3 *quarters* and 17 *pounds*, is 1 Ton, and $\frac{9}{20}$ and $\frac{3}{80}$ and $\frac{7}{2240}$ of a Ton. Now let the farmer, or any other man undertake to reckon the worth of the laſt mentioned quantity of hay, or any other article of produce valued by weight, at the price of 4 Dollars, 44 Cents and 4 Mills *per* Ton, without decimalizing thoſe vulgar fractions, and he would find it a troubleſome buſineſs. He muſt do it in one or the other of theſe two ſeveral ways, *viz.*

1. Add all the vulgar fractions of the given quantity together, by multiplying each

numerator and all the denominators but its own together, and taking the sum of those several products for a new numerator; under which for a new denominator, write the product of all the denominators multiplied together, by which the several fractions are added into one simple fraction—Then,

Multiply the given price and the Numerator together; divide their product by the Denominator, and that quotient add to the given price of a Ton.—Or,

2d. Multiply the given price three times successively, once by each of the several Numerators, and divide their products by their respective Denominators, and then add together all those quotients and the given price of a Ton.

For the satisfaction of the curious and the conviction of all, let the business be exemplified, and the operation of each of the foregoing rules drawn out in figures at length in answering the question,

What is the worth of 1T. 9Cwt. 3Qrs, 17lb. of hay, at 4 Doll. 44 Cents and 4 Mills per Ton? from which every one may the better judge, for himself, of the conveniency of our present weights and measures—of the practical utility of Vulgar Fractions, and how much they are deserving of attention.

By the 1st Rule:

1 Ton & $\frac{9}{20}$ and $\frac{3}{80}$ and $\frac{17}{2240}$

```
Mult. by    3   Mult. by  17      Mult. by  80
           ---            ---               ------
           60            560              179200
         -----            80         by        9
         2240            ---               -------
Mult. by   60           1360   Several  ( 1612800
         ------  Mul. by  20   products (   27200
         134400          ----- add. tog.(  134400
                        27200              -------
                  New Numerator            1774400
```

Denominators Multiplied

```
      2240
By      80
    ------
    179200
By      20
    ------
New Den. 3584000
```

The whole Fraction

$\frac{1774400}{3584000}$

```
Then Mult. the Numerator 1774400
                 By Doll.  4.444  price of a Ton.
                     -----------
                         70976
                        70976
                       70976
                      70976                    doll. c. m.
Divide by 3584|000)7885|433.600( 2. 20. 0
                     7168        Add   4. 44. 4
                    -----             -----------
                     7174      Answ. 6. 64. 4
                     7168
Fraction thrown away -----
                        633600
```

By the 2d Rule:

1 Ton $\frac{9}{20}$, $\frac{3}{80}$, $\frac{17}{2240}$ at 4*d.* 44*c.* 4*m.*

```
                                 4.444  |                        4.444
1st Numr. Multr.                     9  | 2d Numr. Multr.            3
1st Deno.Divs. 2|0)3|9.996              | 2dD.Di.8|0)1|3.332(.16.6
Price of 9 Cwt. D. 1.99.9 16/20         | Prc.of 3qrs. D 0. 16. 6

                                 4.444  | Prc. of a Ton. 4d. 44c. 4m
3d Numr. Multr.                     17  |    of 9 cwt.  1. 99. 9
                                 31108  |    of 3qrs.   0. 16. 6
                                 4444   |    of 17lb.   0. 02. 3
3d Den. divr. 224|0)7|5.548(.03.3       |    Answ.      6. 64. 2
                     672
                     834
                     672
                    (1628)
Price of 17lb. Doll. 0. 03. 3 1628/2240
```

Now let us compare the foregoing operations with the same example wrought by Decimals.

Rule. Multiply the commodity by the price; from the product point off as many right hand figures as there were Decimals in the Multiplier and Multiplicand together, and the rest are Dollars.

```
        9cwt.  =  .45       |        Answers.
        3qrs.  =  .0375     | By 1st Rule,  D.6. 64. 4
        17lb.  =  .0075     | By 2d ——          6. 64. 2
                 ———————    | By Decimals       6. 64. 4
The whole }                 |               very nearly.
 quantity } Ton   1.495     |
Multiply by Doll. 4 444     |
            ———————————
                  5980
                 5980
                5980
               5980
            ———————————
            6.64.3.780 Answer.
```

This laſt method of operation by decimals may ſtill be ſhortened more than one half, by the aforementioned mode of Croſs-multiplication, explained at large in the following work.

But ſtill this mode of operation does not reach the higheſt pitch of improvement to which it might be carried by decimals. An inconvenience will ariſe from the difficulty of readily changing theſe compound vulgar fractions into decimals. The man of buſineſs may not always have his decimal table by him, or may be difficulted to remember the decimal ratio among ſo many various rules of decimal reduction; and ſo be obliged to divide all the numerators by their denominators, in order to find the decimals: and this inconvenience, though ſmaller than the former, will ever continue to operate in a greater or leſs degree, until this *vulgar* evil is plucked up by the very roots—all theſe ſurd, untoward fractional numbers baniſhed from practice and the ſeveral denominations in all commercial tables of mixed quantities conformed to our Federal money, and eſtabliſhed upon a decimal ſcale. To accompliſh all this is a taſk too great for any individual in a republican government. It requires the arm of Congreſs to effect it; and it is equally to be hoped as expected, that their wiſdom and patriotiſm will not be inattentive to ſo important an object of legiſlation.

These considerations, however, have induced me to suggest some hints for this kind of arithmetical improvement, in a work denominated Federal Arithmetic, and to come forward as a *projector* simply, in exhibiting to public view a plan of federalizing weights and measures, as well as money, upon a decimal scale; and illustrating their utility by a variety of practical examples under each. As none of them excepting Federal Troy-weight alters the quantity of the ultimate integer, they might, if approved, be reduced to practice by merchants and others, even without legislative aid. This would enable them to keep their books, both as to commodities and prices, in decimals; and the practice, I am persuaded, would abundantly realize the benefits of the mode.

The following scheme is therefore humbly submitted to the judgment of every candid American.

AVOIRDUPOIS-WEIGHT.—Of this we have two kinds in use, tho' both weighed by the same steelyards and weights. These are commonly distinguished by the terms *gross* weight and *neat* weight. The former, which makes an hundred pounds weight to consist of 112, I must confess, appears perfectly needless, childish and nonsensical, and to be continued in practice merely thro' the force of blind habit and arbitrary custom, without a single good reason for it existing. Liability to waste is the most plausible, and perhaps the only reason which can be affigned : but many articles, fuch as metals, which are the leaft liable to wafte, are weighed by this ftandard. If this were a juft reafon, why would not the fame end be better anfwered by deducting $\frac{12}{112}$ from the *price* of a hundred weight, and thereby avoid this inconvenient mode of reckoning, and the abfurdity of calling 112 only 100. Thus, for inftance, whatever article fells for 1 dollar *per cwt.* grofs; take 11 from an hundred, which is about the proportion, and call the price 89 cents; then let the fame pound upon the fteelyards be divided into *ten* inftead of fixteen notches; and omitting the ufelefs denomination of quarters, we might form, as follows, the Table of

FEDERAL AVOIRDUPOIS.

10 drams make		1 ounce
10 ounces	-	1 pound
100 pounds	-	1 hundred weight
10 hundreds	-	1 thoufand.

TROY WEIGHT, *federalized*.

Let the weight of a Dollar in American, Britifh, and Portuguefe Gold, which according to the Act of Congrefs, paffed February 9, 1793, is 27 grains, be the pennyweight, divide this into ten equal parts for grains—divide the grains decimally alfo, and call the parts Cents—Cents might be divided into Mills, but it is probable there would not be occafion for that minutenefs in practice: Therefore, I fhall not defcend to it, but proportion the ſeveral denominations according to the following Table :—*viz.*

10 Cents	- - - -	1 Grain,
10 Grains	- - -	1 Pennyweight,
10 Pennyweights	-	1 Ounce,
10 Ounces	- - -	1 Pound.

Then the value of Federal, Britiſh, and Portugueſe gold by weight, would ſtand thus in Federal Money, *viz.*

1 Cent is	- -	1 Cent,
1 Grain	- - -	1 Dime or 10 Cents,
1 Pennyweight		1 Dollar,
1 Ounce	- -	1 Eagle, or 10 Dolls.
1 Pound	-	10 Eagles, or 100 Dolls.

Then, after the weight of any quantity of ſtandard Gold is aſcertained and written down in figures, its value in Federal money is already found, no other reduction being needed, but only to point off all the figures below Pennyweights for the decimal parts of a dollar, and all the reſt are dollars, and to be read as one whole number.—Take the following for an example.—

What is the value in Federal money, of the following weight of Federal, Britiſh, or Portugueſe gold, *viz.*

lb. Oz. dwt. gr.

1 . 2 . 3 . 4 . 5 *cents?*

Anſwer Dolls. 123. 45 *cents.*

By ſuch a table as this, it is plain that a child might weigh and determine the value of gold, with the utmoſt eaſe and accuracy.

FRENCH and SPANISH GOLD.

This ſtandard being leſs in value by $\frac{4}{274}$

in the Federal pennyweight, the proportions will be as follow, *viz.*

	Dolls.	*C.*	*M.*
1 Cent equals	0	00	9.854
1 Grain - - -	0	09	8.54
1 Pennywt. - -	0	98	5.4
1 Pound - - .	93	54	

The exchange of this gold into Federal money, may be eaſily performed in either of the ſeveral following methods.

1. Take the actual weight in cents multiplied by 270, and divide by 274, the quotient will be Federal money.—Or,

2. From the actual weight ſubtract its product, when multiplied by 146, obſerving to ſet the left hand figure of the product under the third from the left hand in the ſubſtratum or given weight.—Or,

3. From the given weight taken in grains, ſubtract the quotient made in dividing it by 685.

Let us take the former example to trace the operation of each of theſe rules.

Required the value in Federal money of

lb. oz. dw. gr. cents.

1 . 2 . 3 . 4 . 5 of French or Spaniſh Gold.

1ſt Rule.

lb. oz. dw. gr. cts.

1. 2. 3. 4 . 5. = 12345 *Cents.*

Multiply by 270

86415

24690

———— *Cents.*

Divide by 274)3333150(12164.7

or *Dollars* 121.64.7

2d *Rule.*

lb. oz. dw. gr. cts.

```
1 . 2 . 3 . 4 . 5.          12345 . . . .
Multiply by 146               1802370
---------------            -----------
        74070              121647630
       49380       Dol. 121.64.8 nearly
      12345
      -------
      1802370
```

3d *Rule.*

lb. oz. dw. gr. cts.

```
1. 2. 3. 4. 5.   =   123 4.5 grains.
Divide by 685)123.45(   1.8
              685 D.121.65
              ---
              5495
              5480
              ----
                15
```

But a more concise and convenient rule than either of the foregoing, the reader will find in the *Second Part* of the following work, where the same subject is more particularly treated and explained.

LIQUID MEASURE.—*The Gallon unaltered.*

10 Pints make 1 Gallon
10 Gallons - 1 Federal Barrel
10 Barrels - 1 Hogshead.

FEDERAL CLOTH MEASURE.

For the purpose of mercantile convenience, let the Yard be the only denomination used, and the parts of the yard expressed in decimals. The yard divided into ten equal parts, and theſe again ſub-divided into twentieths of a yard, as parts of a hundred, are as minute diviſions as will ever be needed in Cloth meaſure. It would be convenient to make uſe of a meaſure upon the plan of the following

Federal Yard-Stick.

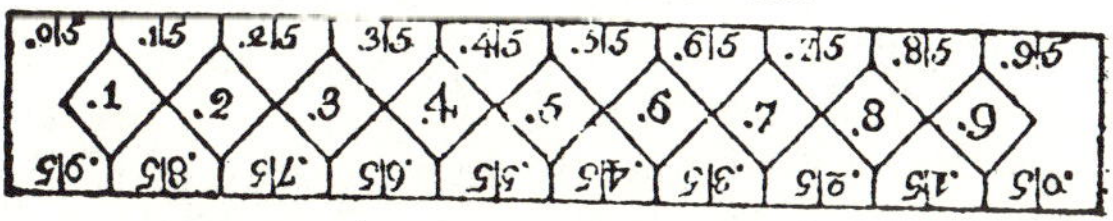

FEDERAL DRY MEASURE.

Let the Buſhel according to its preſent ſtandard be the unit or integer; and the only denomination uſed; and the parts of a Buſhel, as it is now divided by pecks and gallons, be expreſſed in decimals of a buſhel and marked upon the meaſures according to the following Table.—*viz.*

An half peck or 1 gallon	.125	of a Buſhel.
1 Peck or 2 gallons	.25	
1½ Peck or 3 gallons	.375	
½ Buſhel or 4 gallons	.5	
2½ Pecks or 5 gallons	.625	
3 Pecks or 6 gallons	.75	
3½ Pecks or 7 gallons	.875	

FEDERAL APOTHECARY-WEIGHT.

The common Grain unaltered.

10 Grains equal 1 Scruple,
10 Scruples - 1 Dram,
10 Drams - - 1 Ounce,
10 Ounces - 1 Pound.

This decimal table bears the following proportions to the vulgar table in general uſe, by which the reduction might be eaſily performed, *viz.*

Decimal Table.	*Gr.*	*Vulgar Table.*
1 Grain	=======	1 Grain,
1 Scruple	=======	10 Grains,
1 Dram	= 100 =	1 Dram and 2 Scruples,
1 Ounce	= 1000 =	2 Ounces and 2 Scruples,
1 Pound	= 10000 =	1 pound, 8 ounces, 5 drams.

Note. This table, perhaps, might be found rather inconvenient to the Apothecariſt, in compounding his ſimples, until the Diſpenſatory could be conformed to this ſtandard.

Federal Board Measure.

The common Foot unaltered.

10 Pepper-Corns make 1 Inch,
10 Inches - - - - 1 Foot,
10 Square Feet - - 1 Pannel,
10 Pannels - - 1 Gang,
10 Gangs - - - 1 Thouſand feet.

Federal Table of things accounted by the *Tale.*

10 Particulars make 1 *Deſm,*
10 Deſms - - 1 Groſs,
10 Groſs - - - 1 Great Groſs.

It may yet be an object of further inquiry whether the foregoing propoſed reform in the doctrine of weights, might not be carried to a ſtill higher pitch of ſimplicity and improvement; whether it might not anſwer a more beneficial purpoſe, not only to conform the ſeveral different tables of weights to our federal money, but alſo to each other, and reduce them all to one ſingle ſtandard, *viz.* the propoſed Federal Troy weight. It is plain that an unneceſſary multiplication of the tables of compound quantities will not facilitate the ſtudy or practice of Arithmetic, but have a contrary effect: And, let me aſk, what *real* neceſſity can there be of having ſuch a diverſity of weights? What even *imaginary* neceſſity, abſtract from the current of arbitrary cuſtom and habit? What benefit ariſes from it to ſociety in general, or to the tuition of ſchools in particular? What good purpoſes are anſwered by it in the tranſaction of any kind of buſineſs, or in the operation of any arithmetical calculation whatever, which would not be as well, and on the whole much better anſwered, by reducing them all, in practice, to a ſingle ſtandard; and aſcertaining the gravity of gold, iron, medicines, and all kinds of ſubſtances, now claſſed under three different ſorts of weights, by one common table of weight, diſtinguiſhed and dignified by the name of *American weight?* This might be made to aſcend to as large, and deſcend to as ſmall denominations, upon the decimal ſcale, as could ever be needed or wiſhed. But, on the contrary, the inconveniences of the preſent eſtabliſhed mode are obvious. It renders the practice complicated, and ſets the knowlege of Arithmetic, inſtead of nearer, at a farther diſtance from the common reach.—The boy is, perhaps, disgusted and discouraged, at his very outset, in travelling thro' such a thorny wild, such a dreary constellation of mixed quantities, in which he sees no particular reason nor propriety—in learning the names and uses of so many different tables—the several denominations of each, with their respective proportions; and then, as he proceeds, finding them repeated upon him in each of the first rules successively, by the operation of a variety of practical examples under each; and thus, as it were, meeting them at every corner. His memory is fatigued—his patience tried; and in short, his time and pains, and his parents' money, offered a thankless sacrifice at the shrine of arbitrary custom. At the best, he is retarded in the pursuit of real knowlege and improvement, by attending to what is intrinsically needless.

The same arguments, I think, may be applied in support of such a reform in the doctrine of weights, as in that of federal money; and similar good ends be answered by it, as in that of establishing an uniform money standard, and abolishing those absurd and idle diversities existing in pounds, shillings and pence. And, in this age of improvement, shall we stop short at the threshold, and content ourselves with but a partial reform?

The dissimilarity between us and some foreign nations, effected by such a reform, I do not conceive would operate essentially as a clog to our commerce, any more than our actual money establishment. Our own internal convenience and happiness is to be viewed as the first object of our national policy; and a servile compliance with the manners, usages and customs of foreign nations, the last. Our chief interest lies at home; and foreign intercourse has been found to be an inlet of *evils* as well as *goods*. Whatever dissimilarity, therefore, may operate, in its remotest conceivable tendency or smallest degree, as a guard against the bane of foreign influence, is to be regarded as a national blessing.

I need not be reminded, that it becomes not a private individual, in a great Republic, to dictate rules and reforms of this kind: I am not so weak as to aspire to it; but only to exercise the republican private privilege of *proposing* what the more enlightened public may judge of, and candor will not reject without reason.

In the Second Part of the following work, I have particularly attended to the rules of Reduction (commonly so called) between the several tables of mixed quantities; and especially between each and all the various money

NOTE. *The rules of Reduction, applying to the* proposed American weight, *are made out, and illustrated by examples, as the substance of a distinct Lesson, in the* Second Part.

currencies which run in pounds, ſhillings and pence, and Federal money—together with the exchange between the various foreign and federal gold coins by weight, and their value in each of the various currencies reſpectively; endeavoring to fix upon the conciſeſt mode of operation in all caſes; with a variety of examples wrought at large under each: and explanations added, where neceſſary, for the more eaſy inſtruction of Schools, and the benefit of young gentlemen, who may have unfortunately miſſed of a competent early ſchool education.

Decimal Practice, in which I include all operations by decimal fractions, is the title of the Third Part, and therein made the ſubject of a pretty extenſive treatment. A variety of original rules are introduced—their reaſons explained, and their uſe and benefit illuſtrated by numerous examples. I have attempted, by a ſeries of decimal rules, to conform the whole ſyſtem of commercial arithmetic to a Decimal Practice, with a view to evince the ſpecial utility of decimal fractions, in facilitating arithmetical calculations of every kind. How far I have ſucceded, every one will judge for himſelf.

The principles of the art of Book-Keeping form another diviſion of the Third Part. This is a deviation from the uſual method of moſt, if not all the authors who have gone before me in writing general treatiſes of Arithmetic. They have uniformly omitted, altogether, that important branch of knowlege, or but ſlightly touched only upon ſome of its out-works, and minuteſt parts; leaving the young ſtudent, either by mercantile apprenticeſhip, or the dint of neceſſity in tranſacting buſineſs for himſelf upon the ſtage of life, to acquire (in the habit of any mode, however unapt, which he may happen firſt to embrace) the practice of the art, without ever having the knowlege of its firſt principles. This appears to me an error, deſerving of correction; for, tho' the old adage, that *practice makes perfect*, is emphatically true in this article, yet if practice be denied the advantage of theory, the road to perfection muſt ſurely be found more difficult and uncertain. There are many branches of practical knowlege whoſe firſt principles muſt be learnt at ſchool, and which, if the foundation be not well laid, by proper inſtruction in early life, will excite the regret, whilſt they mock the wiſhes of riper years. The art of accomptantſhip appears to belong to this claſs; and, were it introduced as a ſubject of inſtruction, among the higher branches of Arithmetic uſually taught in common ſchools, I am perſuaded that the practice would evince its utility, by laying a foundation in the mind of the young ſtudent, for a more eaſy and advantageous entrance upon buſineſs, in every ſtation in life.

Book-keeping is an art of daily uſe in life, and of the higheſt importance in all commercial dealings. To be well acquainted with it, therefore, is a neceſſary qualification to every man of buſineſs. It enables him readily, and at any time, to aſcertain the exact ſtate of his affairs, and alſo eaſily to make an equitable, preciſe and honeſt adjuſtment of all his accompts with his cuſtomers. Succeſs in buſineſs materially depends upon a thorough underſtanding of the art, and a ſtrict attention to its rules. Ignorance and inattention in this article, are rocks upon which thouſands have ſplit, and made ſhipwreck not only of fortune, but of honeſty and good conſcience. Indeed, without the knowlege and practice of this art, a man's intereſt is ever in a blind, uncertain and hazardous ſituation, and that too in proportion to the variety and extent of his buſineſs.

In addition to a compendium of the Italian mode of Book-keeping agreeably to Gordon's ſyſtem of accomptanſhip, I have propoſed a new method, and called it *The Farmer's Book-keeping*—which I think may be an uſeful improvement to people in the common walks of life—to farmers, mechanics, and many merchants in the country, and all whoſe buſineſs and connections are not very extenſive. It is intended to ſuperſede the neceſſity of a Blotter, Day-book, or Alphabet diſtinct from the Ledger, and the laborious drudgery of poſting books, and looking up particular names and entries in the Day-book or Journal by references in the Ledger, commonly practiſed in the ſettlement of accompts.

CLERKSHIP is ſo interwoven, in practice, with Book-keeping, that I have not diſconnected them in theory. Clerkſhip, in its moſt extenſive ſenſe, includes Book-keeping. The latter is limited by its literal ſignification: the former extends to all the various written forms, and every exerciſe of penmanſhip in the draughting of *notes of hand*, *diſcharges*, *orders*, *receipts*, *bills*, *bonds*, *deeds*, *mortgages*, &c. which enter into the tranſaction of commercial buſineſs. I truſt, therefore, it will not be expected, in a compendium of Arithmetic, that I ſhould minutely trace a ſingle branch, in a meaſure foreign from the reſt, and in itſelf ſufficiently copious for the ſubſtance of a volume; but only to ſketch out the general outlines, with ſome particular directions, and a few of the moſt uſual and neceſſary written forms of doing buſineſs in the common dealings of mankind.

Upon the ſubject of Book-keeping, in this place, I have only to add a ſingle word of advice to every man in every ſtation. *Be as careful and as faithfully exact in making entry upon your Book of every article of* CREDIT, *as you are in that of* DEBT.

This method will enable you, at any time, the more eaſily to reckon, not only with others but with *yourſelf*. It will alſo greatly tend to prevent ſome of the bittereſt evils in life, ſuch as vexatious lawſuits, confuſed and quarrelſome arbitrations, loſs of property—loſs of friendſhip and good neighborhood.

The rules of operation in computing interest is another principal object of the Third Part. There is hardly any part of Arithmetic more practical, or of more daily use; yet the subject is neither so generally nor so thoroughly understood as could be expected, or wished. It is true, that in ordinary cases, interest for a round term of time, may be ascertained with tolerable precision, by the help of printed Interest Tables; and this is a method practised by many. But it will ever be found both more convenient and more respectable for the man of business to carry this knowlege in his *head* than in his *pocket-book*. And what parent would not chuse to give his son that independence in point of education, as might place him above the necessity of applying to his School-master or Stationer for assistance, whenever he has an accompt or note of hand to be adjusted?

Without attempting to dictate any particular mode of reckoning interest upon endorsed notes and bonds, as there is a diversity of practice in this business, I have selected two particular methods, which I believe are the most generally used, and contented myself with adapting to each the best rules of operation I could devise.

1. The rule established by the Superior Court of the State of Connecticut and adopted in practice in various other parts of the Union, *viz.* To subtract each payment from the amount of principal and interest up to the

time of payment; and so taking the remainder for a new principal, make as many several casts as there are payments.

2. A mode considerably practised, and strenuously contended for by many, *viz.* to cast interest upon the whole principal for the whole time, then separately upon each endorsment for its respective time, and subtract the whole amount of the one from that of the other.

But objections are raised to each of these methods; and it is much to be wished that a greater uniformity in this point, were established. This difference, as far as it essentially operates, is disadvantageous to commerce, by placing it on uncertain ground, and hence, has been a source of litigation and lawsuits. There was, a few years since, in the state of Connecticut, an important action at law, by reviews and appeals, carried and tried through all the judicatories, from the commencing Interior to the Supreme Court of Errors; in which action, the whole dispute arose from this difference in the mode of casting interest. The action was brought on a bond of a considerable number of years standing, having a variety of payments, of different dates, endorsed upon it. The plaintiff reckoned his interest by the former mode, and claimed £.1500 or upwards, upon the bond: the defendant reckoned the interest by the latter mode, and plead *full payment*. Judgment finally went in favor of the defendant, upon proof made that that mode by which he reckoned, was the mode of computing intereſt commonly practiſed among merchants and men of buſineſs in the State where the plaintiff lived, and where the contract was made.

Tho' the latter mode of computing intereſt appears to be on the ground of ſimple intereſt ſtrictly, and its variation from the other mode, in common caſes, will not be very material; yet, the following objection, upon a little attention, will be found moſt clearly to lie againſt it, *viz.* that the intereſt will, in a courſe of years, completely expunge, or, as I may ſay, eat up the debt, while no part of the principal is paid.

This may need ſome explanation. The following example, I think, will be concluſive illuſtration: A. lends B. £.100, at 6 *per cent.* intereſt, and takes his note of hand. B. does no more than come and pay A. at every year's end £.6, and has it endorſed upon his note. At the end of ten years B. takes up his note: and what is the ſum he has to pay? It is reckoned thus: The principal £.100, on intereſt 10 years, amounts to £.160: There are *nine* endorſements, of £.6 each, upon which the debtor claims intereſt; one for 9 years, the ſecond for 8, the third for 7, and ſo along down: the whole aggregate amount of the ſeveral endorſements, and their intereſts (as any one may ſee, who will take the pains to reckon it) is £.70 : 0 : 2½: This ſubtracted from £.160, the amount of the debt, principal and intereſt, leaves, in favor of A. the creditor, the balance of £.89 : 19 : 2½— £.10 : 0 : 9½ leſs than the original principal; of which he has not received the ſmalleſt fractional part, but its annual intereſt ſolely. This ſum he completely loſes by this mode of reckoning intereſt.

If the ſame note ſhould lie 20 years in the ſame way, B. would owe but £.38 : 12, without paying a farthing of the £.100 borrowed. Extend it but to 23 years, and A. would fall in debt to B. £.2 : 1 : 7—The intereſt, like Pharaoh's lean kine, has completely eaten up the principal: Whereas, by the former mode, A. would receive, at the payment of the note, the exact ſum which he was intitled to receive, *viz.* £.106, being the principal and its intereſt for the laſt year.

The objections againſt the Connecticut mode are theſe:

1. It is a complicated operation, and tedious in its length, where there are a great many endorſements.

Anſwer. Motives of intereſt are paramount to thoſe of lazineſs or ignorance. A man might afford to cover a ſheet with figures, and even to hire a clerk, if neceſſary, to aſſiſt him, in order to ſave ten pounds in a hundred.

2. *Objection.* It is in ſome caſes, in a degree *compound* intereſt; that is, whenever the

principal is not diminifhed as much as the whole fum paid.

Anfwer. This depends intirely upon circumftances. If it be the intent of the law, or the agreement of the parties, either, or both, that the intereft fhould be annually payable; it is not *compound* intereft, but ftrictly fimple; becaufe the fame rule alfo further provides, that the intereft is not to be added to the principal for a fubftratum or minuend, where the payment is lefs than the intereft then due.* But,

If, by the agreement of parties, the intereft be not payable under a plurality of years, then, befure, it ought not to be reckoned by a plurality of periods; and whatever the debtor pays in the *interim*, would be a juft deduction from the fimple intereft only. In this inftance the Connecticut mode, (tho' it is over-ruled by the agreement of parties, and cannot apply) would be in a fmall degree compound intereft, and in the fame degree work injuftice to the debtor; merely, however, by being a departure from the original contract.

As to the formidable objection, founded upon the moral diftinction of *lawful* and *unlawful* intereft, I would afk, what moral evil there is in a man's underftandingly, and, by agreement, either giving or receiving compound intereft? The crime of ufury, when

---

* *See the rule ftated more at Large, under the head of* Intereft, *in the* Third Part.

consisting not in extortion or exorbitant interest, but in exceeding a certain established rate *per cent.* is perhaps a mere creature of the law, and some of the remaining dregs of ancient superstition. It was once thought, by our pious forefathers, a great sin for a man to receive interest for the loan of money; it was, in the smallest degree of it, reprobated as *usury*. By degrees they relaxed from the severity of this sentiment. As it was found convenient and necessary, interest for money began to be allowed, and in the same degree the conviction prevailed of its being morally right and just. After the lapse of some few centuries, and several fluctuations in the *ratio* of interest, it has progressed to the state in which we find it at the present day; being, in most of the United States, established at the rate of six *per cent. per annum*. But interest upon interest is still viewed as usurious and wrong—and why? Perhaps for the same reason that interest upon *principal* was formerly.

If, by the most moderate calculation, by using my money myself, I might increase it at the rate of 6 *per cent. per annum*, and the amount be my capital, or principal, for the second year, and so on in the geometrical progression of compound interest, at the rate of doubling in 12 years—why should I not receive an annually-increasing benefit from the use of my money, when in the hands of another person, who is more immediately benefited by it? And if the interest for service done, goods sold, or money lent, becomes, at the year's end, a part of the debt, and as honestly due as the principal; why should not the forbearance of that, and especially if by the *lache* of the debtor, equally intitle the creditor to *its* interest, as the further forbearance of the original principal, or as a second sum lent upon a new contract? And, upon what principles of casuistry, would it be less consistent with equity and good conscience?

And upon what reasonable ground, the use of *pecuniary* property should be restricted by *legislative* authority, whilst that of all others is left open to be regulated by contracting parties, and the existing state of commerce; I am also equally difficulted to conceive. Can there be any good reason for the one, which does not equally well apply to the other? Does not experience prove, that both the circulating quantity and current value of money, are as fluctuating as those of any other kind of property, and equally subject to the rise and fall of *market price*? A man may be as extortionous in lending other property, as in the loan of money; but is that a reason for the legislature to affix a price upon the use of my horse, and by law enact that I shall forfeit all demand, and even the horse too, if I require any more, let the circumstances of the contract be as they may? It is not uncommon for the farmer to let his sheep, and other live stock, to be returned at an hundred *per cent.* interest in four years; and such contracts are affirmed by legal adjudications: but ſhould he diſpoſe of his cattle for *money*, and loan it at the ſame rate of intereſt, however benefited might be the borrower, or how great ſoever the riſque and inconvenience of the lender, alas! it would be quite a different caſe—the contract would be illegal, yea uſurious; and the borrower intitled to the privilege of returning the kindeſs of his benefactor, by defrauding him of the moſt equitable demand, *in due courſe of law.*

If the deſigned operation of this be to prevent one man from making another's neceſſity his opportunity of extortion, will it not rather operate to add inſult to wretchedneſs, and take from neceſſity the opportunity of *relief?* For the monied man, if acting from no other motive than intereſt, would ſooner put two locks upon his cheſt, than unlock one, to loan his money at 6 *per cent.* upon the beſt ſecurity given.

But it is time for me to cloſe this ſubject with an apology for proceeding thus far. It is not my intention or wiſh, to act the part of a cenſor or dictator, but that of an humble individual, exerciſing the freedom of enquiry. In this light I wiſh to be viewed in the preceding obſervations. I undertake not to preſcribe at what rate *per cent.* any one ſhall loan his money; but merely to aſſiſt him, by the moſt convenient rules, to calculate the uſe of it, at whatever rate he pleaſes—whether by the *firſt* or *ſecond* mode juſt conſidered—and whether at *ſimple* intereſt, or *compound*. If the purchaſer ſhould receive this benefit from the book, my wiſhes will be gratified—my pains compenſated—and he will loan his money more advantageouſly than at *compound intereſt*.

BURLINGTON, *(Vermont)*
January 31, 1797.

The American Accomptant, &c.

P A R T I.

L E S S O N I.

A R I T H M E T I C,

IN GENERAL.

Q. WHAT *is* Arithmetic?

A. It is the art of computing by numbers, either whole or in fractions.

Q. *What is* Number?

A. It is one or more quantities anſwering to the queſtion "how many."

Q. *What is* Arithmetic *in* whole *numbers?*

A. That which treats of intire quantities, or integral numbers, not divided into parts.

Q. *What is* Arithmetic *in* fractions?

A. That which ſuppoſes its numbers to be the parts of ſome intire quantity or number, leſs than a whole.

Q. *What is the nature of all Arithmetical operations?*

A. By ſome numbers or quantities that are given, to find out others before unknown.

Q. *What are the Fundamental Rules in Arithmetic?*

A. Theſe five, viz. Notation, Addition, Subtraction, Multiplication and Diviſion.

LESSON II.

NOTATION.

Q. WHAT *is* Notation?

A. It is the art of expreſſing numbers, by certain characters or figures.

Q. *What is the* uſe of *Notation?*

A. Notation teaches to write and read numbers by their true value.

Q. *By how many kinds of characters are numbers expreſſed?*

A. By two, viz. the *Arabian* figures, and the *Roman Letters*, called *Numerical Letters.*

Q. *How many different characters of the Arabian figures are uſed in Arithmetic?*

A. Ten.

Q. *How are they formed?*

Thus	1	One.
	2	Two.
	3	Three.
	4	Four.
	5	Five.
	6	Six.
	7	Seven.
	8	Eight.
	9	Nine.
	0	Nought, or Cypher.

Q. *How far may the uſe of theſe figures be extended?*

A. To expreſs all manner of numbers, from the leaſt, to the greateſt that can be named, or conceived.

LESSON III.

Of the Numerical Letters.

Q. WHICH *are the* Roman Letters *uſed to expreſs numbers?*

A. These following, with their numbers expressed both by figures and words in the opposite columns.

Figures.	*Letters.*	*Names.*	*Figures.*	*Letters.*	*Names.*
1	I	One	30	XXX	Thirty
2	II	Two	40	XL	Forty
3	III	Three	50	L	Fifty
4	IV	Four	60	LX	Sixty
5	V	Five	70	LXX	Seventy
6	VI	Six	80	LXXX	Eighty
7	VII	Seven	90	XC	Ninety
8	VIII	Eight	100	C	One hundred
9	IX	Nine	200	CC	Two hundred
10	X	Ten	300	CCC	Three hundred
11	XI	Eleven	400	CCCC	Four hundred
12	XII	Twelve	500	D	Five hundred
13	XIII	Thirteen	600	DC	Six hundred
14	XIV	Fourteen	700	DCC	Seven hundred
15	XV	Fifteen	800	DCCC	Eight hundred
16	XVI	Sixteen	900	DCCCC	Nine hundred
17	XVII	Seventeen	1000	M	One thousand
18	XVIII	Eighteen	1796	MDCCXCVI	One thousand, seven hundred and ninety six.
19	XIX	Nineteen			
20	XX	Twenty			

Q. *How many different letters of the Alphabet are used in expressing every number from* one *to the highest set down in the above Table?*

A. Seven only, *viz.* I, V, X, L, C, D, M. These Letters may be divided into the following classes, *viz.* The single units, I, II, III; the Unit-Cardinal V, and its forerunner IV; 2. The Decimal-Cardinal X, with its forerunner IX; 3. The Half-Century Cardinal L, and its forerunner XL; 4 The Century Cardinal C, and its forerunner XC; 5. The Semi-millenary Cardinal D; and 6. the Millenary Cardinal M. The two last have no distinguishing forerunners.

Q. *What are the Rules of Notation?*

A. The *forreunners* are distinguished by prefixing the last letter of the foregoing number to its Cardinal, which imports that the value of the left hand letter is subtracted from that of the Right hand one—thus

IV is V less by I, or 4. IX is X less by I, or 9, XL is L less by X, or 40. XC is C less by X, or 90.

2. All the intermediate numbers between each ten and the next ten, are a repetition of the same letters in the same order—they are all annexed to the Decimal-Cardinal, and are to be read by adding their value, or number to that of the preceding number of tens—thus XVIII is X, more V. more III, or 10 and 5 and 3, which equals 18.

3. All the tens under forty, are expressed by as many X's; all the tens over 50 and below 90, by annexing to L as many X's as tens over 50.

Lastly, All the numbers between each hundred, are expressed by the same letters, as the numbers under the first Hundred.

Q. *To what special uses are these Numerical Letters applied?*

A. They are of but very little *real* use, or practical benefit—are totally unfit, or certainly the most inconvenient, for any Arithmetical calculation—The use they are applied to, is principally in typography, (besides the mill-marking of boards) to divide Verses or Chapters in Books; and seldom are used to express any higher number, than that of the year of Salvation at the bottom of the Title page.

LESSON IV.

Of the Numeration Table.

Fourth Period.			Third Period.			Second Period.			First Period.		
Hun. of Tho. of Mil.	Tens of Tho. of Mil.	Tho. of Mil.	Hun. of Mil.	Tens of Mil.	Mil.	Hun. of Thous.	Tens of Thous.	Thous	Hund.	Tens.	Units.
											9
										8	9
									7	8	9
								6	7	8	9
							5	6	7	8	9
						4	5	6	7	8	9
					3	4	5	6	7	8	9
				2	3	4	5	6	7	8	9
			1	2	3	4	5	6	7	8	9
		9	1	2	3	4	5	6	7	8	9
	8	9	1	2	3	4	5	6	7	8	9
9	8	9	1	2	3	4	5	6	7	8	9

Q. *What is the use of the foregoing Numeration Table?*

A. It teaches how to read any sum or number expressed in figures.

Q. *Explain it?*

A. Beginning at the uppermost figure of the right hand column, which is so many single units or *ones*, as that figure expresses, I read it, *Nine.*

2d. Row. *Two places of figures.* Beginning, as before, with the right hand figure, and enumerating towards the left, according to the denominations written at the top, I say, 'units, tens:' the left hand figure is therefore so many tens, as when standing alone, it would express single units; that is eight tens or eighty.— Accordingly I read towards the right hand and say, *Eighty nine.*

3d Row. *Three places of figures.* Say, 'units, tens, hundreds;' the left hand figure being so many hundred single units, read the whole, *Seven hundred and eighty nine.*

4th Row. *Four places of figures.* Say, 'units, tens, hundreds, thousands'—the last figure is so many thousand single units—read the whole, *Six thousand, seven hundred and eighty nine.*

5th Row. *Five places of figures.* Say, 'units, tens, hundreds, thousands, tens of thousands'—which figure is so many times ten thousand, as it expresses single units when standing alone—or fifty thousand—Read the whole number, *Fifty six thousand, seven hundred and eighty nine.*

6th Row. *Six places of figures.* Enumerate, 'units, tens, hundreds, thousands, tens of thousands, hundreds of thousands;' read, *Four hundred and fifty six thousand, seven hundred and eighty nine.*

Note. *Let the learner commit to memory the names and numerical order of the several denominations in the Numeration Table, so that he may readily apply them to any number without the help of the Index.*

7th Row. *Seven places of figures.* You now begin to count millions—the left hand figure being next to hundreds of thousands, is so many millions, or thousands of thousands, as when standing alone it would express single units—Therefore read, *Three millions four hundred and fifty six thousand, seven hundred and eighty nine.*

8th Row. *Eight places of figures.* The last place, or left hand figure being tens of millions, read *Twenty three million, four hundred and fifty six thousand, seven hundred and eighty nine.*

9th Row. *Nine places of figures,* which brings you, in enumerating, to hundreds of millions—read it, *One hundred and twenty three millions, four hundred and fifty six thousand, seven hundred and eighty nine.*

10th Row. *Ten places of figures,* which brings you to thousands of millions—read it, *Nine thousand, one hundred and twenty three millions, four hundred and fifty six thousand, seven hundred and eighty nine.*

11th Row. *Eleven places of figures,* amounting to tens of thousands of millions; Read, *Eighty nine thousand, one hundred and twenty three millions, four hundred and fifty six thousand, seven hundred, and eighty nine.*

12th Row. *Twelve places of figures.* The last left hand figure, standing in the place of *Hundreds of thousands of millions,* read it, *Seven hundred and eighty nine thousand, one hundred and twenty three millions, four hundred and fifty six thousand, seven hundred and eighty nine.*

LESSON V.

The same subject continued.

Q. IN *what proportion do numbers increase from the units place towards the left hand?*

A. In a tenfold proportion.

Q. *Why is the Numeration Table made to consist of* twelve *places of figures, rather than ten or eleven only?*

A. Becauſe they make four even periods.

Q. *What do you mean by a* Period ?

A. A number expreſſed by three figures, of which the right hand one ſignifies ſo many units ; the ſecond, ſo many tens : and the third, ſo many hundreds.

Q. *Why are three figures called a period ?*

A. Becauſe, if the number be increaſed above three places, there is ſtill the ſame periodical return of the value of thoſe places, and every third figure to the left hand will always be *hundreds*, if it be ever ſo far extended.

Q. *What are the figures in the Numeration Table called, in diſtinction from the cypher ?*

A. They are called *ſignificant* figures or *digits.*

Q. *What is the uſe of the* cypher *in Notation ?*

A. 1. When ſtanding in units' place in connection with ſignificant figures, it always expreſſes an even decimal number ; or ſuch a number as may be divided by ten, without leaving any remainder.

2. It increaſes the value of its left hand ſignificant figure tenfold—as 7 ſeven, 70 ſeventy, which is ten times 7.

Q. *Does the Cypher have any effect upon its* right *hand figure ?*

A. None at all in whole numbers—but otherwiſe in decimal fractions, as will be ſeen in its proper place.

Q. *What is the effect where there are* two, *or more cyphers together ?*

A. They increaſe the value of the firſt left hand ſignificant figure, by a tenfold proportion, as many times as there are cyphers, thus 4, written 400, 4000 becomes four hundred—four thouſand. Cyphers are alſo uſed for the ſame purpoſe, when occupying vacant denominations, between ſignificant figures. As 4009, is four thouſand, no hundreds, no tens, and nine units—or four thouſand and nine.

LESSON VI.

Numeration farther extended.

Q. IS *the expression of numbers, by figures, limited to twelve places of figures only?*

A. No. It may be continued and increased without end towards the left hand, in the same decimal ratio, by substituting a new collective name at every sixth place of figures from millions, instead of millions of millions, &c. Tho' there is very rarely, if ever, occasion for more than 12 places of figures in ordinary practice.

Q. *By what other names, besides those already mentioned in the Table, would you extend numeration beyond 12 places of figures?*

A. Names are but arbitrary signs of ideas, and it is pretty immaterial indeed, what names are used to express a number beyond all human conception; and where, in fact, the name conveys no adequate idea to the mind: but the names which are usually applied to every 6th place of figures from units, and their order of arrangement, are as follow, viz. Millions, Billions, Trillions, Quatrillions, Quintillions, Septillions, Octillions, Nonillions, Decillions, Undecillions, Duodecillions, &c. Each of these are millions so many times involved, as their indices, or number of remove from the place of units, counting by periods of six figures, point out. So that between either two of these, taken in the order that they stand, there is the same proportion, which there is between a million and a single unit—a million, is a single unit repeated a thousand thousand times—a billion is a thousand thousand millions, or a million of millions, and so on, according to the following

SCALE.

Quintil.		Quatril.		Trillions		Billions		Millions		Units.	
th.	un.	th.	un.	th.	un.	th.	un.	th.	un.	th.	un.
	5		4		3		2		1		
143000		750 026		653 912		973 908		604012		763921	

LESSON VII.

Examples for exercise.

IT *is required of you to write down, in proper figures, the following numbers ?*

Nineteen.

Six hundred and forty two.

Three thousand and forty three.

Seventy six thousand, five hundred and seventy three.

Eight hundred and twenty one thousand and four.

Two millions, twenty seven thousand and nine hundred.

Ninety millions, ninety thousand and nine.

Five hundred millions, sixty seven thousand and three.

Four thousand and seventy one millions, three hundred and forty three thousand, four hundred and fifty two.

Thirty seven thousand million, eighty four thousand and eight.

One hundred and twenty thousand, four hundred and six millions, one hundred and twenty nine thousand, seven hundred and sixty three.

Now write down in words at length the following numbers :

5	734	409070	4916743	7467934857
14	1030	600978	70049048	68198136194
137	60567	5087194	195847096	700004890005

LESSON VIII.

Notation of mixed quantities.

Q. WHAT *is meant by a* mixed *quantity ?*

A. It is a quantity compoſed of ſeveral denominations of the ſame ſpecies or ſort of things, of which all the lower denominations are, according to their numbers, fractional parts of the higheſt denomination, as Pounds, Shillings, Pence; Dollars, Cents and Mills—Tons, Hundreds, Quarters, &c. &c.

Q. *How are the Tables of mixed quantities divided ?*

A. Into thoſe of Money, Weight, Meaſure, Motion, Time, and Tale.

Q. *How are the ſeveral denominations in each Table further diſtinguiſhed ?*

A. The higheſt denomination may be called the ultimate or grand integer—the loweſt denomination the ultimate fraction—the intervening denominations, the *meſne* integers and the *meſne* fractions, according as they reſpect the higher, or the lower denominations.

2. The number expreſſed in the higheſt denomination is unlimited—that of all the others is bounded—each one by the particular number of its *Terminus.*

Q. *What do you mean by* Terminus ?

A. That number which in each of the lower denominations makes an unit, or one in the next higher denomination, and is therefore a bound which the number in that denomination muſt not equal—for inſtance, as twenty Shillings make one Pound—*Twenty* is therefore the *Terminus* of Shillings, and the number, in that denomination, can orderly ariſe no higher than 19.

Q. *In what order and form are the ſeveral denominations to be placed, in expreſſing a mixed quantity by figures ?*

A. Begin by writing the higheſt given denomination at the left hand, placing its characteriſtic, either over it, or at its left hand; then, proceeding towards the right hand, ſet the numbers in each denomination, in the order of the rank or value of its denomination, at a ſmall diſtance apart, and ſeparated, if it be a vulgar table, by two commas thus (,,) but if a Decimal Table, by the Decimal point or dot, thus (.) between the higheſt and the lower denominations.

Q. *What do you mean by a* Characteriſtic?

A. A certain appropriate character, or one or more letters, which repreſent and point out the particular denomination of any number to which it is applied.

Q. *Are theſe to be applied to every denomination in a given mixed quantity?*

A. It is not neceſſary to expreſs any other characteriſtic, than that of the higheſt denomination in the given quantity; unleſs for the greater eaſe of the young beginner, and until he is become well verſed in the order of the denominations.

Q. *What if there be a vacant denomination in the given quantity, as ſeven pounds, and ſeven pence?*

A. Fill up the vacant denomination with as many Cyphers, as it will admit of ſignificant figures: as £ 7,,00,,7.

Q. *What do you mean by a Vulgar Table, and a Decimal Table?*

A. A Decimal Table of mixed quantities, has the terminus of each denomination a decimal number, ſuch as ten, hundred, &c. A Vulgar Table is that which has any other number as Terminus.

LESSON IX.

The Tables of Money—different currencies—ſtandard value of Gold—names and value of foreign and Federal coins.

The Vulgar Table of Money.

		Characteriſtics.
4 Farthings (q) make	1 Penny.	*d*
12 Pence	1 Shilling.	*ſ*
20 Shillings	1 Pound.	£

Q. *Are there not ſeveral currencies in this Table, which differ in their value?*

A. Yes, there is,

1. Sterling money, which is the money of account in England.

2. Iriſh money—uſed in Ireland.

3. Halifax money—the currency of Nova Scotia and the two provinces of Canada.

4. South Carolina and Georgia currency.

5. The currency of New-Hampſhire, Maſſachuſetts, Connecticut, Rhode-Iſland, Virginia, Vermont and Kentucky, commonly called the Lawful Money of New-England.

6. New-Jerſey, Pennſylvania, Delaware and Maryland currency.

7. New-York and North-Carolina currency.

Q. *What are the proportionate values of theſe different currencies?*

A. They may be ſeen by the following tables, valuing 1 Pound of each currency in Federal money, and 1 Dollar of Federal money in thoſe ſeveral currencies.

One Pound,	*Dollars.*		
1. Sterl. money	= 4.44 4	One Dollar Federal money, is	4/6 *Sterl.*
2. Iriſh do.	= 4.81 4		4/10½ *Iriſh.*
3. Halifax do.	= 4.00 0		5/0 *Halifax.*
4. S.C. &c. do.	= 4.98 7		4/8 *S.C. &c.*
5. N.H. &c. do.	= 3.33 3		6/0 *N.H. &c.*
6. N. J. &c. do.	= 2.66 6		7/6 *N. J. &c.*
7. N.Y. &c. do.	= 2.50 0		8/0 *N.Y. &c.*

But all the above different currencies that are uſed in the United States, are giving way to one uniform currency of the *Federal Money.*

Of Federal Money.

		Characteristics.
10 Mills (//) make	1 Cent.	//
10 Cents - - -	1 Dime.	[illegible]
10 Dimes - -	1 Dollar.	[illegible]
10 Dollars - -	1 Eagle.*	E.

Q. *What are the names of the ſeveral foreign and ſederal gold, ſilver and copper coins, circulating in the United States, and their value in Federal Money?*

A. *Gold Coins.*

Foreign.	A Double Johannes is	16.00 0
	A Single ditto, - -	8.00 0
	An Engliſh Guinea, -	4.66 7
	A Half ditto, - -	2.33 3
	A French Guinea, -	4.59 8
	A half ditto, - - -	2.29 9
	4 Piſtoles, - - -	14.45 2
	2 Piſtoles, - - -	7.22 6
	1 Piſtole, - - -	3.61 3
	A Moidore, - -	6.05 8
Federal.	An Eagle, - - -	10.00 0
	A Half ditto, - - -	5.00 0
	A Quarter ditto, - -	2.50 0

Silver Coins.

A French Crown is	1.10
A Half ditto, - -	0.55
A Piſtareen, - - -	0.20
A Half ditto, - -	0.10
Spaniſh & Federal Dol.	1.00

Its parts are in proportion.

---

* *The* Eagle *is the largeſt* Gold Coin *of the* UNITED STATES. Dimes *are annexed to Cents, and only the*

Copper Coins.

The Cent, one hundredth part of a Dollar.
Half Cent, or five Mills.

Q. *At what rate, according to their present standard, are the Gold coins of Great Britain, Portugal, France and Spain, made a lawful tender in the United States, by act of Congress?*

A. Those of Great Britain and Portugal, at the rate of 100 Cents, or 1 Dollar for every 27 grains actual weight: Those of France and Spain at 27 grains and two fifths of a grain actual weight.

Q. *What is the standard of all gold coins of the United States?*

A. Eleven parts fine, or pure gold, to one part of alloy; so that, eleven parts in twelve of the entire weight of the said coins must consist of pure gold, and the remaining one twelfth part of alloy.

Q. *Of what is the alloy composed?*

A. Of silver and copper—not exceeding one half silver.

Q. *What is the proportionate value of gold to silver in all coins current in the United States?*

A. It is as *fifteen to one*, according to quantity in weight of pure gold, or pure silver; that is to say, every fifteen pound weight of pure silver is, by act of Congress, to be of equal value, in all payments, with one pound weight in pure gold; and so in proportion.

Q. *What is the standard for all silver coins of the United States?*

A. One thousand, four hundred and eighty parts fine, to one hundred and seventy-nine parts alloy; and the alloy must be wholly of copper.

---

denominations of Dollars, Cents and Mills *expressed, in reckoning Federal money:* the Dollar being the money unit. *For the names and values of foreign coins, see the* Rules of Exchange, *in the* Second Part.

LESSON X.

The mixed quantities of Weight, Measure, &c.

VULGAR TROY-WEIGHT.

		Characteristics.
24 Grains *(gr.)* make	1 Pennyweight.	*dwt.*
20 Pennyweights -	1 Ounce.	*oz.*
12 Ounces - - -	1 Pound.	*lb.*

Q. WHAT *things are weighed by this weight?*

A. Gold, silver, jewels, electuaries, and all liquors.

FEDERAL TROY-WEIGHT.*

10 Cents *(ct.)* make 1 Grain.
10 Grains - - 1 Pennyweight.
10 Pennyweights - 1 Ounce.
10 Ounces - - 1 Pound.

See this Table more particularly explained in the Introductoin, page 10.

VULGAR AVOIRDUPOIS-WEIGHT.†

		Characteristics.
16 Drams *(dr.)* make	1 Ounce.	*oz.*
16 Ounces - -	1 Pound.	*lb.*
28 Pounds - -	1 Quarter Hund.	*qr.*
4 Quarters - -	1 Hundred wt.	*cwt.*
20 Hundred wt. -	1 Ton.	*T.*

---

* *The new-proposed Federal Tables, tho' already recited in the Introduction, are re-inserted in this Lesson, for the sake of orderly arrangement.*

† *By Avoirdupois are weighed all coarse and dry goods, grocery and chandlery wares, bread, and all metals excepting gold and silver.*

Federal Avoirdupois-Weight.

10 Drams *(dr.)*	make	1 Ounce.	*oz.*
10 Ounces	- - -	1 Pound.	*lb.*
100 Pounds	- - -	1 Hundred wt.	*cwt.*
10 Hundreds	- -	1 Thousand do.	*mwt.*

See the Introduction, page 10.

Apothecary-Weight.* *(Vulgar Table.)*

20 Grains *(gr.)*	make	1 Scruple.	℈
3 Scruples	- -	1 Dram.	ʒ
8 Drams	- - -	1 Ounce.	℥
12 Ounces	- -	1 Pound.	*lb.*

Federal Apothecary-Weight.

10 Grains	equal	1 Scruple.	*Characteristics the same as in the Vulgar Table.*
10 Scruples	- -	1 Dram.	
10 Drams	- -	1 Ounce.	
10 Ounces	- -	1 Pound.	

Long Measure.†

3 Barley-Corns *(b. c.)*	make	1 Inch.	*in.*
4 Inches	- - - - - -	1 Hand.	*hd.*
12 Inches	- - - - -	1 Foot.	*ft.*
3 Feet	- - - - - -	1 Yard.	*yd.*
6 Feet	- - - - - -	1 Fathom.	*fa.*
5 Yards and a half	-	1 Rod, Pole or Perch.	*po.*
40 Rods, or 220 Yards,	-	1 Furlong.	*fu.*
8 Furlongs, or 1760 Yards,		1 Mile.	*m.*
3 Miles	- - - -	1 League.	*l.*
60 Miles	- - -	1 Degree.	*deg.*

---

* *All the weights now used by Apothecaries, above grains, are Avoirdupois.*

† *The use of Long Measure is to measure the distance of places, or any other thing, where length is considered, without regard to breadth.*

Federal Board Measure.

10 Pepper-Corns (*pc.*) make	1 Federal Inch.	*in.*
10 Federal Inches - - - -	1 Common Foot.	*ft.*
10 Square Feet - - - -	1 Pannel.	*p.*
10 Pannels - - - -	1 Gang.	*g.*
10 Gangs - - - - -	1 Thousand Feet.	*td.*

Cloth Measure. (*Vulgar Table.*)

2 Inches and a Quarter make	1 Nail. Marked	*na.*
4 Nails - - - - -	1 Qr. of a Yd.	*qr.*
4 Quarters, or 36 Inches -	1 Yard. - -	*yd.*
3 Quarters of a Yard -	1 Flemish Ell.	*Fle.*
5 Quarters of a Yard - -	1 English Ell.	*Eng.*

See the above Table *federalized*, in the *Introduction*, page 24.

Land Measure.

9 Square Feet make	1 Yard. Marked	*y.*
30 Yards & a Quarter	1 Pole. - -	*po.*
40 Square Poles -	1 Rood. - -	*r.*
4 Roods, or 160 Poles	1 Acre. - -	*a.*

Liquid Measure. (*Vulgar Table.*)*

4 Jills (*j.*) make	1 Pint. Marked	*pt.*
2 Pints - - -	1 Quart. - -	*qt.*
4 Quarts - -	1 Gallon. - -	*gal.*
$31\frac{1}{2}$ Gallons - -	1 Barrel. - -	*bar.*
42 Gallons - -	1 Tierce. - -	*t.*
63 Gallons - -	1 Hogshead. - -	*hhd.*
84 Gallons - -	1 Puncheon. -	*pu.*
2 Hogsheads - -	1 Pipe, or Butt. -	*p.*
2 Pipes, or 4 Hogsheads,	1 Tun. -	*tu.*

---

* *All Brandies, Spirits, Perry, Cyder, Mead, Vinegar and Oil, are measured by this measure, which is usually called* Wine-measure.

LIQIUD MEASURE. (*Federal Table.*)

10 Federal Pints (*pt.*)	make	1 Common Gallon.	*gal.*
10 Common Gallons	- -	1 Federal Barrel.	*f. b.*
10 Barrels	- - -	1 do. Hogſhead.	*hhd.*

DRY MEASURE.

2 Pints (*pt.*)	make	1 Quart.	Marked *qt.*
4 Quarts	- -	1 Gallon. - -	*gal.*
2 Gallons or 8 Qts.		1 Peck. - -	*p.*
4 Pecks	- -	1 Buſhel of the U. S.	*u. b.*
5 Pecks or 40 Qts.		1 Canada Buſhel. -	*c. b.*

See this Table *federalized*, page 25, *Introduction.*

TIME.

60 Seconds (*ſec.*)	make	1 Minute.	Marked *min.*
60 Minutes	- -	1 Hour. - -	*hr.*
24 Hours	- - -	1 Day. - - -	*da.*
7 Days	- -	1 Week - -	*wk.*
4 Weeks	- - -	1 Month - -	*mo.*
13 Months, 1 Day and 6 Hours		1 Common or Julian Year. -	*yr.*

Q. *What is a* Solar *Year?*

A. 365 days, 5 hours, 48 minutes and 55 ſeconds.

Q. *How is the year divided by the* Calendar?

A. Into 12 months, each containing the number of days which follow, *viz.*

Months	Days	Months	Days
September, April, June, November	30	October, December, January, March, May, July and Auguſt	31

February hath but 28 days, excepting the addition of 1 day in every fourth year; which year is called *Biſſextile*, or *Leap Year.**

---

* *The* Anno Domini *which may be divided by four, without any remainder, is* Biſſextile, *or* Leap Year.

B

MOTION, *(in the Heavenly Bodies.)*

60 Seconds (″) make	1 Minute.	Marked	′.
60 Minutes - -	1 Degree.	- -	°.
30 Degrees - -	1 Sign.		

12 Signs, or 360 Degrees, make the whole great Circle of the Zodiac.

Of things accounted by the Tale.

12 Particulars *(p.)* make	1 Dozen.	Marked	*doz.*
12 Dozen - -	1 Groſs.	- -	*gr.*
12 Groſs, or 144 Dozen	1 Great Groſs.		*g. gr.*

Federalized.

10 Particulars *(p.)* make	1 Deſm	Marked	*dm.*
10 Deſms - -	1 Groſs.	- -	*gr.*
10 Groſs, or 100 Deſms -	1 Great Groſs.	-	*g. gr.*

LESSON XI.

Explanation of ſundry Marks and ſigns uſed in this Compendium.

= TWO horizontal parallel lines are the ſign of equality; as $ 1 = $$ 10 = // 100 = / 1000; *i. e.* 1 dollar equals 10 dimes, which equals 100 cents, which equals 1000 mills.

+ A rectangular croſs is the ſign of Addition; as 10 + 7 + 5 = 22; *i. e.* 10 and 7 and 5, added together, equal 22.

{ The perpendicular brace, placed at the left or right hand of two or more ſimple or mixed quantities, combines them together, and ſignifies that their aggregate, or ſum total, is to be taken—thus: { 153
426
738

This is more eſpecially uſed in the compound rules, hereafter explained.

⏞ The horizontal brace. This connects all the numbers over which it is placed, and ſignifies that that number is to be taken, which is produced from one or more operations of thoſe numbers, agreeably to the ſigns with which they are connected—thus: $\overbrace{15+12}$ is the ſame as 27; and, by the brace, are ſequeſtered from any preceding or following numbers. This ſign is more eſcecially uſed in Proportion.

—— A ſtrait line, or daſh, is the ſign of Subtraction. It may be placed between any two or more ſingle or aggregate numbers which are ſet down either horizontally or perpendicularly; as 25—12, or $\frac{25}{12}$, ſignify, in the firſt caſe, that the right hand number is to be taken from the left; and in the ſecond, that the lower number is to be ſubtracted from the upper.

× The *oblique* croſs, or *ecks*, is the ſign of Multiplication. This may be placed between numbers ſet down either horizontally or perpendicularly; as 25×5 =125, or

$$\begin{array}{r} 25 \\ \times 5 \\ \hline 125 \end{array}$$

÷ &) (} Are ſigns of Diviſion. The former is uſed in compendious ſtatements; the latter, or inverted parentheſes, in formal operations, where the example is to be wrought at large. Thus 125 ÷ 5 expreſſes the Quotient of 125, divided by 5; but 5)125(directs to the formal operation of Diviſion.

·· & :: Are the ſigns of proportion: the firſt (··) ſeparates the firſt and ſecond terms, and the third and fourth; the ſecond (::) ſeparates the ſecond and third terms: The firſt may be read by the words *is to*; the ſecond by the words *ſo is*: thus, 3 ·· 5::6 ·· 10; that is, as 3 *is to* 5, *ſo is* 6 to 10.

———— A ſingle line between two lines, is uſed to divide the ſtatement from the work, and alſo the ſeveral ſteps of the operation into its proper diviſions or parts.

( ) Is a ſign, when uſed in explanations, to ſignify that the figure or figures, incloſed by it, are actually ſet down in the work. When it incloſes a figure or figures, in ending the operation of diviſion, thus, 224)448(2, it ſhews what remainder there is.

448
(0)

X The capital *ecks*, uſed in proving operations in Multiplication and Diviſion, as will be explained in its proper place.

═══ The double line, drawn under a row of figures, ſhews that the operation is finiſhed, and the anſwer ſtands over it.

Note. *The Decimal Signs will be explained, under that branch of Arithmetic.*

LESSON XII.

ADDITION, IN GENERAL.

Q. WHAT *is the uſe of* Addition?

A. It teaches to bring ſeveral particular numbers, either of one or more denominations, into one total ſum.

Q. *What is the* aggregate *quantity called?*

A. The ſum total.

Q. *How is* Addition *divided?*

A. Into Simple and Combined; and each of theſe ſubdivided into that of whole numbers and mixed quantities.

Q. *What is the* general rule *of ſetting down ſeveral numbers or quantities, ſo as to prepare them for the work of Addition?*

A. It is indifferent which number you ſet down firſt; but obſerve to place all the figures of the ſame value or denomination in a perpendicular line; that is to ſay, place units under units, tens under tens, &c. pounds under pounds, ſhillings under ſhillings, &c. dollars under dollars, cents under cents, &c.

LESSON XIII.

ADDITION OF WHOLE NUMBERS.

Q. WAHT *is the rule of operation?*

A. After the numbers are ſet down, as directed in the former Leſſon, begin at the unit figure of the lowermoſt number, and add it to all the figures ſtanding directly above it.

Q. *What is the next ſtep?*

A. 1. Set down the amount of thoſe unit figures directly under them, having firſt drawn a line of ſeparation under the ſtatement.

2. If the amount of the figures added exceed *ten*, then ſet down only its number of complete tens, and add *one*, for every of thoſe tens, to the next left hand column; but if the ſum of a right hand column be any number of exact *tens*, in that caſe ſet down a cypher in the ſum total, and carry for the tens to the next column as before.

3. Continue this operation thro' all the columns, obſerving to ſet down the whole amount of the left hand column, which will complete the operation.

Q. *What is the reaſon of this rule of carying* one *for every* ten, *to the next place of figures?*

A. It ſprings from the principle of the Numeration Table, and the decimal ratio of increaſe in the riſing ſcale, which is from right hand to left, in all the denominations or places of figures expreſſing whole numbers: *ten* in the units' place make *one* in the *tens'* place; and ten *tens* make *one* in the place of *hundreds;* and ſo on.

Q. *How is the work of Addition proved?*

A. By adding the figures downwards, and finding the ſame ſum total.

ADDITION TABLE.

1								
2	2							
3	4	3						
4	5	6	4					
5	6	7	8	5				
6	7	8	9	10	6			
7	8	9	10	11	12	7		
8	9	10	11	12	13	14	8	
9	10	11	12	13	14	15	16	9
10	11	12	13	14	15	16	17	18

Q. *How is this Table to be read?*

A. By the figures ſtanding upon the ſteps; each of which added to itſelf is the number ſtanding the next under it; and if you would add any two different numbers upon the ſteps, note the number ſtanding the next under that check where their perpendicular and horizontal rows meet, and that is their ſum; for inſtance, in adding 8 and 4, the number ſtanding the next under their common angle of meeting is 12.

EXAMPLES.*

3	34	456	5607	82596
4	45	523	6391	97403
7	79	979	11998	179999

* *Let the learner be accuſtomed in each Example to read correctly each number expreſſed in the ſtatement before he performs the addition; and afterwards the ſum total.*

Dollars.	*Yards.*	*Pounds.*
4734736	46431734	347312484
3474312	72261374	268126312
4161321	12612714	718126190
7369138	31371262	731618192
3143618	74147312	312134716
4732216	47312641	171216198
27615341		

Explanation of the last sum wrought.

Beginning with the unit figure of the lowermost number, I say 6 and 8 is 14 and 8 is 22 and 1 is 23 and 2 is 25 and 6 is 31: I therefore set down 1 directly under the column, and for the thirty carry 3 to the next column: the *second* column by adding I find to amount to 14—I set down 4 and carry 1—the *third* column amounts to 23—I set down 3 and carry 2; the fourth column amounts to 25, here I set down 5 and carry 2; the *fifth* column amounts to 31, set down 1 and carry 3; the *sixth* column amounts to 26, set down 6 and carry 2; the *last* column amounts to 27, I set down the whole, and find the sum total to be *twenty seven millions, six hundred and fifteen thousand, three hundred and forty one dollars.*

Received of several persons the following sums of Money; what is the total sum received, viz.

Of	A.	$3575
	B.	1846
	C.	297
	D.	2954
	E.	1328

Note. *The Instructor may, both in this and the following Rules, add as many practical examples, as he judges necessary for the exercise of his student.*

LESSON XIV.

Addition of Federal Money, and of the other Federal Tables.

Q. WHAT *is the Rule of Operation?*

A. Juft the fame as that in addition of whole numbers; obferving only to place the feperating point between the feveral denominations.

EXAMPLES.

FEDERAL MONEY.

1	2	3
$ 17.35 5	$ 175.75 0	$ 571.57 4
15.21 3	241.39 4	142.92 0
19.19 6	142.93 5	78.00 6
12.12 2	87.00 9	241.39 1
9.65 8	325.55 2	513.65 9
24.33 3	532.44.4	235.66 6
97.87 7		

Explanation of the firft example, which will virtually explain the operation of the others, and of all the examples in each of the Federal tables following.

Say 3 and 8 is 11, and 2 is 13, and 6 is 19, and 3 is 22, and 5 is 27; fet down 7 and carry 2. Next, 2 I carry to 3 is 5, and 5 is 10, and 2 is 12 and 9 is 21, and 1 is 22, and 5 is 27, (7) and carry 2; next 2 I carry to 3 is 5, and 6 is 11, and 1 is 12, and 1 is 13, and 2 is 15, and 3 is 18; fet down 8, and carry 1; next 1 I carry to 4 is 5, and 9 is 14 and 2 is 16 and 9 is 25 and 5 is 30, and 7 is 37, fet down 7, and carry 3. Laftly, 3 I carry to 2 is 5, and 1 is 6, 1 is 7, 1 is 8, 1 is 9; which, fet down, completes the operation, and makes the fum total *ninety feven dollars, eighty feven cents, and feven mills.*

A Merchant's Bill.

Bought of Anthony Brotherton, Dec. 18, 1796.

9	yards of Silk at	2.33	20.97
14	ditto Broad cloth at	4.50	63.00
9	ditto Holland at	75	6.75
10	ditto Shalloon at	55	5.50

Federal Troy Weight.

1	2	3
lb.oz.dw.gr.	*lb.oz.dw.gr.*	*lb.oz.dw.gr.*
19.7 5 6	44.8 3 2	325.9 8 7
21.6 5 7	32.6 9 4	436.8 7 6
34.8 3 9	57.7 6 5	547.7 6 5
45.3 9 8	84.5 4 1	658.6 5 4

Federal Avoirdupois Weight.

1	2	3
mwt.c.lb.oz.		*mwt.c.lb.oz.dr.*
33.5 64 3		754.6 78 9 0
48.7 57 7		643.5 67 8 9
27.6 28 8		532.4 56 7 8
54.9 61 2		421.3 45 6 7

Apothecary Weight.

1	2
℔.℥.ʒ.℈.*gr.*	℔.℥.ʒ.℈.*gr.*
4.6 7 7 3	17.7 7 7 7
5.8 6 5 4	16.6 6 6 6
6.4 5 6 8	15.5 5 5 5
7.3 4 8 2	14.4 4 4 4

Note. *The other Federal Tables are upon the same principle.*

LESSON XV.

SUBTRACTION

Of Whole Numbers.

Q. WHAT *is the nature and uſe of Subtraction?*

A. It takes a leſs number from a greater, and ſhews the difference between them.

Q. *What are the parts of Subtraction?*

A. 1. The larger number from which the ſubtraction is to be made, called the Subſtratum.

2. The Subtrahend, or ſmaller number, to be taken out of the Subſtratum.

3. The Remainder, or the difference found after the work is performed.

Q. *How are the numbers to be ſet down, to prepare them for the work of Subtraction?*

A. In the ſame manner as in Addition, obſerving only to place the *Subſtratum*, or larger number, the uppermoſt.

Q. *What is the rule of operation?*

A. Draw a line under the Subtrahend, and then, beginning at the right hand, ſubtract the value of each figure in the lower number, from that of the one ſtanding directly above it, ſetting down the difference in a third row, directly under it, for the Remainder.

Q. *What if the upper figure be a larger number than the lower one?*

A. 1. In that caſe you will ſubtract the lower number from the upper, made larger by ten. If, for example, you have to take 7 from 6, ſay 7 from 16, and ſet down the difference between thoſe two numbers.

2. Read the next left hand fiure 1 leſs in the operation than what it ſtands for in the numeration; and if it be a cypher, read it 9; and if there be two or more cyphers ſtanding together, read them all nines, and the firſt left hand ſignificant figure 1 leſs than what it ſtands for.

Q. *What is the reason of this Rule?*

A. It is because your annexing a left hand unit figure, or adding 10 to the smaller Substratum figure, is borrowing or taking away 1 from its next left hand figure, which leaves it one the less; and in case of one or more cyphers, as they make their left hand significant figure a decimal number, taking away 1, reduces the first significant figure 1 less than its nominal value, and places the cyphers, be there ever so many intervening, at 1 less than a decimal number, which is 9; thus, take 1 from 500, will leave 499.

Q. *Is there not another method of performing Subtraction?*

A. Yes: the common method is, in the case above, to borrow ten from which to subtract, and to the difference add the upper number, carrying 1 to the next Subtrahend figure; but this is only a circuitous way of adding *ten* to the upper figure in the first instance.

Q. *How do you prove the operation of this Rule?*

A. By adding the Remainder to the *Subtrahend*, and finding it equal the *Substratum*.

EXAMPLES.

	1	2	3
From	8645	75679	978675
Take	6543	54362	976330
	2102		

	4	5	6
From	654006	8492653	73165841
Take	584567	4738062	56241792
	69439		

Explanation of the example last wrought.

Beginning at the right hand, I say 7 from 16 leaves 9: this assumption changes the three next left hand figures, 400, into 399; therefore I go on with the next figures in the Subtrahend, and say 6 from 9 leaves 3; 5 from 9, 4; 4 from 13, 9; 8 from 14, 6; 5 from 5, 0; and the subtraction is completed—leaving for a remainder, sixty-nine thousand, four hundred and thirty-nine.

LESSON XVI.

Subtraction of Federal Money, and the other Federal Tables.

1. MONEY.

Q. HOW *do you subtract* Federal Money?

A. The rule of operation and of proof, in this and all the other Federal Tables following, is precisely the same as that of whole numbers, observing only to keep the denomiationns distinct by the seperating Points.

	1	2	3
	$ // /	$ // /	$ // /
From	17.35 5	175.75 0	571.57 4
Take	15.21 3	142.95 5	523.65 9
Rem.	2.14 2		

	4	5	6
	$ // /	$ //	$ // /
Borr.	43.6 4 3	59.7 4	48.3 3 3
Paid	37.9 3 7	43.8 3	22.6 6 6
Due			

	7	8
	$ // /.	$ // /.
Received	728.56 3	8765.89 3
Paid out	628.56 4	957.75 8
	$	$

	9
I lent my friend	$525.50 0
Received in part pay	270.16 6
What is the balance due me?	
	$

Troy-Weight.

1	2	3
lb. oz.dw.gr.	*lb. oz.dw.gr.*	*lb. oz.dw.gr.*
45.3 9 8	84.5 4 1	658.6 5 4
34.8 3 9	32.6 9 4	325.6 9 7
=====	=====	=====

Avoirdupois Weight.

1	2	3
mwt.c.lb.oz.	*mwt.c.lb.oz.*	*mwt.c.lb.oz.dr.*
54.9 61 2	48.7 57 7	754.3 45 6 7
33.5 64 3	27.6 28 8	421.6 78 9 0
=====	=====	=====

Apothecary Weight.

1	2
℔ ℥ ʒ ℈ *gr.*	℔ ℥ ʒ ℈ *gr.*
7.3 4 8 2	17.4 4 4 4
4.6 7 7 3	14.7 7 7 7
=====	=====

BOARD MEASURE.

1		2
td.g.pan.ft.		td. g.pan.ft.in.pc.
5.8 9 2		86.1 4 7 3 2
2.5 6 4		48.9 6 8 5 4

CLOTH MEASURE.

1	2	3
yds.dec.pts.	yds.dec.pts.	yds.dec.pts.
42.25	72.85	340.25
19.7	17.35	172 35

LIQUID MEASURE.

hhds.b.gal.pts.	hhds.b.gal.pts.
7.3 7 5	64.4 3 1
5.6 4 3	35.4 6 9

DRY MEASURE.

Bu. dec.pts.	b. dec.pts.
8. 115	65. 625
5. 875	48. 845

LESSON XVII.

ADDITION and SUBTRACTION *combined.*

Q. WHAT *is the nature and effect of this Rule?*

A. It is finding the difference between two quantities, whereof either one or both are aggregate numbers, by the operation of Addition and Subtraction compounded in one process, instead of several distinct processes by those Rules.

Q. *What do you mean, in this place, by an* Aggregate *number?*

A. It is the whole amount of several numbers expressed in the statement, whose sum total is not to be set down in the operation.

Q. *How do you prepare the numbers for the work?*

1. Set them down as in Addition and Subtraction, units under units, &c. &c. the Substratum the uppermost.

2. Place the sign of Subtraction between the numbers, and distinguish the aggregate by extending the perpendicular brace to each of the particular numbers of which it is composed.

CASE I.

Q. *Where the Substratum is a single number, and the Subtrahend an aggregate, what is the rule of operation?*

A. 1. Add the right hand column of the aggregate, and subtract the unit figure of its sum from the figure above it in the Substratum.

2. If you have to borrow ten in the subtraction, add that to the number of tens you have to carry in addition.

Q. *How is the work proved?*

A. By adding up the several numbers of the aggregate, setting down their sum total, and subtracting it from the upper number.

EXAMPLES.

1.

From	98762
Take	7654
	3842
	5763
Remains	81503

Explanation.

Say 3 and 2 is 5, and 4 is 9; 9 from 12 (viz. 2 with the addition of 10 borrowed) leaves 3:—

Next, 1 that I borrowed, to 6, makes 7, and 4 is 11, and 5 is 16; 6 from 6 leaves 0.

Next, 1 that I carry (for the 10 in addition) to 7 is 8, and 8 is 16, and 6 is 22; 2 from 7 leaves 5, which alſo ſet down.

Next, 2 that I carry to 5 is 7, and 3 is 10 and 7 is 17; 7 from 8 leaves 1.

Laſtly, 1 from 9 leaves 8.

2.

	Borrowed $2546.66 6		Lent $2668.40 3
Paid at ſeveral times.	43.51 3	Received at ſeveral times	41.86 3
	57.32 9		65.41 3
	53.59 0		58.36 3
	70.34 6		48.51 2
	65.30 0		65.36 0
	88.93 3		48.61 6
	39.92 0		57.69 6
	45.60 3		12.21 0
Unpaid.		Remains due.	

The general rule of operation is the ſame in the two laſt examples as in the two former.

Theſe examples are judged ſufficient to be inſerted in this place. The Inſtructor or Practitioner can at his pleaſure extend them to all the other tables of mixed quantities, the ſame general rule of operation applying to them all.

CASE 2.

Where the Subſtratum is an aggregate and the Subtrahend a ſingle number.

Rule. Make the ſubtraction from the ſum of each column in the aggregate, ſetting down the unit figure of the remainder, and adding the figure in the tens' place, to the next column of the aggregate, and if there ever be occafion to borrow 10 in the fubtraction, take 1 from the number of tens to be carried in the next addition or from the fum of the next column.

The work may be proved by comparing the fum total of the aggregate fet down, with that of the Subtrahend and Remainder.

EXAMPLES.

1.

96857	
75869	*Explanation.*
13541	1+9+7=17—3=14(4); 1+4+6+
—	5=16 —4=12 (2); 1+5+8+8=
87543	22—5=17(7); 1+3+5+6=15—7=
——	8 (·); 4+7+9=20 —8=12 (12)
Rem. 128724	

2.

Lent to B. at feveral times	℔ 35.45 0
	53.54 5
	28.75 6
	47.63 8
	—
Received	99.90 0
Remains due	

3.

Borrowed of W. at feveral times.	℔ 152.91 6
	133.26 6
	288.76 3
	184.99 0
	—
Paid	491.96 6
Remains due	

CASE 3.

Where the Subftratum and Subtrahend are both aggregates.

Rule. 1. Take the unit figure of the fum of the right hand column in the Subtrahend, from that of the column directly above it in the Subftratum, and fet down the difference below it.

2. If the *unit* figure of the Subtrahend be the larger, borrow 10 as in Simple Subtraction, and add 1 to the number of tens in the fum of the Subtrahend.

3. After this, balance the *tens* of each part ; if they are equal in number there is none to carry to the next

column in either of the aggregates—if they are unequal, carry the balance to that aggregate which has the most.—Continue this operation thro' all the columns from the right hand to the left.

Q. *How is the work proved?*

A. By doing it at large; that is, finding the sum total of each aggregate and subtracting the one from the other.

Examples.

1.

Explanation.

97823 45641 37298	7+2+5=14: 8+1+3=12: 12—4=8 (8) balance of tens 1 in favor of the Subtrahend, therefore say 1+8+4+6=19: 9+4+2=15: 15—9=6 (6) balance of tens again 1 to the Subtrahend, therefore 1+3+7+3=14: 2+6+8=16: 6—4=2 (2) balance of tens even. 5+8+4=17: 7+5+7=19: 9—7=2 (2) balance even. 4+3+7=14 : 3+4+9=16—14=2 (2).
74365 38742 45387	
22268	

Practical Examples in the last Case.

2.

George Maxwell to *Robert Cochran* *Dr.*

1796,				
Jan. 3.	To 5 yds. black Kersimer,	at 2.55 7	12.78 5	
10.	To 25 do. Holland,	at .75	18.75	
Feb. 19.	To 14 lb. Loaf Sugar,	at .29	4.06	
	To 7 do. Hyson Tea,	at 1.75	12.25	
	To 4 gall. Brandy,	at 2.33	11.32	
1796,	*Credit.*			
March 1.	By 10 bush. Wheat,	at .75	7.50	
15.	By 3 cwt. Iron,	5.	15.00	
April 4.	By 150 lb. Cheese,	at .08	12.00	
11.	By 63 do. Flax,	at .133 3	8.37 9	

Balance due,

3.

Archibald Spiggot borrowed of *Anthony Hotspur*, at several times, the following sums of money, *viz.*

1793,	February 14,	419.19 7
	May 30,	621.60 0
	September 3,	881.11 5
1794,	March 23,	634.42 5
	August 1,	1074.88 2

Paid at several times, *viz.*

1793,	December 5.	919.54 0
1794,	February 12.	1490.58 2
	October 11.	349.99 0

What remains due, exclusive of interest ?

LESSON XVIII.

MULTIPLICATION.

Q. WHAT *is Multiplication ?*

A. It is a concise method of Addition.

Q. *What are the parts of Multiplication ?*

A. 1. The *Multiplicand* or the sum to be multiplied.

2. The *Multiplier* or the sum multiplied by.

3. The *Product*, or answer to the question ; which is the sum total of the Multiplicand added to itself as often as there are units in the Multiplier.

Q. *What are these several parts of Multiplication called, taken collectively ?*

A. The Multiplicand and Multiplier are called Factors, and the Product, the Fact, Rectangle or Square.

Q. *How is Multiplication generally divided ?*

A. Into two kinds, viz. Simple, or Single, and Compound, or Combined.

Q. *What is the definition of Simple Multiplication, as treated in this Compendium ?*

A. It is where neither of the Factors exceed the number 12, and the Product is found by a single process of Multiplication simply, and without the combined operation of Addition; as 4 times 6 is 24.

Q. *How are the parts to be arranged in Single Multiplication?*

A. In a horizontal line, with the sign of *Multiplication* placed between the Factors, and the sign of *Equality* between the Factors and the Product; thus 4 × 4 = 16.

Note. *Single Multiplication is a necessary preparation to combined Multiplication, and the whole of it is to be learnt perfectly by heart by the student, before he proceeds to the latter.*

SINGLE MULTIPLICATION, *commonly called the* MULTIPLICATION TABLE.

2 × 2 = 4	4 × 7 = 28	11 × 2 = 22
2 × 3 = 6	4 × 8 = 32	11 3 = 33
2 × 4 = 8	4 × 9 = 36	11 4 = 44
2 × 5 = 10	5 × 5 = 25	11 5 = 55
2 × 6 = 12	5 × 6 = 30	11 6 = 66
2 × 7 = 14	5 × 7 = 35	11 7 = 77
2 × 8 = 16	5 × 8 = 40	11 8 = 88
2 × 9 = 18	5 × 9 = 45	11 9 = 99
3 × 3 = 9	6 × 6 = 36	12 × 2 = 24
3 × 4 = 12	6 × 7 = 42	12 3 = 36
3 × 5 = 15	6 × 8 = 48	12 4 = 48
3 × 6 = 18	6 × 9 = 54	12 5 = 60
3 × 7 = 21	7 × 7 = 49	12 6 = 72
3 × 8 = 24	7 × 8 = 56	12 7 = 84
3 × 9 = 27	7 × 9 = 63	12 8 = 96
4 × 4 = 16	8 × 8 = 64	12 9 = 108
4 × 5 = 20	8 × 9 = 72	
4 × 6 = 24	9 × 9 = 81	

The number 10, I have not noticed in the above Table, because it does not change the figures of its multiplicand in the product; and whenever you would multiply any number by 10, you have only to annex the cypher to it, and the product is found.

LESSON XIX.

MULTIPLICATION *combined with* ADDITION.

Q. HOW *are the factors in this Multiplication, to be placed to prepare them for the work?*

A. Place the Multiplier under the Multiplicand, so that units shall stand under units, tens under tens, &c. as in Addition; and put the sign of Multiplication at the left hand of the Multiplier.

Q. *What is the general rule of operation?*

A. Begin to multiply with the unit figure of the Multiplier, and with that multiply each figure in the Multiplicand from the right hand to the left; in each single product, in the multiplication of whole numbers, set down only the overplus of complete tens, and add the number of tens last found to the product of the next multiplicand figure.

Q. *In what order are the particular products to be set down, where there are two or more figures in the Multiplier?*

A. The first figure in each product is to be placed directly under it Multiplier.

Q. *What is the reason of this rule?*

A. It is because the first figure in each product is ever of the same numerical denomination as its Multiplier; units produce units, tens tens, hundreds produce hundreds; therefore the product of the figure standing in hundreds' place in the Multiplier, must be thrown back into the place of hundreds in the product; and so of the other denominations.

Q. *What is the next step?*

A. After the process of Multiplication is completed then add all the particular products together, and their sum total will be the total product, or answer to the question.

Q. *How do you prove Multiplication?*

A. In ſeveral ways, as

1. By inverting the factors, and multiplying them together ſo as to make the ſame total product as before.

2. By dividing the product by either of the factors, and finding the quotient juſt equal to the other factor. (The learner, however, is not yet ſuppoſed capable of this mode of proof.) Or

3. By a croſs, which is the moſt eaſy and compendious method: viz. firſt add together all the figures in the multiplicand, caſting out all the nines as you proceed—then add the figures of the multiplier in the ſame manner, and ſet the overplus of each on two ſides of the Ecks, thus 7X6—then multiply thoſe two figures together, and caſting the nines out of the product, ſet the overplus at the top of the Ecks for a ſtandard figure, thus 6 *Laſtly*, add together all the

7X6

figures in the total product, in the ſame manner; place the overplus at the bottom of the Ecks, and if it be the ſame with the ſtandard, or topmoſt figure, the work is proved.

Q. *What is the reaſon of this mode of proof?*

A. It ariſes, I conceive, from theſe peculiar properties in the number 9, viz. that whatever number it is multiplied by, the figures of its product added together will invariably make one, or more complete nines—and *ſecondly*, the product, in ſuch caſe, will always lack juſt the number of the multiplier of being ten times its number.

CASE 1.

Examples.

1.	2.	3.
47613127	47613171	71261312
×2	×3	×4
95226254		

4.	5.	6.
71261312	73126184	71312674
×5	×6	×7

7.	8.	9.
31261267	47612312	31261731
×8	×9	×11

10.	11.	12.
76138126	82365243	65423789
×12	×11	×12

CASE 2.

The Multiplier larger than 12.

EXAMPLES.

1.

```
   691861
     ×978
  -------
  5534888
 4843027
6226749
---------
676640058
```

Explanation. 8×1=8(8)8×6=48(8)8×8=64+4=68(8)8×1=8+6=14(4) 8×9=72+1=73(3) 8×6=48+7=55 (55) 7×1=7(7)7×6=42 (2)7×8=56+4=60(0)7×1=7+6=13 (3) 7×9=63+1=64 (4)7×6=42+6=48 (48) 9×1=9 (9) 9×6=54 (4)9×8=72+5=77(7)9×1=9+7=16 (6)9×9=81+1=82(2)9×6=54+8=62 (62)

Laſtly, add all theſe particular products, and the total product is found, viz. 'ſix hundred and ſeventy ſix millions, ſix hundred and forty thouſand, and fifty eight.'

PROOF.

$$\begin{array}{ccc} & 6 & \\ 6 & \times & 4 \\ & 6 & \end{array}$$

Explanation. 6 and 1 (the 9 being thrown away) is 7 and 8 is 15, cast out 9 leaves 6, and 6 is 12, 9 out leaves 3 and 1 makes 4, which set upon the right side of the Ecks.

Multiplier. 9 is nothing : 7 and 8 make 15, 9 out leaves 6. Set it upon the left side of the Ecks—multiply those two numbers together, and the product is 24 ; cast out the nines, and the remainder is 6, which set at the top.

Total Product. Add the figures together the same way as in the factors, casting out all the nines, and the remainder will be 6, which set at the bottom of the Ecks and it being the same with the figure atop, the operation is proved.

2.	3.	4.	5.
129186	2812216	181281	5437764
×98	26	763	239
12659428	73116616	138317403	1299595596

6.	7.	8.	9.
269181	261986	812617	281691
4629	7638	43859	76286
1246038849	2001049068	35640569003	21489079626

Q. *Are there no exceptions to the foregoing case?*

A. Yes. 1. When these figures, 1 and 1, or 1 and 2, happen together in any part of the multiplier, you may multiply by both at once, as in Case 1.

EXAMPLES.

1.	2.	3.	4.
761312	671612	963158	843126
×412	×114	×912	×119
9135744			
3045248			
313660 44			

2. Exception. When any other number between 12 and 20 happens, as 13, 14, 15, &c. then multiply by the figure in the units' place, and, as you multiply, add to the product of each single figure, that of the multiplicand which stands next on the right hand.

EXAMPLES.

1.	2.	3.	4.
5497623	8413574	9364326	8128521
×16	×17	×18	×19

3d Exception. When there is any number between 20 and 30, the multiplier, you may multiply in the same way, only add double the right hand figure.

EXAMPLES.

1.	2.	3.
527392	643897	798346
×25	×26	×27

CASE 3.

Q. *What is the particular rule in the third case of Multiplication ?*

A. 1. Such Factors as have cyphers at the ends must be set down as if there were no cyphers.

2. Pay no attention to the cyphers until the multi-

plication is performed, and then annex the ſame number of cyphers to the total product, as there are in both the factors.

EXAMPLES.

1.
476000
×170

80920000

2.
180120
×48100

8663772000

3.
461210
×81900

37773099000

4.
760000
×4800

3648000000

5.
461200
×72000

33206400000

6.
618010
×74210

45862522100

CASE 4.

Q. *What is the particular rule in the fourth caſe of Multiplication?*

A. When cyphers are placed between the ſignificant figures in the Multiplier, omit them in the operation, obſerving to place the firſt figure of every particular product as before.

EXAMPLES.

1.
128121
×72001

128121
256242
896847

9224840121

2.
128128
×70043

8974469504

3.
246145
×66012

16248523740

CASE 5.*

Q. *How do you multiply any whole number by a sum in Federal Money, in order to find the price or value of the whole?*

A. 1. Set down the factors as before; for the sake of convenience, placing that for the Multiplier which has the fewer figures.

2. Multiply the factors together as if they were both whole numbers, according to the general rule in Lesson XIX.

3. Point off, in the total product, as many right hand figures, as there were figures in the factor or price below dollars, for cents and mills—the rest are Dollars.

EXAMPLES.

Q. *What is the amount of* 3257 *yds. of Velvet, at* $ × 3.55 7 *per yard?*

```
        22799
       16285
      16285
      9771
      --------
Answer, 11585.14 9
```

By this single example, and still more by that in the next Case, the instructor, the merchant, and eve-

* *This and the following Case properly belong to Decimal Arithmetic, in the* Third Part: *But as the multiplication of Federal Money must be of such daily practical use; as its operation is plain and easy to the young beginner, and performed in exactly the same method as the multiplication of whole numbers, it was considered best to insert a short sketch of the subject in the First Part of the work. This may also serve as a specimen, both in rule and example, of all the other (proposed) Federal Tables, without their being particularly noticed in Multiplication.*

ry man possessed of the knowledge of practical Arithmetic, will readily discern the simplicity and superior excellency of our Federal currency, in all the various branches of money calculation.

CASE 6.

Q. *How do you multiply a mixed quantity of any of the (proposed) Federal Tables, by any sum in Federal money, in order to determine its value or price?*

A. 1. Place the Factors, and multiply them as before.

2. From the total product, point off as many right hand figures as there were figures in both the Factors, below their ultimate Integers, or the highest denomination in their respective Tables; then the figures standing upon the left hand of the point, are *dollars*; the two figures next upon the right hand of the point are *cents*; the third *mills*; and if there be any more they are cast away, being less than the ultimtae fraction, one mill.

EXAMPLE.

mwt. c. lb.

A farmer sold 34.70 65 of Hay,
at $ × 4.33 3 per thousand weight: *What did he receive in the whole?*

```
      104295
     104295
    104295
   139060
  ------------
Answer, 150.63 6(745
```

This example, I conceive, evinces the practical utility that would result from having all our Commercial Tables of mixed quantities conformed to our Federal money, and established upon a decimal *scale.*

Questions for exercise, in the two last Cases.

1. Q. *What is the price of* 37543 *acres of Land, at* $4.75 ℔ *acre?* Answer, 178329.25.

2. Q. *What would be the impost duty on* 1538 *bushels of Salt, at* //15 ℔ *bushel?* Answer, ✕230.70.

3. Q. *A merchant bought* 756 *gal. of Rum, at* ✕1.34 ℔ *gallon; what sum did he have to pay?* Anf. 275.04.

4. Q. *How much is* 23*mwt.* 1*c.* 25*lb. of bloomery Iron, worth, at* ✕40.26 ℔ *mwt.?* Answer, 935.61 6.

5. Q. *A silver-smith purchased* 34*lb* 5 *oz.* 6*dw.* 7*grs. Federal Troy weight, of old Silver, for* 58 *cents* ℔ *oz. how much did he give for the whole?* Anf. ✕200.49.

6. Q. *A gentleman built him an house, which required* 47*td.* 5*g. and* 75 *feet of boards, to complete it, for which he paid at the rate of* ✕5.45 ℔ *thousand feet; how much did that article enhance the expence of the building?*

Answer, ✕271.28.

7. Q. *A pedlar bought of a printer,* 3 *gr.* 6 *desm and* 5 *Almanacks, for* ✕6.50 ℔ *gross; how much did the whole cost him?* Answer, 23.72.

8. Q. *He retailed them, by the single, at* //12; *what did he receive for them, and what were his neat gains?*

Answer, ✕ 43.80 received in the whole.
20.07 his neat gain.

LESSON XX.

CROSS MULTIPLICATION, or DIAGONAL INVOLUTION.

Q. IS *there not a shorter method of performing Multiplication, both of whole numbers and the mixed quantities of the Federal Tables?*

A. Yes. A method which saves all the figures in the operation, after the factors are stated, but those of the total product, let the multiplier be ever so large.

Q. *What is it called?*

A. Cross Multiplication, or Diagonal Involution.

Q. *What is the benefit of this rule?*

A. After the learner is well versed in the common method of multiplication, he may easily attain the knowledge of this; which by a little uſe will become equally familiar and eaſy; and as it greatly ſhortens the operation, it will be found proportionably advantageous in practice.

Q. *What is the principle of the operation?*

A. I is the ſame as that in the 2d and 3d exceptions in the 2d caſe of Leſſon XIX, and is in reality but extending the ſame rule to a multiplier of the ſame, or any larger number of figures.

Q. *How is the operation performed?*

A. 1 Set down the factors as before.

2. Multiply the two unit figures of the factors together, and ſet down the unit figure of the product according to the common rule.

3. As you proceed with the unit figure of the multiplier, carry the work in your mind, and add the product of the firſt figure of the multiplier and ſecond of the multiplicand, with that of the ſecond figure of the multiplier and firſt of the multiplicand; ſetting down and carrying as before.—At the next ſtep, add the product of the ſecond and third figures of the multiplier, with the firſt and ſecond of the mulplicand, to that of the firſt figure of the multiplier, and third of the multiplicand—multiplying both ways from corner to corner. Proceed in the ſame manner with all the remaining figures, taking in another left hand figure in both factors, at every new ſtep of the proceſs; ſo that if there be an equal number of figures in the factors, you will multiply the right hand figure of the multiplier, with the left of the multiplicand, and the left of the multiplier with the right of the multiplicand and add their products with thoſe of all the intermediate figures multiplied in this way, at the ſame ſtep.

The following example with diagonal lines drawn between the figures, together with the explanation ſubjoined, will clearly illuſtrate the operation of the rule; whilſt the ſame example wrought at large, will prove its truth, and brevity.

3 4 5 6

3 4 5 6

11943 9 3 6

The same wrought at large.

$$\begin{array}{r} 3456 \\ \times 3456 \\ \hline 20736 \\ 17280 \\ 13824 \\ 10368 \\ \hline 11943936 \end{array}$$

Explanation.

6×6=36 (6); 6×5=30+3=33; 5×6=30+33=63 (3); 6×4=24+6=30; 4×6=24+30=54; 5×5=25+54=79 (9); 6×3=18+7=25; 3×6=18+25=43; 4×5=20+43=63; 5×4=20+63=83 (3): *The* unit *figures of the factors are now dismissed.* 5×3=15+8 to carry=23; 3×5=15+23=38; 4×4=16+38=54 (4): *The* tens *are now dismissed.* 4×3=12+5 to carry=17; 3×4=12+17=29 (9): *The* hundreds *are now dismissed.* 3×3=9+2 to carry=11 (11.)

The operation is now closed; producing *eleven millions, nine hundred and forty-three thousand, nine hundred and thirty six.* Compare this example with the work done at large in the common method, and it is found to save 20 figures in this small sum.

CASE 2.

Q. *How do you perform Cross Multiplication, where the factors consist of unequal numbers of figures?*

A. 1. Set the factors as before, the smallest for the multiplier.

2. Multiply in the same manner as before, and after you have multiplied the unit, or right hand figure of the multiplier, into the one standing immediately over its left hand figure, continue the process with each remaining figure of the multiplicand, just as if all the figures of the multiplier were, at every step, removed one figure farther towards the left hand; and,

for convenience ſake, you may ſet a point over each figure of the multiplicand, ſtanding on the left hand of the multiplier, when you multiply it by the right hand figure of the multiplier, and under each right hand figure, as ſoon as it is diſmiſſed.

EXAMPLES.

1.	2.
59271 acres of Land,	7854362
at × $5.75 ℘ acre?	× 5268
340808.25 *Anſwer.*	41376779016

Explanation of Example 1.

5×1=5 (5); 5×7=35; 7×1=7+35=42 (2); 5×2=10+4=14; 5×1=5+14=19; 7×7=49+19=68 (8): *Now diſmiſs the* unit *figure of the* multiplicand, *and ſet the multiplier under the figures* 927. 5×9=45+6 to carry = 51; 5×7=35+51=86; 7×2=14+86=100 (0): *Now diſmiſs the* tens *in the multiplicand, and ſet the multiplier under* 592. 5×5=25+10 to carry =35; 5×2=10+35=45; 7×9=63+45=108 (8): *Now diſmiſs the* hundreds *in the multiplicand, and the* units *in the* multiplier. 7×5=35+10 to carry=45; 5×9=45+45=90(0): *Diſmiſs the* thouſands *in the* multiplicand, *and* tens *in the* multiplier. 5×5=25+9 to carry=34 (34). This finiſhes the multiplication.

Laſtly, point off the two right hand figures for cents, becauſe there were cents in the multiplier, and the whole work is finiſhed, producing *three hundred and forty thouſand, eight hundred and eight dollars, and twenty five cents.*

CASE 3.

Q. *How do you improve this Rule in Book-keeping?*

A. Place the factors, which are the commodity and price, at each entry, in a horizontal line; then multiply them together as before; carefully obſerving not to take a wrong figure in the multiplicand, and carry out the product in a right hand column.

2. Cast away in the operation, without setting them down, all the right hand figures in the product, next to the three below dollars.

EXAMPLES.

Thomas Baxter to *Joseph Manly* Dr.

		$	/	/
To 325 yds. Coating,	at $2.33 3	758	22	5
To 75 do. Satin,	at 3.25	185	25	

Explanation of the first Entry.

5×3=15 (5 mills and 1 cent to carry); 5×3=15+1 =16; 2×3=6+16=22 (2 in the units' place of cents); 5×3=15+2=17; 3×3=9+17=26; 2×3=6+26 =32 (2 in the dimes' place) 5×2=10+3=13; 3×3= 9+13=22; 2×3=6+22=28 (8 in the units' place of dollars); 2×2=4+2=6; 3×3=9+6=15 (5 in the tens' place of dollars); 3×2=6+1=7 (7 in the hundreds' place of dollars,--making *seven hundred and fifty-eight dollars, twenty-two cents and five mills.*

LESSON XXI.

DIVISION, IN GENERAL.

Q. WHAT *is* Division?

A. It is a concise method of performing many Subtractions. It shews how many times one number is contained in another, and how many remains.

Q. *How many parts are there in* Division?

A. Four; *viz.*

1. The *Dividend*, or number to be divided.

2. The *Divisor*, or number by which the division is made.

3. The *Quotient*, or the number of times that the divisor is contained in the dividend, which is the answer to the question.

4. The *Remainder*, or the number left after the work is performed, which is always less than the divisor, and of the same kind with the Dividend.

Q. *Which of these are certain, and which not?*

A. The three first are certain and necessary—the *remainder* is uncertain, as in the operation of some numbers there is none left.

Q. *How many sorts of division are there?*

A. Division may be generally divided into Simple or Single Division, and Combined Division.

LESSON XXII.

SINGLE DIVISION, *or the* DIVISION TABLE.

Q. WHAT *is Single Division?*

A. Single Division is where the quotient is found by the operation of Division simply, without the combination of any of the other first rules, and without having any remainder.

CASE 1.

Q. *What is peculiar in the 1st case of Single Division?*

A. The quotient is found by one single process of the divisor.

Q. *How are the parts to be arranged in this case?*

A. In a horizontal line—the dividend first, the devisor next, with the *statement* sign of division between them, and then the quotient separated by the sign of equality. This is just the reverse of the Multiplication Table, and may be usefully learned by heart.

EXAMPLES.

18 ÷ 2 = 9	30 ÷ 5 = 6	24 ÷ 8 = 3
16 ÷ 2 = 8	25 ÷ 5 = 5	16 ÷ 8 = 2
14 ÷ 2 = 7	20 ÷ 5 = 4	81 ÷ 9 = 9
12 ÷ 2 = 6	15 ÷ 5 = 3	72 ÷ 9 = 8
10 ÷ 2 = 5	10 ÷ 5 = 2	63 ÷ 9 = 7
8 ÷ 2 = 4	54 ÷ 6 = 9	54 9 = 6
6 ÷ 2 = 3	48 ÷ 6 = 8	45 9 = 5
4 ÷ 2 = 2	42 ÷ 6 = 7	36 9 = 4
27 ÷ 3 = 9	36 ÷ 6 = 6	27 9 = 3
24 ÷ 3 = 8	30 ÷ 6 = 5	18 9 = 2
21 ÷ 3 = 7	24 ÷ 6 = 4	99 ÷ 11 = 9
18 ÷ 3 = 6	18 ÷ 6 = 3	88 11 = 8
15 ÷ 3 = 5	12 ÷ 6 = 2	77 11 = 7
12 ÷ 3 = 4	63 ÷ 7 = 9	66 11 = 6
9 ÷ 3 = 3	56 ÷ 7 = 8	55 11 = 5
6 ÷ 3 = 2	49 ÷ 7 = 7	44 11 = 4
36 ÷ 4 = 9	42 ÷ 7 = 6	33 11 = 3
32 ÷ 4 = 8	35 ÷ 7 = 5	22 11 = 2
28 ÷ 4 = 7	28 ÷ 7 = 4	108 ÷ 12 = 9
24 ÷ 4 = 6	21 ÷ 7 = 3	96 12 = 8
20 ÷ 4 = 5	14 ÷ 7 = 2	84 12 = 7
16 ÷ 4 = 4	72 ÷ 8 = 9	72 12 = 6
12 ÷ 4 = 3	64 ÷ 8 = 8	60 12 = 5
8 ÷ 4 = 2	56 ÷ 8 = 7	48 12 = 4
45 ÷ 5 = 9	48 ÷ 8 = 6	36 12 = 3
40 ÷ 5 = 8	40 ÷ 8 = 5	24 12 = 2
35 ÷ 5 = 7	32 ÷ 8 = 4	

The number ten is omitted as a divifor in the above Table; becaufe whenever 10 is the divifor, you have only to cut off the right hand figure of the dividend for a remainder, and the other figures are the quotient fought.

CASE 2.

Q. *How are the parts to be arranged in this cafe?*

A. Set the divifor firft, and the operation fign between it and the dividend, and the quotient either at the right hand, or underneath, without the fign of equality.

EXAMPLES.

1.	2.	3.	4.
2) 24	3) 6390	4) 48884	5) 205555
12	2130		

5.	6.	7.	8.	9.
6) 546	7) 4907	8) 72808	9) 6399	10) 8569|0

L E S S O N XXIII.

DIVISION *combined with* MULTIPLICATION *and* SUBTRACTION.

Q. HOW *is this rule generally divided?*

A. Into Short and Long Diviſion.

Q. *How are theſe diſtinguiſhed?*

A. In Short Diviſion, the diviſor does not exceed 12: In Long Diviſion, it conſiſts of any greater number.

SHORT DIVISION.

Q. *What is the rule of operation?*

A. Inquire how often the diviſor is contained in the firſt left hand figure of the dividend, and if that be too ſmall to contain it, take the two firſt; ſet that number down for the firſt left hand figure of the quotient—*next*, multiply the diviſor by the quotient figure, and ſubtract the product from the figure or figures taken in the dividend, and to the remainder annex the next figure of the dividend for a new dividend (performing this operation in your mind only) and extend the ſame proceſs to each remaining figure of the dividend ſucceſſively, ſetting down only the quotient.

Q. *How do you dispose of the final remainder?*
A. Annex it fractionwise to the quotient, with the divisor under it, as in the first example following.

EXAMPLE.

5) 61231280 ——— 12246256 ———	*Explanation.* 5 in 6, 1 (1) 1 left; in 11, 2 (2) 1 left; 5 in 12, 2 (2) 2 left; 5 in 23, 4 (4) 3 left; 5 in 31, 6 (6) 1 left; 5 in 12, 2 (2) 2 left; 5 in 28, 5 (5) 3 left; 5 in 30, 6 (6) and 0 left.

2)71367413	6)312610851	11)7312613107
3)42310812	7)713126719	12)38126173I4
4)13812612	8)701267131	11)1622728131
5)61231281	9)126713108	12)1731261712

LESSON XXIV.

LONG DIVISION.

CASE 1.

Q. WHAT *is the general rule in Long Division?*
A. Set down the parts as in Short Division—multiply the divisor by the quotient figure, and set down the product at large; subtract it from the dividend, and to that remainder annex the next right hand figure in the dividend, for a new dividend. This operation must be repeated for every remaining figure in the dividend.

Q. *How do you prove division?*
A. It may be proved in two several ways, viz.

1. By multiplying the quotient by the divisor, and adding the remainder, if there be any, to the product—if this equal the dividend, the work is proved.

2. It may be done with less trouble and equal certainty, with an X, by a rule similar to that of proving multiplication. *First.* Add together all the fi-

gures in the divisor, casting out the *nines*, and set down the overplus upon the right side of the character. *Secondly*, do the same with the quotient, and set the overplus upon the left hand of the *Ecks*. *Thirdly*, multiply those figures together, and casting the nines out of the product, set down the everplus at the top, for a standard figure.—*Lastly*, add all the figures of the dividend in the same manner, and set the overplus at the bottom, which if equal to the standard figure the operation is right.

Q. *What must be done in this case, if there be a remainder?*

A. Add all the figures of the Remainder, as in the other parts, and subtract the overplus from that of the Dividend, and that remainder will be the same number as the standard figure if the work be right. But if the overplus of the remainder, be larger than that of the Dividend, then borrow 9, which is the *terminus* figure, instead of 10, to substract from; and to that difference add the overplus of the Dividend, which will equal the standard figure.

EXAMPLES.

```
91)72165871(793031
   637
   ---
    846
    819
    ---
     275
     273
     ---
       287
       273
       ---
        141
         91
        ---
        (50)
```

Proof, *with its Explanation.*

```
   5
5  X  1
   5
```

Divisor 9=0+1=1 (1)
Quotient 7+3=1+3+1 (5)
Standard 1×5=5 (5)
Dividend 7+2=0+1+6+5=3+8=2+7=0+1=(1)
Rem. 5+0=5 Lastly 1+9−5=5 the proof figure.

82)31712617(19)73261714(3164)31917352(
73)27342694(381)73247231(6528)42697326(
64)47342637(773)32756373(2932)52436237(
55)73582063(947)23489734(33408)27364432(
46)76535754(762)32846273(73246)94264824(
37)34235772(7628)28937432(6257)37431749(
28)73264624(3247)34937352(23724)34285362(

CASE 2.

When cyphers ſtand at the end of the diviſor, they muſt be cut off, and the ſame number of figures muſt be cut off from the dividend.

The figures cut off in the dividend, muſt be annexed to the remainder at laſt.

EXAMPLES.

625|00)712653|52(528|000)75556|075(
426|00)713524|74(452|000)75653|585(

LESSON XXV.

Q. IS *there not a ſhorter method of performing Long Diviſion?*

A. Yes; a method which ſaves one half the number of figures.

Q. *How is it done?*

A. 1. When you multiply the diviſor by the quotient figure, ſubtract the figures of the product immediately from the dividend, without ſetting them down, according to the method of Compound Subtraction; and ſet down only the remainders.

2. When you have to borrow ten in the ſubtraction, add one, to the number of tens which you have to carry in the multiplication, to the product of the next diviſor figure.

This method, by a little exercise, will become equally familiar and eaſy to the learner, and will be found very uſeful in practice.

Take the Example, wrought at large in Leſſon XXIV, *for an Example of this Rule.*

91)7216587 1(79303

816

275

287

141

(50)

Comparing this Example with the ſame wrought at large, we find 14 figures ſaved in 28.

LESSON XXVI.

Diviſion of Federal Money, by a Diviſor not exceeding 12.

Q. HOW *is the operation performed?*

A. 1. In the ſame manner as Short Diviſion of Whole Numbers; only obſerving to point off by itſelf the quotient of dollars in the dividend, for the ſame denomination in the quotient.

2. Where the higheſt denomination expreſſed in the dividend does not contain the diviſor, the firſt denomination in the quotient will be the ſame as the ſecond in the dividend.

EXAMPLES

$ 1.	$ 2.	// 3.	// 4.
7)3.55 5(	6)45.25 8(	5)3.3(	5)44 4

$ 5.	$ 6	$ 7.	$ 8.
9)672.07 7(	8)817.72 6(	4) 5.66 6(	3)88.22 3(

\$ 9.	\$ 10.	\$ 11.	\$ 12.
11)576.16 7(	12)83.54 9(	11)100.83 3(	12)3.67 2(

CASE 2.
Long Division of Federal Money.

Q. *How is the operation performed?*

A. 1. Place the parts, and divide, juſt as in the diviſion of whole numbers.

2. The placing of the ſeparating point in the quotient, is by the ſame rule as in the former caſe of Short Diviſion.

EXAMPLES.

\$ // / // /
82)31.71 2(38 6

711

552

Rem. (60)
leſs than a mill.

\$	\$
95) 743.15 9(	2345)28754.19 6(
323) 826.60 0(	5432)69245.78 9(
147)8968.07 0(	3254)89694.45 7(
183)5096.00 9(	4523)48962.87 5(
212(9125.00 0(	1765)98765.43 2(

For the mutual diviſion of Decimal mixed quantities, the learner is referred to the diviſion of Decimal Fractions, *in the* Third Part.

LESSON XXVII.
Addition of Mixed Quantities of the Vulgar Tables.

Q. WHAT *is the general rule of operation in the Addition of mixed quantities?*

A. After the ſeveral numbers in the ſtatement are ſet down, according to rule in Leſſon XII, add together all the numbers of the ſame denomination, beginning with the loweſt denomination expreſſed in any of the given quantities, and set down underneath it, in the sum total, the surplus which it contains over and above the complete number of its terminus; and for every time its terminus is contained, carry one to the next higher denomination.

2. The highest denomination in every table of mixed quantities consists of whole numbers, and is to be added as such.

3. Set down the amount of the last left hand denomination, in the highest denomination which it will admit.

Q. *What are the* PENCE TABLES, *so called?*

A. These following, viz.

20*d*. = 1/8	80*d*. = 6/8	2*s*. = 24*d*.	8*s*. = 96*d*.
30*d*. = 2/6	90*d*. = 7/6	3*s*. = 36*d*.	9*s*. = 108*d*.
40*d*. = 3/4	100*d*. = 8/4	4*s*. = 48*d*.	10*s*. = 120*d*.
50*d*. = 4/2	110*d*. = 9/2	5*s*. = 60*d*.	11*s*. = 132*d*.
60*d*. = 5/0	120*d*. = 10/0	6*s*. = 72*d*.	12*s*. = 144*d*.
70*d*. = 5/10		7*s*. = 84*d*.	

Note. *This Table is to be learned by heart.*

EXAMPLES.

1. MONEY.

1. £. *s*. *d*.	2. £. *s*. *d*.	3. £. *s*. *d*.
44,, 12,, 6¼	25,, 11,, 11½	47,, 12,, 6½
31,, 18,, 1½	16,, 12,, 6	31,, 17,, 3
47,, 12,, 4	11,, 9,, 10½	17,, 13,, 11¼
14,, 12,, 10¼	16,, 12,, 4¼	18,, 14,, 10½
16,, 14,, 11	34,, 1,, 10	16,, 15,, 11
19,, 12,, 2	17,, 14,, 11¼	17,, 14,, 4½
£. 175,, 2,, 11½		

Explanation of the Example wrought.

I first add up the *farthings*, and find their amount to be 6; this being 2 over its *terminus*, or making *one penny halfpenny*, I ſet down only the halfpenny, and carry the one to the place of pence: the amount of the pence I find 35, which, by the Pence Table, is 2/11; I therefore ſet down the 11 pence, and carry 2 to the place of ſhillings: the amount of the ſhillings I find 82, which being £.4,,2, I ſet down the 2 ſhillings, and carry 4 to the place of pounds: the number of pounds being added, I find the whole ſum total to be *one hundred and ſeventy-five pounds, two ſhillings and eleven pence halfpenny.*

2. Troy Weight.

1. lb. oz. dw. gr.	2. oz. dw. gr.	3. lb. oz. dw. gr.	4. lb. oz. dw. gr.
4,,11,,13,,14	7,,13,,12	4,,10,,12,,13	7,,10,,12,,10
8,,6,,9,,2	6,,10,,14	3,,10,,16,,12	3,,4,,16,,13
	9,,12,,17	4,,9,,16,,14	4,,13,,16,,12
13,,6,,2,,16	16,,13	3,,3,,19,,13	4,,3,,16,,13

The operation of the above examples being wrought by the ſame general rule with thoſe in the former Table, it is judged unneceſſary to inſert a particular explanation in this and the following Tables.

3. Avoirdupois Weight.

T. c. q. lb.	T. c. q. lb.	c. q. lb.	lb. oz. dr.
4,,12,,3,,16	7,00,,1,,16	17,,3,,12	14,,10,,12
3,,15,,1,,13	1,,12,,3,,10	26,,2,,19	26,,12,,10
	3,,4,,3,,17	24,,1,,12	29,,12,,12
8,,8,,1,,1	3,,1,,2,,12	26,,3,,9	27,,2,,3

4. Apothecary Weight.

lb. ℥ ʒ ℈ gr.	lb. ℥ ʒ ℈ gr.	lb. ℥ ʒ ℈ gr.
3,,11,,7,,2,,19	7,,3,,3,,2,,10	7,,3,,4,,2,,10
6,,3,,4,,2,,3	3,,2,,2,,4	6,,2,,7,,2,,4
2,,7,,2,,9	2,,3,,4,,2,,8	3,,7,,2,,4,,9
4,,2,,2,,2,,8	6,,2,,3,,2,,10	2,,3,,4,,0,,10

5. Cloth Measure.

1.	2.	3.	4.
yds.qr.na.	*ells.qr.na.*	*yds.qr.na.*	*yds.qr.na.*
37,,2,,2	44,,0,,2	27,,2,,3	37,,2,,3
20,,3,,3	27,,3,,2	36,,3,,3	37,,2,,3
35,,3,,3	55,,4,,3	34,,1,,2	45,,3,,3
39,,3,,3	49,,3,,3	39,,4,,0	16,,2,,0

6. Land Measure.

1.	2.	3.
A. r. p.	*A. r. p.*	*A. r. p.*
27,,3,,22	37,,2,,32	26,,3,,36
32,,2,,23	35,,3,,33	43,,2,,33
35,,0,,20	16,,3,,37	34,,3,,35
36,,1,,34	39,,3,,36	46,,2,,28

7. Liquid Measure.

1.	2.	3.
Tier. g. q.	*Hhd. gal.qts.*	*T.hhd.gal.qts.*
37,,34,,3	27,,21,,2	7,,2,,46,,3
46,,40,,2	47,,13,,3	6,,3,,35,,2
66,,10,,3	49,, 8,,2	7,,1,,41,,2
89,,31,,2	29,,12,,3	6,,2,,16,,1

8. Dry Measure.

1.	2.	3.	4.
Gal. qt. pt.	*Pe.gal.qt.*	*B. p. qt.*	*Can.b. p. qt.*
16,,3,,2	6,,1,,2	89,,3,,6	98,,2,,3
47,,1,,0	9,,0,,3	47,,2,,6	9,,3,,6
69,,3,,0	1,,1,,0	35,,3,,7	79,,3,,2
88,,0,,1	2,,0,,3	42,,0,,4	14,,3,,6

9. Long Measure.

M. fur. p.	*Yds. f. in.*	*Le. m. fur. p.*	*Yds. f. in. b.c.*
17,,7,,19	44,,2,, 7	56,,2,,7,,30	16,,1,,0,,0
26,,1,, 9	16,,0,, 4	48,,1,,2,,18	56,,2,,0,,1
60,,3,,16	80,,1,,10	54,,2,,1,,20	48,,1,,4,,2
40,,4,,19	46,,2,, 4	90,,2,,7,, 9	45,,2,,8,,2

10. Time.

M. w. d.	*H. m. sec.*	*M. w. d.*	*D. h. m. sec.*
46,,1,,6	47,,10,,32	34,,2,,1	27,,19,,40,,45
24,,2,,5	27,,44,,43	23,,3,,6	19,,20,,16,,28
16,,3,,6	24,,44,,54	56,,2,,4	47,,10,,43,,40
39,,3,,5	4,, 6,, 5	50,,3,,7	40,,30,,49,,54

11. Motion.

° ′ ″	° ′ ″	° ′ ″
47,,40,,54	47,,56,,49	47,,13,,32
46,,25,,36	27,,10,,31	70,,59,,44
47,,56,,59	56,,54,,35	98,,56,,54
54,,45,,56	90,,45,,34	44,,36,,59

LESSON XXVIII.

SUBTRACTION *of Mixed Quantities.*

Q. WHAT *is the rule of operation?*

A. After the given quantities are ſet down according to the rule in the Leſſon XII, begin the ſubtraction in the loweſt denomination expreſſed in either of the given ſums or quantities, proceeding towards the left hand, ſubtracting each quantity in the ſubtrahend from that of the ſame denomination ſtanding directly above it in the ſubſtratum, and ſetting down the difference directly underneath, in a third row, for the remainder; first drawing a line between the statement and the work, and observing to keep the several denominations separated by the proper marks.

2. If the quantity in any of the lower denominations in the *subtrahend* be smaller than the one standing above it in the *substratum*, take the upper number so many more than its *terminus*, and read the next denomination in the substratum one the less; but if it be a vacant denomination, or there are several vacant denominations coming together, call each and all of them in the work one less than its terminus, and the next left hand quantity one less than its figures. In the highest given denomination, the subtraction is ever the same as that of whole numbers.

If this mode of subtracting mixed quantities prove more unhandy to the young beginner than the common mode, the instructor can direct him to that, which is performed by subtracting the lower quantity from the terminus of its denomination, and to this difference adding the upper quantity for a remainder; add one in such case to the next left hand quantity in the sub trahend.

Note. *Proof is by the same method as in whole numbers.*

EXAMPLES.

1 MONEY.

	£. *s*. *d*.	£. *s*. *d*.	£. *s*. *d*.	£. *s*. *d*.
From	14 10,6½	41,15.3	76,11,4½	73:7,6
Take	3.17.7½	19,17,1½	13,17,7	19,14½
Rem.	£ 10,12,11			

2 TROY WEIGHT.

	oz. *dw*. *gr*.	*oz*. *dw*. *gr*.	*oz*. *dw* *gr*.	*lb*. *oz*. *dw*. *gr*.
From	78,10 12	78, 5,20	23,16,12	84, 4,11,12
Take	2,10,19	10, 4.19	5.19,14	17,10,11,17
Diff.				

Avoidrupois-Weight.

	C.qr.lb.	C.qr.lb.	T.c.qr.	T.c.qr.lb.
Bought	71,2,18	17,2,13	17,10,2	12,2,3,20
Sold	3,1,26	10,2,13	20,19,3	5,3,2,20
Unſold				

4. Apothecary-Weight.

	℥.ʒ.℈.gr.	℥.ʒ.℈.gr.	lb.℥.ʒ.℈.gr.
From	65,4.2,10	47.5,1,16	48,2,2 0,19
Take	7,7.2,12	2.1,2.18	10,1,2,2,17

5. Long-Measure.

	L.m.f.p.	Yd.f.in.b.c.	L.m.f.p.
From	71,1.3.10	40 0,3.2	64.0,3.4
Take	25,2.5,20	26,0,2,2	23.2 3,20

6. Cloth-Measure.

	Yds.qr.na.	Yds.qr.na.	Yds.qr.na.
From	71,3,1	52,2,3	148.0.0
Take	14,2,3	16.1,3	86,0.3

7. Land-Measure.

	A. r. p.	A. r. p.	A. r. p.	A. r. p.
Purchaſed	12,1,12	25,3,17	28,1, 7	32,0, 9
Plowed	5.3,17	12,3,23	19,1,28	16,2,24
Rem. Unpl.				

8. Liquid-Measure.

	T.hhds.gal.	T.hhds.gal.	Gal.qts.pts.	Gal.qts.pts.
From	3, 2, 10	7, 2, 10	19, 2, 1	67, 1, 1
Take	1, 3, 19	1, 2, 28	12, 3, 0	12. 3, 0

9. DRY-MEASURE.

	B.p.qts.	*B.p.gal.qts.pts.*	*C.b.p.qts.*
From	45,2.4	67 0. 1, 3. 0	23.2, 5
Take	29 3,6	38,3, 0, 2, 1	7.4, 6

10. TIME.

	D. h.m. sec.	*W.d. h. m. sec.*	*W. d. h. m. sec.*
From	41,13.22,12	144,10,30.34	35.3,23,13.30
Take	22,35.44.34	30.3,19.48,26	10,3,14, 6,35

11. MOTION.

	° ′ ″	° ′ ″	° ′ ″
From	48,20,24	47, 2,30	63,34,35
Take	35.33.34	20,24,56	49,34,44

LESSON XXIX.

Multiplication of the Mixed Quantities in the Vulgar Tables.

WHAT *do you observe in this kind of Multiplication?*

A. Multiply by a whole number; carry for the particular *terminus* of each denomination in the given quantity, as in Addition, and set down only the overplus.

In CASE 1, The multiplier does not exceed 12.

In CASE 2, Take two figures, which multiplied together, will make the multiplier, and multiply the given quantity by one of those figures, and that product by the other; as where the multiplier is 35, multiply by 7, and that product by 5.

CASE 1.

£. s. d.	lb.oz.dw.gr.	T. c. qr.lb.	Yds.f.in.b.c.
25,7,6¼	57,5,12,16	2,13,3,14	37,2,3,1
×4	×5	×6	×7

Yds.qr.na.	G.qt.pt.	A. r. p.	D. h. m. sec.	° ′ ″
56,3,2	28,3,1	26,3,36	57,51,14,45	30,16,20
×8	×9	×11	×12	×5

CASE 2.

£. s. d.	lb. oz. dw. gr.	T. c. qr. lb.
47,,14,,9½	39,,10,,17,,8	18,,6,,3,,15
×35	×48	×72

yds.qr.n.	T. gal.qr.	A. r. p.	D. h. m.	H. m. sec.
28,,2,,3	29,,17,,3	26,,3,,13	14,,19,,21	47,,13,,32
×56	×88	×63	×132	×144

LESSON XXX.

Division of Mixed Quantities in the Vulgar Tables.

Q. HOW *do you perform this Division?*

A. Place the parts as in Division of Whole Numbers; multiply the remainder in the division of each denomination, by the terminus of the next lower denomination, and to the product add the given quantity of that denomination for a new dividend.

F

£. s. d.	lb. oz. dw. gr.	T. c. qr. lb.
2)48,,12,,6½	3)14,,10,,3,,6	4)17,,1,,1,,14
£. 24,, 6,,3¼		

lb. oz. dr.	M. f. p.	Yds. f. in. b.c.
5)46,,12,,10	6)38,,2,,14	7)46,,0,,10,,2

Yds. qr. n.	Mo. w. d.	D. h. m. sec.	° ′ ″
8)16,,2,,2	9)48,,2,,2	12)46,,16,,12,,30	12)33,,4,,7

END OF THE FIRST PART.

The American Accomptant, &c.

PART II.

LESSON I.

COMMUTATION, IN GENERAL.

Q. WHAT *is* Commutation?

A. It is the changing of numbers or quantities of one or more denominations, into others of different denominations, but of the same value.

Q. *How is Commutation generally distributed?*

A. Into Reduction* and Consolidation; and each of these again into those *direct* and *indirect*.

Q. *What is* Reduction?

A. Changing greater names into smaller, as pounds into shillings, dollars into dimes, days into hours, &c.

Q. *What is* Consolidation?

A. It is the reverse of Reduction, or changing small-

* *The old division of this rule into* Reduction ascending *and* Reduction descending, *is discarded as an abuse of language: The first of these is a* self-contradiction, *and the latter a mere* tautology: *The one is* descending upward, *and the other* descending downward.

er names into greater, as ſhillings into pounds, cents into dollars; or a lower into a higher currency, as that of the State of New-York into the lawful money of New-England.

Q. *What is Commutation* direct?

A. It is either reducing or conſolidating any given ſum or quantity into other names of the ſame Table, as pounds into ſhillings, or ſhillings into pounds; dollars into cents, and cents into dollars, &c.

Q. *What is Commutation* indirect?

A. It is changing a given quantity in any table of currency, weight or meaſure, into the denominations of a different table—as changing Avoirdupoiſe into Troy weight, Liquid into Dry meaſure, lawful money of New England into federal money, and the reverſe.

LESSON II.

REDUCTION DIRECT.

Q. WHAT *is the general rule of performing* direct *Reduction?*

A. RULE. Multiply the higheſt denomination given by the terminus of the next lower denomination, adding to the product the given quantity of that denomination: This product multiply by the terminus of the next lower denomination, adding as before; and repeat the ſame proceſs until the whole is reduced to the denomination required.

EXAMPLES *in each Table.*

1. Reduce £15,,12,,8½ into farthings.

Terminus of ſhill.	×20
	312
Term. of pence,	×12
	3752
Term. of farth.	×4
Anſwer,	15010

2. In £127,,15,,4 how many pence and groats?

Anſwer, 28984 *pence:* 7246 *groats.*

Note. *The Commutation of Federal Money might naturally be placed under the head of this Lesson: but as it affords some curious and distinguishing rules, and is soon to be the universal Currency of the United States, it is judged best to reserve it as the subject of a distinct Lesson.*

Troy Weight.

lb. oz. dw. gr.

3. Reduce 15,,7,,16,,12 of gold into grains.

Term. of oz. ×12

187

Term. of dw. ×20

3756

Term. of gr. ×24

Ans. 90156 *grains.*

Explanation.

15×12+7=187: 187×20+16=3756: 3756×24+12=90156, the number of grains in *lb.* 15,,7,,16,,12.

Avoirdupois Weight.

T. c. qr. lb.

4. Reduce 25,,17,,3,,15, into ounces.

Term. of cwt. ×20

517

Term. of qr. ×4

2071

Term. of lb. ×28

58003

Term. of oz. ×16

Ans. 928048 *ounces.*

Explanation.

25×20+17=517: 517×4+3=2071: 2071×28+15=58003: 58003×16=928048 ounces.

Apothecary Weight.

lb. ℥ ʒ ℈ *gr.*

5. In 7,,3,,1,,2,,11 how many grains. *Anſ.* 41871.

℥ × 12

87

ʒ × 8

697

℈ × 3

2093

gr. × 20

Anſ. 41871 *grains.*

Explanation.

$\overbrace{7\times 12}+3=87$: $\overbrace{87\times 8}+1=697$: $\overbrace{697\times 3}+2=2093$: $\overbrace{2093\times 20}+11=41871$ grains.

Long Measure.

6. In 75 miles, how many barley-corns?

Term. of r. × 320

24000

T. of f. × 16½

384000

12000

396000

of in. × 12

4752000

of b.c. × 3

Anſ. 14256000 *barley-corns.*

Explanation.

$\overbrace{75\times 320}=24000$ rods: $\overbrace{24000\times 16\frac{1}{2}}$ 396000 feet: $\overbrace{396000\times 12}=4752000$ inches: $\overbrace{4752000\times 3}=14256000$ *b. c.*

CLOTH MEASURE.

Yds qr.na.

7. In 17,,3,,3 how many nails?

Term. of qr. × 4

71

Term. of na. × 4

Ans. 287 *nails.*

LAND MEASURE.

8. In 45 acres, how many square inches?

Term. of r. × 160

7200

in. in a r. × 198

Ans. 1425600 *inches.*

LIQUID MEASURE.

9. A general, upon a field day, gave a puncheon of spirits to his soldiers, to drink his health: it was dealt out in the quantity of half a jill to a man: What was the number of the brigade? *Ans.* 2560 *men.*

DRY MEASURE.

10. A merchant paid out £86,,13,,4 for 325 bushels of wheat: How much did he give ℔ pint?

Ans. 1 *penny per pint.*

TIME.

11. How many seconds in a year, consisting of 365 days, 5 hours, 48 minutes and 55 seconds?

Ans. 30956935.

12. How many hours since the nativity of Christ, to the present hour?

MOTION.

13. How many seconds are contained in the twelve signs of the Zodiac? *Ans.* 129600.

14. A certain city was laid out in a ſquare form, interſected by 13 ſtreets, at right angles, into ſmall ſquares; each ſquare contained 2 acres of ground; each quarter acre an houſe, and each houſe 7 perſons: What was the number of ſquares, of acres, of houſes, and of people. *Anſ.* 144 *ſquares,* 288 *acres,* 2304 *houſes, and* 16128 *people.*

LESSON III.

CONSOLIDATION DIRECT.

Q. WHAT *is* direct *Conſolidation?*

A. It is changing a given ſum or quantity, of a ſmaller, into a *larger* name of the *ſame* Table; as pence into pounds, days into years, &c.

Q, *What is the rule of operation?*

A. RULE. 1. Divide the given number by the *terminus* of its denomination; that quotient by the *terminus* of the next higher denomination, and ſo on, until you arrive to the denomination required; obſerving that the quotient riſes one denomination higher at every diviſion made. Or,

2. Divide the given ſum or quantity by the *grand terminus* of its denomination, *viz.* that number which makes an unit in the denomination required: the quotient is the anſwer; and the remainder, if any, muſt be conſolidated according to the other rule, it being of the ſame denomination as the dividend, or given quantity.

Q. *How is the grand terminus found?*

A. By multiplying all the intermediate *termini* together; or, in other words, finding how many in the denomination of the given quantity, make *one* in the higher denomination required.

EXAMPLES.

1. Consolidate 15010 farthings into pounds.

Rule 1.

```
4)15010(
 ------
12) 3752½ pence.
 ------
20) 31|2 shill. & 8 d.
 ------
Ans. £15,,12,,8½
```

Rule 2.

```
G.t.96|0)1501|0(£15,12,8½
        ----
         541
        ----
         610
        ×20
        ----
96|0)1220|0(12
        ----
         260
        ----
          68
        ×12 &c.
```

2. How many pounds are contained in 89916 grains of gold? *Ans.* 15*lb.* 7*oz.* 6*dwt.* 12 *gr.*

3. In 27856*lb. Avoirdupoise*, how many tons? *A.* 12*T.* 8*cwt.* 2*qrs.* 24*lb.*

4. In 8145*lb.* of wheat, how many bushels, allowing 60*lb* to a bushel? *A.* 135*bush.* & 3*pecks.*

5. Reckoning the aforesaid quantity of wheat at 1 penny 3 farthings per *lb.* how much is it per *bush.* and what is the price of the whole?
A. 8/9 *per bush.* and £59,,7,,9¾ *price of the whole.*

6. In 41871 grains, Apothecary weight, how many pounds? *A.* 7*lb.* 3℥ 1ʒ 2℈ 11*gr.*

7. How many miles are contained in 14256000 barley-corns? *Ans.* 75.

8. In 12376 nails of cloth, how many yards? *A.* 773½ *yards.*

9. In 2560 quarts, how many puncheons? *Ans.* 8.

10. In 59752 quarts, how many bushels, *U. S.* measure, and how many of *Canada* measure?
A. 1867*bush.* 1*peck*, U. S. *measure*:
1493*bush.* 4*pecks*, Can. *ditto.*

11. If a man travels 13246 miles in 225360 min-

utes, improving only 12 hours in a day; what progreſs does he make in a minute; how many hours is he on horſeback, and how many days employed in performing the journey?

A. He progreſſes 18 *rods*, 13 *feet*, $4\frac{1392}{22536}$ *inches* per *min.* He is 3756 hours on horſeback, and is 313 days performing the journey.

LESSON IV.

INDIRECT COMMUTATION, *in general.*

Q. WHAT *is the general rule of operation?*

A. The general rule which applies in all caſes of exchange, between any two different tables of mixed quantities, is founded upon the reciprocal proportion exiſting between the particular kind of currency, weight or meaſure of the given ſum or quantity, and that into which it is to be changed. From the ſame principle alſo ſpring all the particular rules, which, for the benefit of ſhortening the work, may be applied in certain caſes.

Having found this reciprocal proportion, in as ſmall whole numbers as the proportion will admit, it being perhaps as 2 to 5, or 3 to 4, or 1 to 6, or whatever the proportion may be; then, if the operation be *Reduction*, or in the deſcending line of exchange, take the following

GENERAL RULE.

Multiply the given ſum or quantity by the larger proportional number, and divide that product by the ſmaller. If the ſmaller proportional number lack but *one* of the larger, then divide the given quantity by the ſmaller, and add the quotient to the dividend. If the ſmaller be a ſingle unit, then you have only to multiply by the larger.

For the reverse, or CONSOLIDATION.

Multiply by the smaller proportional, and divide by the larger. If the difference between them be but 1, then divide the given quantity by the larger, and subtract the quotient from the dividend. If the smaller be a single unit, then you have only to divide by the larger.

Give Examples under each branch of the aforementioned Rules.

1. REDUCTION.

1. Let it be required to change 75 English ells into ells Flemish.

Here the proportion being as 3 to 5, therefore

Multiply 75
by 5

Divide by 3)375(

Ans. 125 *Flemish ells.*

2. Reduce 56 bushels of wheat, *Canada* measure, into bushels of the *U. S.* *The proportion is as* 4 *to* 5.

4)56(
×14

Ans. 70 *bush. U. S.*

3. Reduce 39 Spanish milled dollars into pistareens. *Proportion* 1 *to* 5.

39
×5

Ans. 195 *pistareens.*

2. CONSOLIDATION.

1. Change 125 ells Flemish into English ells.

```
      125
      ×3
      ---
    5)375(
      ---
Ans.  75  English ells.
```

2. Change 70 bushels *U. S.* into *Canada* bushels.

```
  5)70(
  —14
   —
Ans. 56 Bush. Can.
```

3. In 195 pistareens, how many Spanish dollars.

```
  5)195(
    ---
Ans. 39 Span. doll.
```

Note. *Further Examples may be seen, under the particular Rules, in the following Lessons.*

LESSON V.

The mutual Exchange between each and all the various Money Currencies of *Pounds, Shillings* and *Pence.*

SECT. 1.

STERLING MONEY *exchanged.*

Q. HOW *do you reduce Sterling Money into Irish Money?*

A. RULE. Add one twelfth part.

```
Reduce £100 S. into I. m.       Reduce £49,,18,,8
   12)100, 00, 00                  12)49,,18,, 8
       +8.. 6,, 8                     +4,, 3.. 2½
Ans. £108,, 6,, 8              Ans. £54,, 1,,10½
```

Q. *How do you reduce Sterling into Halifax money?*

A. Rule. Add one *ninth* part. If the given sum be pounds simply, only annex a cypher, and divide by 9.

Reduce £100
9)1000(

Ans. £111,,2,,2½

Reduce £54,,4,,6
9)54,,4,,6(
+6,,0,,6

£60,,5,,0

Q. *How do you reduce Sterling money into the currency of* South-Carolina *and* Georgia?

A. Rule. Add one *twenty seventh* part.

Reduce £100,,00,,0
27)100 (+3,,10,,4½

19 A. 103,,10,,4½
×20

27)380(10
10

×12

27)120(4

12
×4

27)48(1

(21)

Reduce £175,,15,,9
27)175,,15,,9(+6,,10,,2

13 A. 182,, 5,,11
×20

27)275(10

5
×12

27)60(2

(6)

Note. *In the above Examples, the common divisor and the quotient figures are repeatedly expressed: this is only for the sake of greater perspicuity, but is unnecessary to the practitioner.*

Q. *How do you reduce Sterling money into the currency of New-Hampshire, Massachusetts, Rhode-Island, Connecticut, Virginia, Vermont and Kentucky?*

A. Rule. Add *one third.*

Reduce £100 *Sterling.*	Reduce £27,,19,,6 *Sterl.*
3)100(+33,,6,,8	+9,, 6,,6
Anſ. £133,,6,,8	*Anſ.* £37,, 6,,0

Q. *How do you reduce Sterling money into the currency of New-Jerſey, Pennſylvania, Delaware and Maryland currency?*

A. Rule. Multiply the given ſum in Sterling money by 5, and divide the product by 3.

Reduce £100 *Sterling.* to *New-Jerſey,* &c.	Reduce £55,,14,,10 *Sterl.*
100	×5
×5	3)278,,14,, 2
3)500(	*Anſ.* £92,,14,, 0½
Anſ. £166,,13,,4	

Q. *What is the rule of reducing Sterling money into the currency of New York and North-Carolina?*

A. Rule. Multiply by 16, and divide the product by 9.

Reduce £100 *Sterl.* to *New-York,* &c. currency.	Reduce £44,, 4,,4 *Sterl.*
100	×16
×16	9)707,, 9,,4
9)1600	*Anſ.* £78,,12,,1¼
Anſ. £177,,15,,6½	

SECT. 2.

Irish Money *exchanged.*

Q. *How do yon change Iriſh into Sterling money?*

A. Rule. From the given ſum deduct *one thirteenth* part.

Consolidate £100 *Irish* money into *Sterling*.

13)100
—7,,13,,10

Ans. £92,, 6,, 2

Consol. £54,, 1,,10½ *Irish.*

13)54,, 1,,10½
—4,, 3,, 2½

Ans. £49,,18,, 8

Q. *How do you change Irish into Halifax money?*

A. Rule. Add *one thirty-ninth* part to the given sum.

Reduce £100 *Irish*, into *Halifax* money.

39) 100 (2,,11,,3¼
+100

£102,,11,,3¼ *Answer.*

Q. *How do you reduce Irish money into the currency of South-Carolina and Georgia?*

A. Rule. Multiply by 112, and divide the product by 117.

Reduce £100 *Irish* into *S. Carolina* & *Georgia* cur.

100×112=11200
117)11200(£.95,14,6 $\frac{42}{117}$

670

85
20

)1700(

530

62 &c.

Reduce £35,,7,,4 *Irish*, into *S. Car.* &c. currency.

Ans. 33,,17,,1 $\frac{27}{117}$

Q. *What is the rule of reducing Irish money into the currency of New-Hampshire, Massachusetts, &c.?*

A. Rule. Multiply by 16, and divide the product by 13.

Reduce 100*l.* *Irish* into into L. M. of *N. E.*

100
×16
13)1600(*Ans.* 123,,1,,6

Reduce 184,,13,,4 *Irish.*

184,,13,,4
×4×4=16
738,,13,,4
×4
13)2954,,13,,4(
Ans. 227,, 5,,9

Q. *By what method is the value of any sum in Irish money found, in the currency of New-Jersey, Pennsylvania, Delaware and Maryland?*

A. Rule. Multiply it by 20, and divide the product by 13.

Reduce £100 *Irish* into *New-Jersey*, &c. currency.

100
×20
13) 2000(
Ans. 153,,12,,3½

Reduce £48,,15,,3 *Irish.*

48,,15,,3
×5×4=20
243,,16,,3
×4
13)975,, 5,,0
Ans. 75,, 0,,4

Q. *How do you reduce Irish money into the currency of New-York and North-Carolina?*

A. Rule. Multiply the given Irish sum by 64, and divide the product by 39.

Reduce £100 *Irish* into *New-York*, &c. currency.

```
   100
  ×64
  ----
39)6400( Anf. 164,,2
   ---
   250
   ---
   160
   ---
     4
   ×20 &c.
```

Reduce £87,,14,,2 *Irish*.

```
        87,,14,,2
          ×8×8=64
      -----------
       701,,13,,4
               ×8
      -----------
39)5613,, 6,,8(
   ---
   117
    153
    ---  Anf.143,,18,,10
     36
    ×20 &c.
```

SECT. 3.

Halifax Money exchanged.

Q. *How do you change Halifax money into Sterling?*

A. Rule. Deduct one tenth part from the Halifax sum.

Consolidate £100 Halifax into Sterling money.

```
   10)100
     —10
     ---
Anf. 90
     ==
```

Consolidate 60*l.* 5*s.* Halifax into Sterling money.

```
   10)60,,5
     —6,,0,,10
     ---------
Anf. 54,,4,, 2
     ========
```

Q. *How is Halifax money changed into Irish money?*

A. Rule. Deduct one fortieth part.

Change 100*l.* Halifax into Irish money.

```
   4|0)10|0
     —2,,10
     ------
Anf. 97,,10
     ======
```

Consolidate 320*l.* 15*s.* 8*d.* Halifax.

```
40)430,,15,,8(—8,,00,,4¾
              ----------
         Anf. 312,,15,,3¼
              ===========
```

Q. *How do you consolidate this currency into South-Carolina and Georgia currency?*

Rule. Subtract a fifteenth part.

Change 100*l.* Halifax into South-Carolina, &c.

15)100
—6,, 8
———
Ans. 93,, 12
==

Change 125*l.* 15*s.* Halifax.

125,, 15
15)125,, 15(—8,, 9
—
6 *Ans.* 118,, 6
20 &c. ===

Q. *How do you reduce Halifax money into the currency of New-Hampshire, Massachusetts, &c. currency.*

Rule. Add one fifth part.

Reduce 100*l.* Halifax into L. M. of N. E.

5)100
+20
——
Ans. 120
==

Reduce £87,, 15,, 10
+17,, 11,, 2
———
Ans. 105,, 7,, 0
====

Q. *Give the rule of reducing Halifax money into N. Jersey, Pennsylvania and Maryland currency.*

Rule. To the given sum add one half.

Reduce 100*l.* Halifax to N. Jersey, &c. currency.

2)100
+50
——
Ans. 150
==

Reduce £327,, 19,, 8
+163,, 19,, 10
———
Ans. 491,, 19, 6
====

Q. *What is the method of changing Halifax money into the currency of New-York and North-Carolina?*

Rule. Multiply by 8, and divide the product by 5.

Reduce 100*l.* Halifax to N. Y. &c. currency.

100
×8
5)800(
Anſ. 160

Reduce £157,,17,,7
×8
5)1263,, 0,,8
Anſ. 252,,12,,1½

SECT. 4.

SOUTH CAROLINA *and* GEORGIA *Currency exchanged.*

Q. *What is the method of conſolidating this currency into Sterling money?*

RULE. From the given ſum ſubtract one twenty-eighth part.

Change 100*l.* S. Carolina into Sterling money.

28)100
—3,,11,,5
Anſ. 96,, 8,,7

Conſolidate £182,, 5,,11 S. Carolina.
—6,,10,, 2
Anſ. 175,,15,,9

Q. *How do you change South-Carolina, &c. currency into Iriſh money?*

RULE. Multiply the given ſum by 117, and divide the product by 112.

Reduce 100*l.* S. Carol. into Iriſh money.

100×117=11700
112)11700(104,,9,,3 *Anſ.*
500
52
20
)1040(
32
×12 &c.

Reduce £33,,17,,1 S. Car.
37,,17,,1
×9×13=117
304,,13,,9
×13
112)3960,,18,,9(35,,7,,3
600
40
×20 &c.

Q. *How do you change South-Carolina, &c. currency, into Halifax money?*

Rule. Add one fourteenth part.

Reduce 100*l.* S. Carol.

```
        100
14)100(+7,,2,,10
      ----------
      107,,2,,10 A.
      ==========
```

Reduce £118,, 6

```
14)118,,6(+8,, 9
         -------
   Anf. 126,,15
        =======
```

Q. *How do you reduce South-Carolina, &c. currency, into the lawful money of New-England?*

Rule. Multiply the given fum by 9, and divide by 7.

Reduce 100*l.* S. Carol. into L. M. of N. E.

```
 100
×9
 ----
7)900(128,,11,,5 Anf.
      ==========
```

Reduce £132,,13,,4

```
           ×9
  ---------------
7)1194,,0,,0(
  ---------------
Anf. 170,,11,,5
     ==========
```

Q. *How do you reduce this currency into that of New-Jerfey, &c.?*

Rule. Multiply by 45, and divide the product by 28.

Reduce £100 S. Carol.

```
 100×45=4500
28)4500(196,,8,,7 Anf.
   --   ==========
  270
  ---
  180
  ---
   12
  ×20
  ---
  )240(
```

Reduce £234,, 5,,6

```
          ×9×5=45
   ---------------
   2111,,11,,6
           ×5
   ---------------
28)10557,,27,,6(
   ---------------
Anf. 377,, 1,,3
     ==========
```

Q. *How do you reduce the currency of South-Carolina and Georgia into that of New-York and North-Carolina?*

Rule. Multiply by 12, and divide by 7.

Reduce 100*l.* S. Carol. into N. Y. &c. currency.

100 × 12 = 1200

7)1200(

Anf. 171,,8,,6¼

Reduce £125,,15,,5
×12

7)1509,, 5,,0(

Anf. 215,,12,,1

SECT. 5.

LAWFUL MONEY *of* NEW ENGLAND *exchanged.*

Q. *How do you confolidate this currency into Sterling money?*

RULE. From the given fum fubtract one fourth part.

Confolidate 100*l.* N. E. into Sterling money.

4)100
—25

Anf. 75

Confolidate £37,,6

4)37,,6
—9,, 6,,6

Anf. 27,,19,,6

Q. *How is this currency changed into Irifh money?*

RULE. Multiply the given fum by 13, and divide the product by 16.

Change 100*l.* N. H. &c. into Irifh money.

100 × 13 = 1300

16)1300(81,,5 *Anf.*

20

4

×20 &c.

Change £227,, 5,,9 N.H.

227,, 5,,9
×13

16)2953,,14,,9(184,,11,,3

135

73 &c.

Q. *How do you change the currency of New-Hampfhire, Maffachufetts, &c. into Halifax money?*

RULE. From the given fum deduct one fixth part.

Change 100*l.* N. E.

6)100(
—16,,13,,4

Anf. 83,, 6,,8

Confolidate £105,, 7

6)105,,7 (—17,,11,, 2

Anf. 87,,15,,10

Q. *How do you change this currency into S. Carolina, &c. currency?*

RULE. Multiply the given sum by 7, and divide by 9.

Change 100*l.* N. E. into S. Carol. &c. currency.	Change £170,,11,, 5 N. E.
9)700=100×7	×7
	9)1193,,19,,11
Ans. 77,,15,,6	*Ans.* 132,,13,, 4

Q. *How do you change the currency of N. Hampshire, &c. into the currency of N. Jersey, Pennsylvania, &c.?*

RULE. To the given sum add one quarter.

Reduce 100*l.* N. E. into N. Jersey, &c.	Reduce £247,,14,, 4
100÷4=25:100+25=125	¼ is +61,,18,, 7
Ans. 125	*Ans.* 309,,12,,11

Q. *How do you reduce N. Hampshire, &c. currency, into that of N. York and North Carolina?*

RULE. To the given sum add its one third part.

Reduce 100*l.* N. E. into N. York, &c. currency.	Reduce £95,,13,,8
3)100	3)95,,13,, 8
+33,,6,,8	+31,,17,,10½
Ans. 133,,6,,8	*Ans.* 127,,11,, 6½

SECT. 6.

The Currency of NEW-JERSEY, PENNSYLVANIA, DELAWARE *and* MARYLAND, *exchanged.*

Q. *How do you consolidate this Currency into Sterling money?*

RULE. Multiply the given sum by 3, and divide the product by 5.

Change 100*l.* N. J. into Ster. ×3

5)300

Anf. 60

Change £322,,18,,9 N. J. ×3

5)968,,16,,3

Anf. 193,,15,,3

Q. *How do you confolidate this currency into Irifh money?*

RULE. Multiply the given fum by 13, and divide the product by 20.

Change 100*l.* N. J. &c. currency into Irifh money.

2|0)130|0=100 ×13

Anf. 65

Confol. £75,,00,,5 N. J. ×13

2|0)975,, 5,,5

Anf. 48,,15,, $3\frac{1}{4}$

Q. *How do you confolidate N. Jerfey, &c. currency, into Halifax money?*

RULE. From the given fum fubtract one third part.

Change 100*l.* N. J. &c. into Halifax money.

3)100

−33,, 6,,8

Anf. 66,,13,,4

Confol. £491,,19,, 6

3)491,,19,,6(−163,,19,,10

Anf. 327,,19,, 8

In what manner do you confolidate the currency of N. Jerfey, &c. into the currency of N. Hampfhire, &c.?

RULE. From the given fum fubtract one fifth part.

Change 100*l.* N. J. &c. currency, into L. M. of N. E.

5(100

−20

Anf. 80

Confol. £309,,12,,11 N. J.

−61,,18,, 6

Anf. 247,,14,, 4

In what manner do you reduce N. Jersey, &c. currency, into that of N. York and N. Carolina?

RULE. To the given sum add one fifteenth part.

Change 100*l.* N. J. cur. into that of N.Y. & N.C.

15)100
+6,,8
Ans. 106,,8

Reduce £119,,19,, 9 N.J.
15)119,,19,,9(+7,,19,,11¼
Ans. 127,,19,, 8¾

SECT. 7.

NEW-YORK *and* N. CAROLINA *Currency exchanged.*

Q. *In what manner do you consolidate this currency into Sterling money?*

RULE. Multiply the given sum by 9, and divide the product by 16.

Change 100*l.* N.Y, &c. into Sterling money.

100
×9
16)900(56,,5 *Ans.*

Consol. £78,,12,,2 N. Y.
×9
16)707,, 9,,6
Ans. 44,, 4,,4

In what manner do you change N. York and N. Carolina currency into Irish money.

RULE. Multiply the given sum by 39, and divide the product by 64.

Change 100*l.* N. Y. &c. into Irish money.

100
×39
64)3900(60,,18,,9 *Ans.*
60
20 &c.

Conf. £143,,18,,10 N. Y.
143,,18,,10
×3×13=39
431,,16,, 6
×13
64)5613,,14,, 6(87,,14,,3 *Ans.*

How do you change N. York, &c. currency, into Halifax money?

RULE. Multiply the given ſum by 5, and divide the product by 8.

Change 100*l.* N. Y. cur. into Halifax money.

8)500=100×5

Anſ. 62,,10

Conſ. £252,,12,, 2 N.Y.
×5

8)1263..00..10

Anſ. 157,,17,, 7¼

Q. *How do you conſolidate the currency of New-York and N. Carolina into that of S. Carolina and Georgia?*

RULE. Multiply the given ſum by 7, and divide the product by 12.

Change 100*l.* N. Y. &c. cur. into S. Carol. &c.

12)700=100×7

Anſ. 58,,6,,8

Conſol. £215,,12,,2 N.Y.
×7

12)1509,, 6,,2

Anſ. 125,,15,,6

Q. *How do you conſolidate N. York, &c. currency, into that of N. Hampſhire, Maſſachuſetts, &c.?*

RULE. From the given ſum deduct one quarter.

Change 100*l.* N. Y. into L. M. of N. E.

4)100
−25

Anſ. 75

Conſol. £127,,11,,6 N.Y.
1 *quarter* −31,,15,,4½

Anſ. 95,,16.1½

Q. *How do you conſolidate New-York, &c. currency, into New Jerſey, &c. currrency?*

RULE. Deduct one ſixteenth part.

Change 100*l.* N.Y. &c. into N. J. &c. currency.

16)100
−6,, 5

Anſ. 93,,15

Conſol. £127,,19,, 9
1 *ſixteenth* −7,,19,,11¼

Anſ. 119,,19,, 9¼

LESSON VI.

The Exchange between the ſeveral Tables of *Weights* and *Meaſures*.

SECT. 1.

AVOIRDUPOIS & TROY WEIGHT *exchanged.*

Q. HOW *do you change Avoirdupois weight into Troy weight?*

RULE. Take the given weight in one denomination, either pounds, ounces, or drams.

If in pounds, multiply them by 175 and divide the product by 144, and the quotient will be Pounds Troy;

If in ounces, multiply by 175 and divide by 192: the qnotient will be Troy ounces;

If in drams, multiply by 875, and divide by 768, and the quotient will be *penny weights.*

To reverſe the operation, or to bring Troy into Avoirdupois weight, you have only to exchange the Multiplier and the Diviſor and proceed as before.

EXAMPLES.

Change 56 *lb.* 12 *oz.* Avoirdupois into Troy weight.

```
     ×16
     ———
     908 oz.
    ×175
    ———— Tr.oz.  lb.  oz. dw.gr.
192)158900(827 = 68  11..12..2  Anſ.
    ——————       ============
     1530
     ————
     1460
     ————
      116
     × 0
     ————
    )2320(12 &c.
```

The Reverse.

Change 68*lb.* 11 *oz.* 12 *dw.* 2 *gr.* Troy weight, into Avoirdupois ?

NOTE. In changing Troy grains into Avoirdupois weight, you have only to divide by 7000. Thus, 68 *lb.* 11 *oz.* 12 *dw.* 2 *gr* =397250 *gr.*

7|000,397|250(56 *lb.* 12 *oz.* *Ans.*

5250
×16

)84|000(12

SECT. 2.

VULGAR & FEDERAL AVOIRDUPOIS *exchanged.*

Q. *What is the Rule.*

RULE. Pounds being the same in both tables, the exchange is only between the ounces and drams; therefore to change ounces of the vulgar into those of the federal table, multiply them by 10, and divide the product by 16—to exchange them back, multiply by 16 and divide by 10.

EXAMPLES.

Q. *What is the value of* 8 *oz. Avoird. in Fed. Avoird ?*

8
×10

16 80(5 *oz.* *Ans.*

Reverse the operation. 5 *oz.* *Fed. Avoird.*

×16

10)80(8 *oz.* *Vulg. Avoird.*

SECT. 3.

AVOIRDUPOIS *and* FEDERAL TROY *or* AMERICAN WEIGHT *exchanged.*

Q. *What is the Rule ?*

RULE. Change them by making use of the following numbers, as Multipliers and Divisors, *viz.*

	Mult.	Div.	
For Avoirdupois pounds,	70	27	
ditto ounces,	175	108	
ditto drams,	4375	432	*quot. gr.*
In changing Federal Troy Pounds,	27	70	
ditto ounces,	108	175	
ditto penny wt.	864	875	*drams*
ditto grains,	432	4375	*Avoird.*

EXAMPLES.

Change 1 Ton into Federal Troy weight.

1 Ton=2240 *lb.*

×70

	lb.	*oz.*	*dw.*	*gr.*	
27)156800(	5807 .	4 .	0 .	$7\frac{11}{27}$	*Ans.*

218

200

(11)

Change 5807*lb.* 4*oz.* 0*dw.* 7*gr.*$\frac{11}{27}$ Fed. Troy into Avoird.

$5807.407\frac{11}{27}$

27

7|0)15680|0.000

2240 *lb.*=80 *qrs.*=20 *cwt.*=1 *Ton.* *Ans.*

SECT. 4.

VULGAR *and* FEDERAL TROY WEIGHT *exchanged.*

Q. *What is the Rule?*

RULE. To change the vulgar into federal Troy weight, take the given weight in grains, annex a cypher, and divide by 27: the quotient will be Federal Troy weight, and of the same denomination.

2. To change federal into vulgar Troy weight, take the given weight in grains, multiply it by 27, point

off the right hand figure of the product, and the rest will be grains in Vulgar Troy.

EXAMPLES.

Change 57*lb.* 10*oz.* 8*dw.* 3*gr.* into Federal Troy weight.

```
×12           27)3333150(123450 grains.
                              lb. oz. dw.
---            --
694            63             123 . 3 . 5 Anf.
 ×20           --             ===========
----           93
13888          --
  ×24          121
-----          ---
333315         135 &c.
```

The Reverse.

Change 123*lb.* 4*oz.* 5*dw.* federal, into vulgar Troy weight.

```
123450
  ×27
-------
33331|50           lb. oz. dw.gr.
333315 grains =    57,,10,,8,,3
                   ============
```

SECT. 5.

FEDERAL AVOIRDUPOIS *and* FEDERAL TROY *exchanged.*

Q. *What is the Rule?*

RULE. To change federal Avoirdupois into federal Troy weight, multiply the given weight, in pounds, by 70, and divide the product by 27.

To change the other way, multiply by 27, and divide by 70.

EXAMPLES.

Change 100*lb.* fed. Avoird. into fed. Troy weight.

```
100×70=7000   lb. oz. dw. gr.
   27)7000( 259   2 . 5 . 9 7/27 Fed. Troy. Anf.
      --    ===============
      160
      ---
      250
      ---
       (7)
```

lb. oz. dw. gr.
Change 259 . 2 . 5 . 9 $\frac{7}{27}$ Federal Troy.
259 . 259 $\frac{7}{27}$
×27

7|0)700|0 . 000

100 *lb.* Fed. Avoird. *Anſ.*

SECT. 6.

Vulgar Troy *and* Federal Avoirdupois Wieght *exchanged.*

Q. *What is the Rule?*

		Mult.	Div.
Rule. Change	pounds *vulg.* Troy, by	144	175
	Ounces *ditto* by	24	35
	Penny weights into drams	12	35
	Grains into drams	1	70
Change	pounds *fed.* Avoird.	175	144
	Ounces into ounces	35	24
	Drams into grains	70	1

Examples.

Change 100*lb. vulg.* Troy into *fed.* Avoirdupois weight.

100×144=14400 *lb. oz. dr.*
175)14400(82 . 2 . 8 *Anſ.*
400
500
1500
(100)

Change 100*lb.* federal Avoirdupois into vulgar Troy weight.

100×175=17500 *lb. oz. dw. gr.*

144)17500(121 . 6 . 6 . 16

310

220

76

×12 &c.

NOTE. Apothecary weight *is not particularly consider-ed in this Lesson, because* grains *in the vulgar table are precisely of the value with those in the vulgar table of Troy weight.*

SECT. 7.

VULGAR & FEDERAL LIQUID MEASURE *exchanged.*

Q *What is the Rule?*

RULE. To change the former into the latter, reduce the given weight to gallons, which are the same in both tables—then point off the first right hand figure for gallons, the second for federal Barrels, and the rest, if any, are Hogsheads.

2. To reverse the exchange—fill the denominations of Barrels and Gallons with Cyphers, if significant figures are wanting; you have, then, only to remove all the separating points, and the exchange is made.

EXAMPLES.

Change 15 *Hhds.* 1 *Bar.* 15 gallons and an half into federal Liquid Measure.

15
×63

945 gall.
1 Bar. = $31\frac{1}{2}$
Gall. $15\frac{1}{2}$

Hhds.bar.gall.

992 gall. =9 . 9 . 2 *fed. liq. meas.*

Change 9 *Hhds.* 3 Bar. and 2 gallons federal, into vulgar liquid measure.

Hhds. bar. gal.
9. 9. 2 *Hhds, bar. gal.*
992 gal. = 15,,1,,15½ *Vulg. Liq. mea. Anf.*

LESSON VII.

Direct REDUCTION of Federal Money, and the other Federal Tables of *Mixed Quantities.*

Q. WHAT *is the general Rule of direct Reduction in all the Federal Tables.*

RULE. Remove the feparating points, and read all the denominations, as one fimple whole number.—This reduces the given quantity into the loweft denomination which it expreffes—If a lower reduction be required, exprefs the remaining denominations by annexing as many Cyphers.

EXAMPLES.

Reduce 24.7.5.6 into Mills.

Anf. 24756 Mills

Reduce 24 into Dimes, Cents & Mills

Anf. 240
2400
24000

Q. *What if any of the middle denominations in the given fum be wanting, as 5 Dollars and 5 Mills?*

A. Fill each and all of the vacant denominations with Cyphers; thus 5.00.5 and then reduce as before.

Viz. 5005

EXAMPLES of DIRECT REDUCTION *in the other* FEDERAL TABLES.

lb. oz. dw. gr.
Reduce 3. 7. 6. 5 into ounces, into penny weights and into grains.

lb. 3 . 7 . 6 . 5 *Anſ.*
oz. 37 . 6 . 5
dw. 376 . 5
gr. 3765

cwt. C. lb. oz. dr.
Reduce 6 . 5 . 43 . 2 . 1 into *cwt.* pounds, *oz.* & *dr.*
Anſ. C. 65 . 43 . 2 . 1
lb. 6543 . 2 . 1
oz. 65432 . 1
dr. 654321

lb. ℥ ʒ ℈ *gr.*
Reduce 3 . 4 . 0 . 9 . 2 into ounces, into *dr.* into ſcr. & [into grains.
Anſ. 34 . 0 . 9 . 2
340 . 9 . 2
3409 . 2
34092

Hhds. B. gal. pts.
Reduce 9 . 9 . 2 . 5 into barrels, gallons, & points.
Anſ. 99 . 2 . 5
992 . 5
9925

G. gr. gr. doz. part.
Reduce 3 . 4 . 5 . 6 into all the lower denominations.
Anſ. 34 . 5 . 6
3 . 45 . 6 N.B. There is no *direct* Reduction
3456 nor Conſolidation, in the Federal tables of Cloth & of Dry Meaſure.

LESSON VIII.
Direct CONSOLIDATION of Federal *Mixed Quantities.*

Q. WHAT *is the general Rule of operation?*

RULE. From the higheſt given denomination, point off, figure by figure, as many figures upon the right hand, as that denomination is below the denomination sought or required; and these figures thus pointed off will be the lower denominations in their just order.— If you omit *Dimes* in the Table of Federal Money, then point off two figures for *Cents*.

EXAMPLES.

Confolidate 57964 Mills into all the higher denominations.

Anf. //5796.4
579.6.4
.769.6.4

This fpecimen is judged fufficient to exemplify the foregoing Rule; and alfo to fupercede the neceffity of ftating any examples of direct Confolidation, in any of the other Federal tables, inafmuch as they are all upon the fame principle, and performed in precifely the fame method.

Q. *What is the reafon or propriety of the foregoing rules of reducing and confolidating Federal quantities?*

A. Becaufe the feveral denominations in each table ftand conected by a *decimal* ratio; each denomination being a decimal integer of the next lower, and a decimal fraction of the next higher denomination.

LESSON IX.

How to change the various Currencies of Pounds, Shillings and Pence, into Federal Money.

1. STERLING MONEY.

Q. HOW *do you reduce* Sterling *into Federal money?*

RULE. If the given fum be Pounds only, multiply by 40, and divide by 9; the Quotient will be Dollars: if there be any Remainder, reduce it to the lower denominations by annexing Cyphers and dividing.

2. If the given fum confift of Pounds and Shillings, reduce it to Shillings, then double them and divide as before.

3. If there be Pounds, Shillings and Pence, reduce them to pence, and divide by 54, the number of pence in a Dollar.

EXAMPLES.

Reduce 36*l.* Sterling into Federal money.

36
×40

9)1440

Ans. $\$160$

Reduce £36,,9 into Fed. money.
×20

729
×2

9)1458(162 *Ans.*

Reduce £579,,17,,9 Ster. into Federal money.

579,,17,,9
×20

11597
×12

54)139173(2577.27.74. $\$$

311

417

393 &c.

&c.

SECT. 2.

IRISH MONEY *federalized.*

Q. *How do you reduce this currency into Federal money?*

RULE. Reduce the whole sum to half pence, and divide by 117.

EXAMPLES.

Reduce £78,,4,,6 Irish, into Federal money.

78,,4,,6
×20

1564
×12

18774
×2

37548 *Half pence.*

117(37548($\$320.923$ *Ans.*

244

108.0

27.0

36.0

(9)

SECT. 3.

HALIFAX MONEY *federalized.*

Q. *How do you reduce this currency into Federal money?*

RULE. If the given ſum be in pounds only, multiply by 4, and the product will be dollars.

If in ſhillings, divide by 5.

If in pence, divide by 60, and the quotients, in either caſe, will be dollars. The remainders, if any, reduce as in the former Sections, by annexing cyphers and continuing the diviſion.

EXAMPLES.

Reduce £45,,17,,9 Hal. into Federal money.

45,,17,,9
×20

917
×12

6|0)1101|3(183.55 *Anſ.*

Reduce £68,,14 Hal. into Federal money.

68,,14
×20

5)1374(

274.8 *Anſ.*

SECT. 4.

SOUTH CAROLINA & GEORGIA Currency *federalized.*

Q. *What is the Rule?*

RULE. If the given ſum be pounds only, multiply by 30, and divide the product by 7: the quotient will be dollars.

If there be ſhillings, or ſhillings and pence, reduce the whole to pence, and divide by 56: the quotient will be dollars.

EXAMPLES.

Reduce £349 S. Car. &c. cur. into Fed. money.

349
×30

7)10470(

1495.71.4 *Anſ.*

Reduce £765,,3,,9 S.C.

×20

15303
×12

56)183645(3279.37.5 *A.*

SECT. 5.

NEW-HAMPSHIRE, MASSACHUSETTS, CONNECTICUT, RHODE-ISLAND, VERGINIA, VERMONT *and* KENTUCKY currency, *federalized.*

Q. *How do you change this currency into federal money?*

RULE. If the ſum conſiſt of pounds only, annex a cypher and divide by 3, and if *one* remains it is // 33.83 if *two* it is //66.6.

If there be pounds, ſhillings and pence, divide the pounds by 3; take the remainder and the ſhillings in the given ſum, in ſhillings; divide them by 6, and annex the quotient figure to the quotient of the pounds, for dollars, the value of the remaining ſhillings and pence, if any, find by the table in the appendix.

EXAMPLES.

Reduce £ 157 N. E. into Federal money.

3)1570(

// 523.33.3

Reduce £ 575..17..8

3)575(1919.61 *Anſ.*

6) 57(

Remaining 3/8= // 61

DECIMAL RULE*.

Set down the ſhillings, pence, &c. in decimals of a pound; annex the left hand decimal figure to the pounds, and divide by 3, the quotient will be the federal money value complete.

---

* *The decimal rule of Commutation in this, and ſeveral of the other currencies, is of all others, the eaſieſt and beſt for the practitioner, as it ſuperſedes the uſe of a table for the ſmaller denominations. It is therefore hoped that the irregularity of anticipating decimal operations in this part of the work will be excuſed; as the learner may paſs over them, until he has firſt obtained a competent knowledge of decimal Arithmetic.*

EXAMPLES.

Reduce £ 575,,17,,8 L.M. of N. E. into federal money. 17/8 = .883 therefore

3)5758.83(

\$ 1919.61 *Ans.*

SECT. 6.

NEW-JERSEY, PENNSYLVANIA, DELAWARE & MARYLAND currency, *federalised.*

Q. *What is the Rule?*

RULE. If there be pounds only, multiply them by 8 and decide the product by 3; the quotient will be dollars.

If there be shillings, or shillings and pence, reduce the whole to pence, annex a cypher and divide by 9, the quotient will be cents; therefore point off the two right hand figures for cents, and the rest will be dollars.

EXAMPLES.

Reduce £ 345 N. J. currency into Fed. money.

345
×8

3)2760(

\$ 920 *Ans.*

Reduce £ 534,,9,,11 N. J. cur.

× 20

10689
12

9)1282790(

\$ 1425.32.2 *Ans.*

DECIMAL RULE.

Take the given sum in pounds and decimals, multiply by 8 and divide by 3; the quotient will be federal money.

Reduce £534,,19,,11 N. J.

534.996
×8

3)4279.968

\$ 1426.65.6 *Ans.*

SECT. 7.

NEW-YORK *and* NORTH-CAROLINA currency *fed.*

Q. *What is the Rule?*

RULE. If there be pounds only annex a cypher, and divide by 4, the quotient will be dollars; and if there be any remainder, (which will ever be 2) it is half a dollar, or 5 dimes.

If there be ſhillings and pence, divide the pounds as before without annexing a cypher; if there be any remainder it is pounds; reduce them to ſhillings, in your mind only, add them to the ſhillings in the given ſum, and divide them by 8. annexing the quotient figure to the former quotient, for dollars. As to the remaining pence, you may either annex a cypher to them and divide by 96, for dimes and cents; or find their federal money value in the table.

EXAMPLES.

1 Reduce £450. N. Y. currency into Fed. money.

4)4500(

$1125 *Anſ.*

2 Reduce £575 into Federal money.

4)5750

$437.50 *Anſ.*

The remainder 2 being /5 or //50.

3. Reduce £692,,12,,6 N. Y. currency into Fed. money.

8)4)692,,12,,6

1731 & 4/6 left = //56.2

Or 96)54.0 == 56.2

1731.56.2 *Anſ.*

Explanation of the 3d example. Dividing 692 by 4, the quotient is 173 without any remainder. Next divide the 12/ by 8 and the quotient figure 1 annex to 173, making $1731.

DECIMAL RULE.

The given ſum expreſſed in pounds and decimals multiply by 2.5,—the product is federal money. Take the 1ſt and 3d examples in the laſt rule.

Reduce £450 N.Y. cur.
×2.5
\$1125.0 *Ans.*

Reduce £692,,12,,6 N. Y. currency.
£692,,12,,6=692.625
×2.5
Ans. \$1731.56.25

LESSON X.

How to change Federal money into the several Currencies of Pounds, Shillings and Pence.

1. *Into* STERLING MONEY.

Q. WHAT *is the Rule?*

RULE. Multiply the given sum by 4.5 which reduces it to shillings and decimals; to change the decimals into pence, multiply them by 12, and from the product point off the same number of right hand figures; the figure or figures upon the left of the point will be pence.

EXAMPLES.

Consolidate \$183.55 into Sterling money.
183.55
×4.5
2|0)82|5.975
×12
£41,,5,,11.700 *Ans.*

Consolidate \$247.44.5
×4.5
2|0)111|3.5025
×12
Ans. £55,,13,,6.0300

SECT. 2.

Into IRISH MONEY.

RULE. Multiply the given sum by 39 and divide the product by 160; the quotient will be in Irish money, in pounds and decimals.

EXAMPLES.

Confolidate $240 into Irifh money.

```
    240
   ×39
  ————— £
16|0)93|60 (58 . 5
  —       ×20
         ————
Anf. 136 £58,,10|0
    ——   ===
    8.0
    ——
    (0)
```

Confol. $320.924 into Irifh money ×39

```
  ——————————
16|0)1251|6.036
  ——————————
     78.2252
        ×20
     ———————
     4.5040
         12
Anf. £78,,4,,6(0480)
     ============
```

SECT. 3.

Into HALIFAX MONEY.

Q. *How do you change federal money into this currency?*

RULE. Divide the dollars by 4 and the quotient will be pounds; annex the lower denominations to the remainder, if any, and annex a cypher to that number; then halve that number and cut off the left hand figure or figures, lefs than 20. for fhillings; the others multiply by 12, and cut off juft as many right hand figures from the product, the left are pence, &c. Or,

RULE 2, Multiply the given fum by 60, the quotient will be pence Halifax money; which confolidate according to rule in Leffon 3d.

EXAMPLES.

Confolidate $183.55 into Halifax money.

```
4)183.55 £45,,17,,9 Anf.
  ——      ====
 32)550
   ———
   17.75
   ×12
   ————
   9.00
   ————
```

Or, $183.55

```
          ×60
12)11013.00 Pence
2|0)  91|7-9
     ————
  £45,,17,,9 Anf.
     ====
```

SECT. 4.

Into SOUTH-CAROLINA *and* GEORGIA currency.

Q. *What is the Rule?*

RULE. Multiply the given ſum by 7, and divide the product by 30, the quotient will be pounds and decimals; change the decimals as in Section 2.

EXAMPLES.

Conſol. $1495.71.5 into S.C & Georg. cur.

```
  1495.715
        ×7
 ---------
3|0)1047|0.005
 ---------
  £349 Anſ.
```

Conſol. 3279.37.5 into S. C. cur.

```
        ×7
3|0)2295|5.625
     ----
   765.1875
        ×20
     3|7500
        ×12
     ------
Anſ. £765,,3,,9|0000
```

SECT. 5.

Into NEW-HAMPSHIRE, MASSACHUSETTS, CONNECTICUT, RHODE-ISLAND, VIRGINIA, VERMONT & KENTUCKY currency.

Q. *How do you change Federal money into the Lawful money of New-England?*

RULE. Multiply the given ſum by 6; then point off as many right hand figures from the product, as there were figures below dollars—the reſt are ſhillings; the figures pointed off are decimals of a ſhilling, which commute into pence, as in Section 1.

EXAMPLES.

Conſolidate $523.33.4 into L. M. of N. E.

```
   523.334
        ×6
 ---------
2|0)314|0.004
  £157 Anſ.
```

Change $1919.61 into L. M. of N. E.

```
   1919.61
        ×6
 ---------
2|0)1151|7.66
        ×12
 ---------
£575,,17,,7.92 Anſ.
```

SECT. 6.

Into the Currency of NEW-JERSEY, PENNSYLVANIA, DELAWARE *and* MARYLAND.

Q. *What is the Rule?*

RULE. Multiply the given ſum by 3, and divide the product by 8; the quotient will be pounds and decimals.

EXAMPLES.

```
Conſolidate $920 into         Conſol. $1425.32.3 in-
the currency of N.J. &c.      to N.J. &c.        ×3
                                         ----------
     920                              8)4275.969
      ×3                               ----------
   -----                               £534.496
  8)2760(                                    ×20
   -----                                   -----
   £345 Anſ.                               9.920
   =====                                     ×12
                                           -----
                                 £534,,9,,11.04 A.
                                   ==============
```

SECT. 7.

Into NEW-YORK *and* NORTH-CAROLINA *Currency.*

Q. *What is the Rule of changing Federal Money into this Currency?*

RULE. Multiply the given ſum by 8, and the product will be ſhillings, or ſhillings and decimals: commute them as in Section 1. Or,

Multiply the given ſum by .4, and the product will be pounds, or pounds and decimals.

EXAMPLES.

```
Conſolidate $1731.56.2           Or 1731.562
into N. Y. &c. currency.                  ×.4
                                     ---------
      1731.562                       692.6248
            ×8                             20
   -----------                         ------
  2|0)138|5|2.496                     12.4960
           ×12                             12
        ------                         ------
 £692,,12,,5.952 Anſ.           £692,,12,,5.9520
 ===============
```

LESSON XI.

How to change the Ratio of any number of Pence or Shillings upon the Pound, into the equivalent number of Cents upon the Dollar, and the reverse.

Q. WHAT *is the Rule?*

RULE. 1. To change shillings upon the pound, multiply them by 5, and the product will be the equivalent number of cents upon the dollar.

2. To change pence upon the pound into the same ratio of cents upon the dollar, you have only to annex a cypher to the pence, and divide them by 24; the quotient will be the true number of cents.

RULE 2. To reverse the operation, or change cents upon the dollar into pence upon the pound, multiply the given number of cents into 24; then cut off the right hand figure of the product, and the rest are the number of pence sought.

The following Tables will shew the mutual proportions, *viz.*

1 Penny upon the Pound		=	0 . 4	upon the Dollar.
2 *ditto*	*ditto*	=	0 . 8	*ditto*
3 *ditto*	*ditto*	=	1 . 25	*ditto*
4 *ditto*	*ditto*	=	1 . 6	*ditto*
5 *ditto*	*ditto*	=	2 . 1	*ditto*
6 *ditto*	*ditto*	=	2 . 5	*ditto*
7 *ditto*	*ditto*	=	2 . 9	*ditto*
8 *ditto*	*ditto*	=	3 . 4	*ditto*
9 *ditto*	*ditto*	=	3 . 75	*ditto*
10 *ditto*	*ditto*	=	4 . 2	*ditto*
11 *ditto*	*ditto*	=	4 . 6	*ditto*
12 *ditto*	*ditto*	=	5	*ditto*

1 Cent upon the	Dollar	= £.0,,2¼	upon the Pound.
2 *ditto*	*ditto*	= 0,,4¾	*ditto*
3 *ditto*	*ditto*	= 0,,7	*ditto*
4 *ditto*	*ditto*	= 0,,9½	*ditto*
5 *ditto*	*ditto*	= 1,,0	*ditto*
6 *ditto*	*ditto*	= 1,,2½	*ditto*
7 *ditto*	*ditto*	= 1,,4¾	*ditto*
8 *ditto*	*ditto*	= 1,,7	*ditto*
9 *ditto*	*ditto*	= 1,,9½	*ditto*
10 *ditto*	*ditto*	= 2,,0	*ditto*

EXAMPLES.

1. Suppofing a public tax to be levied of 3*d* ½ upon the pound, what would the fame ratio of affeffment be, counting upon dollars?

$$3^d\ \tfrac{1}{2} \times 10 = 35\ //$$

$$24\ )\ 35\ (\ 1 \cdot 4\tfrac{1}{3}\tfrac{4}{4}\ \textit{Anf.}$$

110

2. A merchant made 33 per cent. advance upon the prime coft in the fale of his goods; how much did he advance upon the pound?

$$\begin{array}{r} 33 \\ \times 24 \\ \hline 12)79.2 \\ \hline 6.6 = 6/7\tfrac{1}{5}\ \textit{Anf.} \end{array}$$

3. A bankrupt's eftate was divided among his creditors, at the average proportion of 13/4 upon the pound; what proportion was that in Federal money?

Anf. //66.6 *upon the Dollar.*

NOTE. *The amounts are calculated by the fame rules as thofe of Simple Intereft, in the Third Part.*

LESSON XII.

How to apportion the Price of Avoirdupois Weight, (112 to the *Cwt.*) upon the ſame number of Hundreds in Federal Avoirdupois, or reckoning only 100*lb.* to the *Cwt.*

Q. WHAT *is the Rule?*

RULE. To the number of Dollars in the given price, annex the dimes and cents, or two cyphers if it conſiſt only of dollars, and divide that number by 112: the quotient will be the anſwer. Or,

If there be two or more hundreds in the given weight, multiply the number of hundreds into the given price, increaſed as before, and divide by the whole number of pounds in the given weight of Vulgar Avoirdupois.

EXAMPLES.

1. At 1 Dollar per *Cwt.* (vulg. Avoird.) what is the price of 1 *Cwt.* Federal Avoirdupois?

112)100.0(89.3 nearly. *Anſ.*

1040

320

(96)

2. If a ton of iron coſt $100 what is the price of 1000 *lb. Fed. Avoird.*?

1. Ton = 2240*lb.*)100000(44.642 *Anſ.*

10400

14400

9600

(640)

LESSON XIII.

TARE AND TRET.

Q. WHAT *are we to underſtand by the terms*, Tare, Tret, *and* Cloff ?

A. Certain allowances made by merchants and tradeſmen in ſelling their goods by weight, viz.

TARE is an allowance made to the buyer, for the weight of the box, barrel, or bag, &c. in which the purchaſed goods are contained, and is varied according to circumſtances, being at ſo many pounds *per* box, &c. or at ſo much *per Cwt.* or at ſo much in the groſs weight.

TRET is an allowance of 4*lb.* in every 104*lb.* for waſte, duſt, &c.

CLOFF is allowance of 3*lb.* upon every 3 *Cwt.*

Q. *What are the diſtinctions of* GROSS, SUTTLE, *and* NEAT WEIGHT ?

A. Groſs weight, means the whole weight both of the article of traffic, and the barrel, box, caſk or cheſt in which it is contained, without any deduction.

Suttle weight is when part of the allowance is deducted from the groſs, as when the Tare is taken out and the Tret remains to be deducted—or, when the Tare and Tret are ſubtracted, and the Cloff is ſtill to come out.

Neat weight, is what remains after all allowances are deducted.

Q. *How is the Neat weight found, when either one or all of the foregoing allowances are to be made ?*

RULE. Multiply the Tare, and the weight upon which it is predicated, or the number of cheſts, caſks, &c. together, ſubtract the product from the groſs weight and the remainder will be the neat weight required.

2. When Tret is allowed with Tare—Divide the Suttle by 26, the quotient is the Tret ; ſubtract this from the ſuttle and the remainder is Neat.

3. When Tare, Tret and Cloff are allowed, subtract the Tare and Tret as before, and then divide the suttle by 168, and the quotient will be the Cloff, which subtract from the suttle and the remainder will be the Neat.

EXAMPLES.

In 15 barrels of flour, each weighing 2 *Cwt.* 1 *qr.* 14 *lb.* gross, Tare 12*lb.* per barrel, what is the Neat weight, in each of the three aforementioned cases of allowances?

1. *Tare deducted.*

12×15=180 *lb.* *Cwt. qrs. lb.*
Or *Cwt.* 1,,2,,2 2,, 1., 14 gross *wt.* of 1 *bll.*
×5×3=15

Cwt. 11,,3,,14
×3

35,,2,,14 Gross *wt.* of the whole.
— 1,,2,, 2 Tare subtracted.

Ans. 34,,0,,12 Neat.

2. *Tare & Tret deducted.*

Cwt.
26)34,,0,,12 Suttle.
— 1,,1,, 6,,14,,12 Tret subtracted.

Cwt. 32,,3,,5,,1,,4 Neat.

3. *Tare, Tret & Cloff, allowed.*

Cwt. qrs. lb.
32,,3,,5=3675 *lb.* Suttle.
168)3675(=========21,,14 Cloff subtracted.

315 112)3653,,2

147
×16 &c. *Cwt.* 32,,2,,13,,2 Neat. *Ans.*

NOTE. *It is considered as needless to add any further examples under the foregoing Rule, as the same general principles apply in every case of the kind; and all, in fact, are wrought by the rules of* Direct Proportion.

LESSON XIV.

Commutation between the Federal Troy weight of American, British, Portuguese, French and Spanish Gold, and Federal money.

1. AMERICAN, BRITISH, & PORTUGUSE Gold.

Q. HOW *do you change the federal Troy weight of this standard Gold into federal money?*

RULE. Remove all the separating points on the left of penny-weights, and pounds, ounces and penny-weights are dollars. Remove the point between grains and cents, and they are cents, in federal money.

If there are only pounds given, annex two cyphers. If ounces only, or pounds and ounces, annex 1 cypher, and they are reduced to dollars.

EXAMPLES.

What is the value, in Federal money, of 2*lb.* 3*oz.* 4*dw.* 5*gr.* of American, British, or Portuguese gold?

lb. oz. dw. gr. cts. Reduce 5*lb.* *lb. oz.* Red. 3*oz.*

2 . 3 . 4 . 5 . 0 *Ans.* $500 Red. 5 . 6 *Ans.* $30

Ans. $560

$234 . 50 *Ans.*

2 FRENCH *and* SPANISH Gold.

Q. *How do you change the federal Troy weight of this gold into federal money?*

RULE. 1. Take the given weight in grains, multiply it by 985; from the product point off the four right hand figures, and the rest are dollars. Or,

RULE 2. Subtract the given weight from itself, placing the first left hand figure of the Subtrahend under the third from the left hand in the Substratum— from this remainder subtract one half of the given weight; the second remainder is the federal money value; set the point at the left hand of the figure standing directly under the unit figure of the grains in the given weight, which will separate the dollars and cents.

EXAMPLES.

What is the federal money value of 3*lb*.4*oz*.5*dw*.6*gr*. of French or Spanish gold?

3456	Or, 3456.. 1st substr. or given *wt*.
×985	*—3456 1st Subtrahend.
$ 340.41.6|0 *Ans*.	342144. 1st Rem. & 2d Substr.
	—17280 Half the given *wt*. subt.
	$ 340.41.6|0 *Ans*.

What is the federal value of 1*lb*. of French gold?

1000 grains.	Or, 1000.. 1st Subtra. or given *wt*.
×985	— 1000 1st Subtrahend.
$ 98.50|00 *Ans*.	99000 1st Rem. & 2d Substr.
	—500 Half the given *wt*. subtracted.
	$ 98.50.0 *Ans*.

NOTE. *This last Example will tend to explain the principle of the 2d Rule, as it shews its operation to be in effect the same as that of multiplying the given weight by* 985.

* *This operation may be still further shortened by the Rule of Combined Subtraction, in Part I, Lesson XVII, Case* 1; *setting the figures thus*, viz.

```
 3456..
   3456 }
   1728 }
$ 340.41.6
```

Q. *How do you reverse the foregoing operations, or find the weight, in federal Troy, of any sum of gold accounted in federal money?*

RULE. If it be American, British or Portuguese gold, point off, in the given sum, cents for cents, dimes for grains; the first right hand figure of the dollars for penny-weights, the second for ounces, and the rest, if any, are pounds.

EXAMPLES.

What is the weight of $234.50 in Federal Troy weight?

Ans. lb. 2.3.4.5

What is the weight of 500, of 560, and of 30$.

Ans. 5*lb.* *Ans.* 5*lb.*6*oz.* *Ans.* 3*oz.*

Q. *How do you find the federal Troy weight of any sum of French or Spanish gold, accounted in fed. money?*

RULE. Take the given sum in *mills*, divide by 985, and the quotient wil be penny-weights, federal Troy weight. If there be any remainder, annex a cypher, and divide again for grains and cents.

EXAMPLES.

What is the federal Troy weight of $340.41.6 in French gold?

985)340416(*dw.*345.6=3*ld.* 4*oz.* 5*dw.* 6*gr.* *Ans.*

4491

5516

591.0

(0)

LESSON XV.

Commutation between Vulgar Troy Weight and Federal Money.

Q. WHAT *are the Rules?*

RULE 1. To ascertain the value of the weight of any given quantity of coined gold (expressed in Vulg. Troy weight) in Federal money, *first*, reduce the given weight to Federal Troy weight, by the rule in Lesson VI, Sect. 4: *nextly*, into Federal money by the rules in the last Lesson.

RULE 2. To find the weight of any given sum of Federal money, in coined gold, *first*, change the sum into Federal Troy weight, by the rule in the last Lesson, and *next* into Vulg. Troy, by rule in Lesson VI, Sect. 4.

1. AMERICAN, BRITISH *and* PORTUGUESE Gold, *into* Federal money.

Reduce *lb* 5,,3,,6,,1 into Fed. money.

×12
—
63
×20
—
1266
×24
—
27)30385o(*lb*.11.2.5.3.7 Fed. Troy.
—
33 $ 1125.37 *Anſ.*
—
68 &c.

Reduce *lb.* 5,, 1,, 4,, 9
×12

61
×20

1224
×24

27)293850(10883.3
lb. 10.8.8.3.3 Fed.T.
℥ 1088.33 *Anſ.*

By Rule 2.

What is the Vulg. Troy weight of ℥ 1125.37?
1125.37 is
lb. 11.2.5.3.7 or
gr. 11253.7 Fed. Troy.
×27

1|0)30384|9.9
24)30385 or nearly.
2|0)1266—1 *gr.*

12(63—6 *dw.*

lb. 5,,3,,6,,1 *Anſ.*

What is the Vulg. Troy weight of ℥ 1088.34?
gr. 10883.4 Fed. Tr. wt.
×27

24)293851.8

2|0)122|4—9 *gr.*

12)61—4 *dw.*

Anſ. lb. 5,,1,,4,,9 Vulg. T.

FRENCH *and* SPANISH Gold, *by Rule* 1.

What is the value of 56322 grains, Vulg. Troy weight, of French gold, in Federal money?

```
56322×10÷27=20860gr.
      20860 ..  [Fed.Tr.

         20860 }
         10430 }
      ---------
$2054.71.0 Ans.
```

What is the value, in Fed. money, of 5751 *gr.* (Vulg.Troy) French gold?

```
5751×10÷27=2130 gr.
     2130
     ×985
    ------
$209.80.5'0 Ans.
```

The Reverse, by Rule 2d.

What is the vulgar Troy weight of $2054.71?

```
985)205471 0(2086 dwt. Federal Troy.

    8471         2086
                  ×27
     5910        ----
                 56322grs. Ans.
      (o)
```

What is the vulgar Troy weight of $209.80.5?

```
985)209805 ( 213
               ×27
      1280    ----
              5751 grains.   Ans.
       2955

        (o)
```

LESSON XVI.

Exchange between the Weight of Foreign Gold and each of the currencies of Pounds, Shillings and Pence, which are ufed in the United States.

SECT. I.

SOUTH-CAROLINA *and* GEORGIA Currency.

Q. HOW *do you find the value of any given weight of Britifh or Portuguefe gold, in this currency?*

RULE. Reduce the given weight to grains, and divide by 116; the quotient will be pounds in this currency.

Reverfe.

RULE. Reduce the given fum to pence, then multiply by 29, and divide by 60; the quotient will be grains, Vulg. Troy.

EXAMPLES.

What is the value, in S. Car. &c. currency, of 27*lb.* 5*oz.* 7*dw.* 8*gr.* of Britifh or Portuguefe gold?

```
lb.27,,5,,7,,8          £.  s.  d.
×12          116)158096(1362,,17,,11 5/29
——                ——
329               420
×20               ——
——                 729
6587               ——
×24                336
——                 ——
158096             104
                   ×20 &c.
```

What is the weight of £1362,,17,,11$\frac{5}{29}$ S. Car. &c. currency, in British or Portuguese gold?

1362,,17,,11$\frac{5}{29}$
×20
27257
×12
327095$\frac{5}{29}$

327095$\frac{5}{29}$*
×29
(10)948576|0
24)158096 grains.
2|0)658|7—8gr.
12)329—7dw.
lb. 27,,5,,7,,8 Ans.

FRENCH *and* SPANISH Gold.

RULE. Divide the whole number of grains in the given weight by 124; the quotient will be pounds S. C. &c.

Reverse.

RULE. Multiply the whole number of pence in the given sum by 31, and divide the product by 60; the quotient will be grains, Vulg. Troy.

EXAMPLES.

What is the value of 158069 *grs.* of French or Spanish gold, in the currency of S. Car. &c.

124)158096(1274,,19,,4$\frac{8}{31}$
340
929
616 &c.

What is the weight, in French and Spanish gold, of £1274,,19,,4$\frac{8}{31}$ S. Car.

£. pence.
1274,,19,,4$\frac{8}{31}$=305992$\frac{8}{31}$.
×31
6|0(948576|0
Ans. 158096 *gr.*

* *Multiplying* $\frac{5}{29}$ *by* 29, *makes just* 5; *so that, in all cases of this kind, you have only to add in the Numerator, or upper number in the fraction.*

SECT. 2.

New-England, &c. Currency.

English and *Portuguese* Gold.

Rule. Multiply pounds (weight) by 64; the quotient will be pounds currency.

An ounce being £5,,6,,8, therefore multiply this sum by the number of ounces.

A penny-weight being 5/4, multiply the number of penny-weights into this sum.

Multiply the grains into $2\frac{1}{2}d$, and add the several products together. Or

Divide the whole number of grains in the given weight by 90; the quotient will be pounds, N. E. currency.

Reverse.

Rule. Reduce pounds, or pounds and shillings, to shillings, cut off the right hand figure, and divide by 128; the quotient will be pounds weight: the figure so cut off, bring down to the last remainder. Or

Multiply the whole number of pence in the given sum by 3, and divide the product by 8; the quotient will be grains.

Examples.

What is the value of *lb.*56,,11,,12,,8 *gr.* in the L. M. of N. E.

*lb.*56	£5,, 6,,8	*s.*5,,4	*d.*$2\frac{1}{2}$
×64	×11*oz.*	×12*dw.*	×8 *gr.*
£3584,,00,,0	58,,13,,4	3,,4,,0	1/8
58,,13,,4			
3,, 4,,0			
1,,8			
£3645,,19,,0 *Anſ.*			

Or, *lb.* 56,, 11,, 12,, 8 = 328136 grains.

9|0)32813|6

3645

86

× 20 &c. = £3645,, 19 *Ans.*

What is the weight of £3645,, 19 N. E. in Brittish, &c. gold?

3645,, 19

× 20

128)72919(*lb.* 56,, 11,, 12,, 8 *Ans.*

891

1289

× 12

)1486|8(11

&c.

Or, £3645,, 19 = 875028 pence.

× 3

8)2625084(

Ans. 328135½ grains.

This lacks half a grain, because there was one ninth of a shilling remainder, in the second example.

FRENCH *and* SPANISH Gold.

RULE. Multiply the whole number of grains by 3, and divde the product by 274; the quotient will be pounds, N. E.

Reverse.

RULE. Multiply the whole number of pence by 137, and divide the product by 360; the quotient will be grains.

EXAMPLES.

What is the value in N. F. money, of 56*lb.* 11*oz.* 12*dw.* 8*gr.* *Fr.* or *Sp.* gold?

328136 grains.

×3

274)984408(

Ans. £3592,,14,,7$\frac{25}{137}$

What is the weight, in French or Spanish gold, of £3592,,14,,7$\frac{25}{137}$ N. E.?

862255$\frac{25}{137}$ *d.*

×137

360)11812896|0(328136

328136*gr.*=*lb* 56.11.12.8

SECT. 3.

NEW-JERSEY, *&c.* Currency.

English and *Portuguese* Gold.

Q. *How do you find the value of English gold, in this currency?*

RULE. Divide the whole number of grains by 72; the quotient will be pounds currency.

Reverse.

RULE. Multiply the whole number of pence by 3, and cut off the right hand figure of the product; the rest are grains.

EXAMPLES.

What is the value, in N. Jersey, &c. currency, of 328136*grs.* British or Portuguese gold?

72)328136(4557,,8,,10$\frac{2}{3}$ *Ans.*

What is the weight of £4557,,8,,10$\frac{2}{3}$ N. Jersey, &c. currency, in British, &c. gold?

£4557,,8,,10$\frac{2}{3}$=1093786$\frac{2}{3}$ pence.

×3

32813|6|0

328136 grains=56*lb.* 11*oz.* 12*dw.* 8*gr.* *Ans.*

FRENCH *and* SPANISH Gold.

RULE. Multiply the whole number of grains in the given weight by 75, and divide the product by 26; the quotient will be pence.

Reverse.

RULE. Multiply the pence by 26, and divide the product by 75; the quotient is grains.

EXAMPLES.

What is the value of 328136 *grs.* of French or Spanish gold, in N. Jersey, &c. currency?

328136
×75

26)24610200

12)946546$\frac{4}{26}$

2|0)78871|8—10

£3943,,18,,10$\frac{4}{26}$ *An.*

What is the weight, in French or Spanish gold, of £3943,,18,,10$\frac{4}{26}$ N. J. cur.

946546$\frac{4}{26}$*d.*
×26

75)24610200(328136

328136*gr.*=*lb.*56,,11,,12,,8

SECT. 4.

NEW-YORK *and* NORTH-CAROLINA Currency.

British and *Portuguese* Gold.

RULE. Annex a cypher to the whole number of grains, and divide by 675; the quotient will be pounds currency.

Reverse.

RULE. Multiply the whole number of pence by 9 and divide the product by 32; the quotient will be grains.

EXAMPLES.

What is the value of 328136 *grs.*?

675)3281360(4861..5..5$\frac{7}{9}$

5813

4136 &c.

What is the weight of £486,,5,,5$\frac{7}{9}$ N. Y. &c. in French or Span. gold?

Pence mult. by 9, produce

32)10500352(328136*gr.*

=56*lb.* 11*oz.* 12*dw.* 8*gr.*

FRENCH *and* SPANISH Gold.

RULE. Annex a cypher to the whole number of grains in the given weight, and divide by 685; the quotient will be pounds, New-York, &c. currency.

Reverse.

RULE. Multiply the whole number of pence in the given sum by 137, and divide the product by 480; the quotient will be grains.

EXAMPLES.

What is the value of 328136 *grs.* in N. Y. &c. currency? £. *s. d.*

685)3281360(4790,6,1 $\frac{79}{137}$

What is the weight of £4790,,6,,1 $\frac{79}{137}$ N. York, currency, in *Fr.* or *Sp.* gold?

328136 *grs.* *Ans.*

LESSON XVII.

RECAPITULATION of all the foregoing Rules of Exchange, in one universal Rule, by the help of the following Tables.

TABLE 1.

Shewing the reciprocal proportions between all the different Currencies of Pounds, Shillings, &c. and Federal Money, respectively.

	Ster.	*S.C.*	*Ir.*	*Hal.*	*N.E.*	*N.J.*	*N.Y.*	*Fed.*
Federal.	9/40	7/30	39/160	1/4	3/10	3/8	2/5	
N. York, &c.	9/16	7/12	39/65	5/8	3/4	15/16		5/2
N. Jer. &c.	3/5	28/45	13/20	2/3	4/5		16/15	8/3
N. Eng. &c.	3/4	7/9	13/16	5/6		5/4	4/3	10/3
Halifax.	9/10	14/15	39/40		6/5	3/2	8/5	4/1
Irish.	12/13	112/117		40/39	16/13	20/13	64/39	160/39
S. Carol. &c.	27/28		117/112	15/14	9/7	45/28	12/7	30/7
Sterling.		28/27	13/12	10/9	4/3	5/3	16/9	40/9

TABLE 2.

Shewing the reciprocal proportions between the several Tables of Weight.

		Avoirdupois weight.			Troy weight.			
		lb.	oz.	dr.	lb.	oz.	dw.	gr.
Fed. Troy, or American wt.	lb.	27/70	216/35	3456/35	15/32	45/8	900/8	2700/1
	oz	27/700	108/175	1728/175	3/64	9/16	45/4	270/1
	dw	27/7000	54/875	86[illegible]/875	[illegible]/640	[illegible]/160	9/8	27/1
	gr	27/70000	27/1375	432/4375	3/6400	9/1600	9/80	27/10
Fed. Avoirdupois.	lb.		16/1	256/1	175/144	175/12	875/3	7000/1
	oz.	1/10	16/10	256/10	35/288	35/24	175/6	700/1
	dr.	1/100	16/100	64/2[illegible]	7/576	7/48	35/12	70/1
Troy weight.	lb.	144/175	2304/175	737[illegible]/35		12/1	240/1	[illegible]760/1
	oz.	12/175	192/175	3072/175	1/12		[illegible]0/1	480/1
	dw.	3/875	48/875	768/875	1/240	1/20		24/1
	gr.	1/70[illegible]	2/[illegible]	32/875	1/5760	1/480	1/24	
Avoird. weight.	lb.		16/1	256/1	175/144	175/12	875/3	7000/1
	oz.	1/16		16/1	175/2304	175/192	875/48	875/2
	dr.	1/25[illegible]	1[illegible]		35/[illegible]373	175/3072	87[illegible]/768	875/32

		Fed. Avoirdupois lb.	oz.	dr.	Fed. Troy, or American wt. lb.	oz.	dw.	gr.
Fed. Troy, or American wt.	lb	27 70	27 7	270 7		10 1	100 1	1000 1
	oz.	27 700	27 70	7 7	1 10		10 1	100 1
	dw.	7 7000	2 700	27 70	1 10[illegible]	1 10		10 1
	gr.	27 70000	2[illegible] 7000	[illegible] 7[illegible]	1 1000	1 100	1 10	
Fed. Avoirdupois.	lb.		1[illegible]	[illegible] 1	70 27	700 27	7000 27	[illegible]0000 27
	oz.	1 1[illegible]		10 1	7 27	7[illegible] 27	700 27	7000 27
	dr.	1 100	1 10		7 270	7 27	70 27	700 27
Troy weight.	lb.	144 17[illegible]	28[illegible] 35	[illegible]56 7	32 15	64 3	640 3	6400 3
	oz.	12 175	24 35	48 7	8 45	16 9	160 9	1600 9
	dw.	[illegible] 87	6 175	1[illegible] 3[illegible]	8 900	4 45	8 9	80 9
	gr.	[illegible] 7000	1 [illegible]00	1 70	1 2700	1 270	1 27	10 27
Avoird. weight	lb.		10 1	100 1	70 27	700 27	7000 27	70000 27
	oz.	1 16	10 16	[illegible]00 16	35 216	175 108	875 5[illegible]	4375 27
	dr.	1 256	10 256	25 64	3456 35	175 1728	875 864	4375 432

NOTE. *Read these two pages as one Table.*

TABLE 8.

Proportions between the weight of coined Gold and the several currencies of the United States.

		Fed. money.	S. Carolina and Georgia currency.			N. England, &c. currency.			N. Jersey, &c. currency.			New-York, &c. currency.		
		$	£.	s.	d.	£.	s.	d.	£.	s.	d.	£.	s.	d.
American, British and Portuguese Gold.	lb.	640/3	1440/29	28800/29	345600/29	64/1	1280/1	15360/1	80/1	1600	1928/1	256/3	5120/3	20480/1
	oz.	160/9	120/29	2400/29	28800/29	16/3	320/3	1280/1	20/[illegible]	400/3	1600/1	64/9	1280/9	5120/3
	dw.	8/9	6/29	120/29	2400/29	4/15	16/3	64/1	2/[illegible]	20/3	80/1	16/45	64/9	256/3
	gr.	1/27	1/116	5/29	120/29	1/90	2/9	8/3	1/[illegible]	1/18	10/3	2/135	8/27	32/9
French and Spanish Gold.	lb.	[illegible]/137	[illegible]/137	[illegible]/137	[illegible]/137	[illegible]/137	[illegible]/137	[illegible]/137	[illegible]/137	200000/137	2472000/137	[illegible]/137	229400/137	2752000/137
	oz.	2400/137	560/137	11200/137	134400/137	720/137	14400/137	172800/137	900/137	18000/137	21600/137	960/137	19200/137	230400/137
	dw.	120/13	28/137	560/137	6720/137	36/137	720/137	8640/137	45/137	900/137	10800/137	48/137	960/137	11520/137
	gr.	5/137	7/822	70/411	840/411	3/274	30/137	360/137	5/416	25/104	75/26	2/137	40/137	480/137

Q. *How are the foregoing Tables to be applied?*

RULE. Look the particular currency or weight of the given ſum or quantity, and the particular denomination in which it is taken, in the left hand column; *next*, the particular currency or weight into which it is to be changed, by the index at the top, and the check at their common angle of meeting contains their reciprocal proportion; *then*, multiply the given ſum or quantity by the upper proportional number, and divide the product by the lower one; the quotient will be the anſwer ſought.

EXAMPLES *under each of the Tables.*

1. Reduce £65, Iriſh money, into the currency of N. Jerſey, &c.

By the Table, the proportionals are found be 20 *and* 13.

Therefore £65
×20

13)1300(£100 N. Jerſey, &c. *Anſ.*

2. Reduce 578 drams, Avoird. into grains, Tr. wt.

The tabular numbers are 875 *and* 32.

578
×875

32)505750(15804 *Anſ.*
185
257
150
(22)

3. What is the value, in pence, N. England, &c. currency, of 540 grains of Britiſh gold?

The tabular numbers are 8 and 3.

```
   540
  ×8
  ———
3)4320
  ———
  1440 pence. Anſ.
  ===
```

LESSON XVIII.

Miſcellaneous Queſtions for exerciſe.

1. WHAT is the Federal money value of £5725,, 15,,6 Sterling money? *Anſ.* $25447.88 9

2. An Invoice of goods from Dublin amounts to £7572,,5. Required the ſum in Federal money?
Anſ. $31065.641

3. To what ſum in S. Carolina and Georgia currency, will 4100 Federal dollars amount?
Anſ. £956,,13,,4

4. What ſum in Federal money, equals £137,,18,,4 Halifax currency? *Anſ.* $751.66 4

5. To what ſum in Federal money does the debt of Great Britain amount, eſtimated at £400 000 000 Sterling? *Anſ.* $1777777777.77 7

6. What is the weight of the laſt mentioned ſum of dollars in Engliſh gold coin?
Anſ. 8333333*lb.* 4*oz.* Vulg. Troy.

7. What is the Avoirdupois weight of this ſum of gold? *Anſ.* 3061 *Tons*, 4*Cwt.* 1*qr.* 26*lb.* 13*oz.* 2*dr.*

8. How many cents upon the dollar is 3/6 upon the pound? *Anſ.* //.17.5

9. What is the Federal money value of £268,,12,,8 N. England &c. currency? *Anſ.* $895.44 3

10. What number of dollars muſt I receive in lieu of £432,,15 N. Jerſey, &c. currency? *Anſ.* $1154.

11. I bring my action against Jacobus Van Scheldt of the state of N. York, upon a note of hand given for £237,,12, for what sum must I declare in Federal money? *Ans.* $594

12. A. exchanged with B. 132 bushels of Maize at 2/6 per bushel, for Wheat at 4/6 per bushel; how many bushels of Wheat must A. receive?

Ans. 73 *Bush.* 1 *peck*, 2 *qts.* 1 *pt.*

13. Giles Jackson, farmer, traded with Robert Howard and Co. merchants—delivered 25 bushels of flax-seed at $.88 7, 40 bushels of oats at $.30 3, and 10 bushels of potatoes at $.22; How many yards of cloth may he take up at $2.82 per yard? *Ans.* 39 yds.

14. James Dawson exchanged rum with Job Fullerton, 185 *gal.* at $1.75, for brandy at $2.33 3—how many gallons must Dawson receive?

Ans. 138 *gal.* 3 *qts.*

15. J. Tucker exchanged with Jonathan Olmstead, 47 yards of cambric at $1.52 6 per *yd.* for callicoes at $1.32, and chintzes at $1.52 6 per yard; how many yards must he have of each sort? *Ans.* 31.5 yards.

16. A land jobber purchased 1575 acres at 2/6 the acre; 3240 acres at 2/2; and 725 acres at 3/6; then sold the whole for 12/ per acre—what was the average advance upon the acre, and what the amount of his neat proceeds. *Ans.* 8/11¾ the average advance.

£2491,,5 Neat proceeds.

17. A merchant bought wheat in Vermont for the N. York market, 5526 bushels at 12/ per bushel, expecting to sell it at 20/; but finding the market fast rising he stored it in the city with directions to his factor, not to sell it under 24/; the price arose to 23/10, and then suddenly fell to 8/. What did the merchant lose in his wheat, exclusive of the expence of transportation, storage, wastage, lying out of his property, &c. *Ans.* £1105..4

18. At the close of the American war, the Congress of the United states settled with the officers of the ar-

my, by commuting their half pay for life, theretofore promiſed them, into 5 years full pay in hand. Col. Broadſword received for his commutation money £628 N. England currency—What ſum would he have received in Federal money, upon the other eſtabliſhment, had he lived 30 years? *Anſ.* $6280.

19. John Thimbleton, a monied ſpeculator, bought up old continental ſecurities, in ſoldiers notes, to the amount of £10560, at the depreciated rate of 2/6 upon the pound. Afterwards, under the new Federal government, the credit of thoſe ſecurities was eſtabliſhed at par. *Queſtion.* How much was Mr. Thimbleton enriched at the expence of the war-worn veteran?

Anſ. £9240

20. Daniel Buller borrowed of Jonathan Leaſon £51,,17,,6 Lawful money of N. England, to diſcharge himſelf from the cuſtody of the officer, by whom he was held on execution. About 17 years afterwards, in the time of the American war, Mr. Buller ſold a couple of yearling ſteers for that ſum of money, in bills of public credit, or continental money, ſo called, at the time that it was depreciated 2000 per cent, and very cheerfully made a lawful tender of the money, in diſcharge of his debt to Leaſon. *Queſtion.* How much ought honeſt Mr. Buller to have paid in continental money; what was the real value of what he paid; and what was the diſtance between good conſcience and actual conduct?

Anſ. The real value of what he paid was £2,,16,,10½. What he ought to have paid in continental money was 400 times as much, viz. £1148,,1,,4

His gratitude to his friend, was, to cheat him of £49,,0,,7½ L. M. Or, £1096,,3,,10, Continental money.

LESSON XIX.

The denominations of the Money of Account of various Foreign Nations, with their reſpective values in Federal money.

France.

	$ // /
1 Denier - -	=0.00.08
12 Deniers = 1 Sol. -	=0 00.95
20 Sols = 1 Livre Tournois	=0.19.0

Spain.

	$ // /
1 Marvedie - -	=0 00.3
34 Marvedies = 1 Real Plate	=0.10.0
10 Real Plate = 1 Dollar	=1.00.0

Portugal.

	$ // /
1 Ree - - -	=0.00.124
10 Rees = 1 Half Vintin	=0 01.24
10 Half Vintin = 1 Teſtoon	=0.12.4
10 Teſtoons = 1 Mill Ree	=1.24 0

Russia.

	$ // /
1 Muſcoque - - -	=0.00 5
2 Muſcoques = Copee - -	=0.01 0
10 Copees = 1 Grievener -	=0.10 0
10 Grieveners = 1 Rouble -	=1.00 0

Sweden.

	$ // /
1 Runſtick - - -	=0.00.52
32 Runſticks = 1 Copper Dollar	=0.16 7
6 Copper Dollars = 1 Rix Dollar	=1.00 0

Denmark.

	$ // /
1 Schilling - - -	=0.01.04
16 Schillings = 1 Mark -	=0.16 7
6 Marks = 1 Rix Dollar -	=1.00 0

UNITED NETHERLANDS.

	℔ ß d
1 Penning - - -	=0.00.03
16 Pennings = 1 Stiver - -	=0.01.45
20 Stivers = 1 Guilder -	=0.39 0

HAMBURGH.

1 Phenning - - -	=0.00.13
12 Phennings=1 Schilling Lub.	=0.02 1
16 SchillingsLub.= 1 MarcBancc	=0.33 3

CHINA.

1 Cash - - - -	=0.00.148
10 Cash = 1 Cadarene - -	=0.01.48
10 Cadarenes = 1 Mace -	=0.14 8
10 Mace = 1 Tale - -	=1.48 0

BENGAL.

1 Pice - - - -	=0.00.32
12 Pices = 1 Anas - -	=0.03 9
16 Anas = 1 Rupee - -	=0.55 5

INDIA.

1 Pice - - - -	=0.00 7
8 Pices = 1 Fanam - -	=0.05 4
36 Fanams = 1 Pagoda -	=1.94 0

LESSON XX.

The Weights and Measures of different places.

1 WEIGHT.

One hundred pounds weight, of England, Scotland, Ireland, and America, amount to,	*lb. oz.*
At Geneva,	81,, 7
At Rouen, the viscounty weight,	88,, 0
At Frankfort and Nuremburgh,	89,, 7
At Rochelle,	90,, 9
At Amsterdam, Paris, Bourdeaux, &c.	91,, 8
At Hamburgh,	93,, 5
At Leipsic,	96,, 1

	lb. oz.
At Liege,	96,, 5
At Antwerp, or Brabant,	96,, 8
At Seville, Cadiz, &c.	97,, 0
At Portugal,	104,,13
At Lyons, the city weight,	106,, 0
At Thoulouſe, and upper Languedoc	107,,11
At Marſeilles, and Provence,	113,, 0
At Leghorn,	132,,11
At Genoa,	137,, 4
At Venice,	152,, 0
At Milan,	153,,11
At Naples,	154,,10

2. Cloth Measure.

One hundred yards of America, England, Scotland and Ireland, equal,

Of France, England, Oſnaburg & Geneva,	80 Ells.
Of Amſterdam, Haerlem, Leyden, the Hague, Rotterdam, &c.	$133\frac{1}{3}$ Ells.
Of Antwerp and Bruſſels,	$131\frac{2}{3}$ Ells.
Of Hamburgh, Frankfort, Leipſic, Bern, Baſil, and Cologne,	160 Ells.
Of Breſlau, in Sileſia,	$166\frac{3}{5}$ Ells.
Of Dantzick,	150 Ells.
Of Bergen and Drontheim,	$146\frac{2}{3}$ Ells.
Of Sweden or Stockholm,	154 Ells.
Of St. Gall for Linen,	$114\frac{2}{3}$ Ells.
——— for Cloth,	$149\frac{1}{3}$ Ells.
Of Marſeilles and Montpelier,	$46\frac{2}{3}$ Canes.
Of Thouloufe and Upper Languedoc,	50 Canes.
Of Genoa,	$40\frac{2}{3}$ Canes.
Of Rome,	44 Canes.
Of Caſtile and Biſcay,	107 Vares.
Of Cadiz and Andaluſia,	$109\frac{1}{5}$ Vares.
Of Portugal or Liſbon,	$81\frac{1}{3}$ Vares.
Of Portugal or Liſbon,	$133\frac{1}{3}$ Covedos.
Of Venice,	136 Braſſes.

Of Bergamo, &c.	104⅓ Braſſes.
Of Florence and Leghorn,	154¼ Braſſes.
Of Milan,	171⅓ Braſſes.

3. Dry Measure.

Eighty-two American or Wincheſter Buſhels equal at

Aiguillon 41 Sacks,
Albi 25 Setiers,
Alicant 12 Cahizes,
Alkmaar 36 Sacks,
Amersfort 16 Muddes,
Amſterdam 27 Muddles, or 1 Laſt,
Antwerp 32½ Veertels,
Arles 49 Setiers,
Bayonne 36 Sacks,
Beaucaire 28 Setiers,
Beaumont 36 Sacks,
Bergen-op-Zoom, 63 Siſters,
Bois-le-Duc, 20½ Mouwers,
Bommel 18 Muddes,
Bourdeaux 38 Boiſſeau,
Breda 33 Veertels,
Bruges 17½ Hoedts,
Bruſſels 25 Sacks,
Bueren 21 Muddes,
Cadillac 33⅓ Sacks,
Cadiz 52 Hanegas,
Cahors 100 Cartes,
Campen 24½ Mudd,
Carcaſſone 35 Setiers,
Clairac 34½ Sacks,
Cleves 16¼ Mouwers,
Condom 41 Sacks,
Coningſberg 1 Laſt,
Copenhagen 42 Tuns,
Dantzick 1 Laſt,
Delf 29 Sacks,
Deventer 36 Muddes,

Doesbourgh 22 Mouwers,
Dort, or Dordrecht 24 Sacks,
Dunkirk 18 Razieres,
Edam 27 Muddes,
Elling 1 Last,
Embden $15\frac{1}{4}$ Tuns,
Erfelsteyn 21 Muddes,
Franckfort 27 Malders,
Ghent 56 Halsters,
Genoa 25 Mines,
Gimond 20 Sacks,
Graveline 22 Razieres,
Haerlem 38 Sacks,
Hamburgh $\frac{12}{13}$ths of a Last,
Huesden $17\frac{1}{4}$ Muddes,
Hoorn, or Horn, 44 Sacks,
Ireland 38 Bushels,
La Brille 40 Sacks,
La Reole 30 Sacks,
Lavour 21 Setiers,
Lisle in Flanders, 38 Razieres,
Lisbon 216 Alquiers,
Leghorn 40 Sacks,
Lorrain 27 Muddes,
Lubeck 95 Schepels,
Middlebourgh $48\frac{1}{2}$ Sacks,
Montfort 21 Muddes,
Paris 19 Setiers,
Porto Port 180 Alquiers,
Purmerent 27 Muddes,
Rabastens 17 Setiers,
Rhenen 20 Muddes,
Ruremond 68 Schepels,
Riga 46 Loopens,
Rotterdam 29 Sarks,
St. Giles 40 Charges,
St. Omer $22\frac{1}{2}$ Razieres,
St. Valery 19 Setiers,

M

Saumur 19 Setiers,
Steenbergen 35 Veertels,
Stockholm 23 Tons,
Terveer 39 Sacks,
Thiel 21 Muddes,
Thoulouſe 26 Setiers,
Tongres 15 Muddes,
Tonnington 34 Tons,
Venloo $21\frac{3}{4}$ Mouwers,
Vianden 20 Muddes,
Utrecht 25 Muddes,
Zurick Zee 40 Sacks.

NOTE. *For the operation of exchange between the different monies, weights and meaſures in the two laſt Leſſons, apply the Rule of Three or the rules of Decimal Commutation, in the Third Part.*

END OF THE SECOND PART.

The American Accomptant, &c.

PART III.

DECIMAL PRACTICE.

LESSON I.

General Questions.

Q. WHAT *is meant by a* Fraction?

A. A part or parts of an unit, and is so called in contradistinction to an integer or whole number.

Q. *How many hinds of Arithmetical Fractions are there?*

A. Two; Vulgar* and Decimal Fractions.

Q. *May not the same fractional part of an integer be expressed in either?*

A. Yes.

Q. *What is incidental to all fractions?*

A. Two numbers; one called the numerator and the other the denominator. The former is always expressed; the latter is either expressed or understood.

Explain them.

The Numerator expresses the number of single parts

---

* *As the use of* vulgar *fractions may be advantageously superseded by that of* decimals, *they are viewed as an unnecessary branch of common-school education, and therefore omitted in this Compendium.*

contained in the fraction; the Denominator, the whole number of parts which compose the Integer. Thus $\frac{4}{5}$ and .8, that is, four fifths and eight tenths: Here the first is a Vulgar, and the latter a Decimal fraction; the numbers 4 and 8 are numerators, and 5 and 10 their denominators. Increasing or diminishing the numerator has the like effect upon the value of the fraction, as nine tenths is more, and seven tenths less than *eight* tenths; but to increase the denominator lessens, and to diminish it, augments the fraction; four fourths being an integer, and four sixths less than four fifths.

Q. *In what respects do vulgar and decimal fractions differ?*

A. Principally with respect to their *notation*, their *denominators*, their *mode* of operation, and their *utility*.

In a vulgar fraction, the numerator and denominator are both noted, or written down, and the one set over the other: in decimals, the numerator only is expressed.

In vulgar fractions, the denominator may be any number whatever; in decimal fractions, the denominator is ever a decimal number, or unity, with one or more cyphers annexed.

Vulgar fractions admit of *improper* fractions, or fractions greater than an integer, such as $\frac{8}{7}$; but decimals are always *proper* fractions, or less than an integer.

Their difference in mode of operation and utility, may be better understood by example and practice, than by any particular description.

L E S S O N II.

NOTATION of Decimal Fractions.

Q. IN *what respect does the Notation of decimals differ from that of whole numbers?*

A. 1. Decimal fractions are distinguished by a dot or point, (thus .) set at the left hand of the fractional number, which may be called the *Sinister* point. This is of great and necessary use in decimals, as it supplies the place of the denominator, and designates the magnitude of the fraction. As it divides the fraction from the integral figures, it is termed the *Seperatrix*.

2. Decimal fractions decrease infinitely towards the right hand; whole numbers increase infinitely towards the left; both starting from unity as a fixed central point, according to the following

TABLE.

C Millions	X Millions	Millions	C Thousands	X Thousands	Thousands	Hundreds	Tens	Units	Tenth parts	Hundredth parts	Thous. parts	X Thous. parts	C Thous. parts	Millionth parts	X Millionth parts	C Millionth parts
9	8	7	6	5	4	3	2	1	.2	3	4	5	6	7	8	9

NOTE. *The decimal places, counting from the point towards the right, are also called* Primes, Seconds, Thirds, Fourths, &c.

Therefore it is evident, that,

3, The magnitude of a decimal fraction, compared with another, does not depend upon the number of its figures, but upon the value of its first left hand figure: for instance, a fraction beginning with any figure less than 9, such as, .8573024, &c. if extended to an infinite number of figures, will not equal .9

Q. *How do you enumerate, so as to read a decimal fraction?*

A. The numerator being expressed by the figures actually set down, enumerate and read them as you would the same figures in a whole number. To find the denominator, consider the sinister point as standing for 1, and all the figures upon its right hand for so many cyphers; then, by the common method, enumerate and read them accordingly, which will give you the denominator of the fraction. Thus, the following fractions, .1, .15, .236, .0001, by this rule are to be read, *one tenth, fifteen hundredths, two hundred and thirty six thousandths, one ten thousandth; which, written in the manner of vulgar fractions, would stand,*

$\frac{1}{10}, \frac{15}{100}, \frac{236}{1000}, \frac{1}{10000}.$

Q. *What is the effect of removing the finister point?*

A. If you remove it towards the right hand, it multiplies the fraction by 10 at every figure; thus, .235 being 2.35, becomes two integers and thirty-five hundredths: remove it another figure, and it is 23.5, twenty-three and five tenths: remove it another figure, which is the same as taking it away, and it becomes a simple whole number, 235.

But removing the point towards the left hand has directly the contrary effect: It divides, and makes the quantity ten times the less at every figure it is removed; thus 235 becomes 23.5, 2.35, .235, .0235, and so on.

Q. *What are the effects of cyphers at the right or the left hand of a decimal fraction?*

A. At the right hand they neither increase nor diminish its value; but place them upon the left hand of the fraction, and they make it ten times the less for every cypher so placed.

Q. *What is the reason of this?*

A. Because, in the first case, the numerator is increased just in the same proportion with the denominator, and .1, *one tenth,* becomes .10, *ten hundredths;* but in the other case the denominator only is increased, which diminishes the fraction, and makes .1, *one tenth,* no more than .01, *one hundredth.* Therefore,

Any two or more decimal fractions, however differing in their magnitude, may be expressed by an equal number of figures, and have the same common denominator. So theſe decimals, .8. .05, .456, .0003, may be written .8000. .0500. .4560. .0003.

Q. *How may a whole number be decimally expreſſed?*

A. By annexing one or more cyphers, ſeparated by the ſiniſter point—thus, 39.0, 24.000.

LESSON III.

Exerciſes in Decimal Notation.

Q. HOW *do you read the following decimal fractions? which is the largeſt, and which the ſmalleſt of them?*

.3	.51004	.880
.25	.020304	.000400405
.50	.0070060	.0000060000
.499	.88800001	.99
.0621	.888999002	.0000000009

Q. *How do you write down in figures the following decimal fractions expreſſed in writing,* viz.

Five, hundredths.

Twenty-five, thouſandths.

Three hundred and ſeventy-ſix, ten thouſandths.

Six hundred and four thouſand and ſeventy-one, millionths.

Twenty thouſand, eight hundred and thirty-three, millionths.

One hundred and ninety one, ten thouſandths.

Six thouſand, eight hundred and ſeventy-five, hundred thouſandths.

Two thouſand and eighty-three, millionths.

Forty-one thouſand, ſix hundred and ſixty-ſix, ten millionths.

Seven thouſand and two, hundred thouſandths.

Six thouſand, ſix hundred and ninety-ſix, hundred millionths.

Twenty-ſeven thouſand & nine, hundred thouſandths.

Eight hundred and ſeventy-three, thouſand millionths.

Forty-ſeven, hundred thouſand millionths.

LESSON IV.

Decimal Points.

Q. WHAT *other Decimal Points are uſed in this Compendium, and what are they called?*

A. The *Dexter* point, the *Surdal* point, and the *Antiſurdal* point.

Explain them.

1. The *Dexter* point, placed thus, 5˙, when applied to the dividend, according to the rules of diviſion hereafter given, denotes that the figures upon its left hand will quotient integers, and thoſe upon its right, fractions. It is alſo uſed in reducing a decimal fraction into its proper value, in the lower denominations of a vulgar table; and then it ſhews that the figures upon the left hand only are made uſe of, and thoſe upon its right thrown away, being ſmaller than the ultimate fraction, or loweſt denomination of that table.

2. The Surdal point is a colon, (:) This is a ſign of rejection: It is uſed in Diviſion, in caſe the dividend cannot be exactly meaſured by the diviſor; and being applied to the laſt remainder, (thus, 537:) denotes it to be a ſurd number, of no further account or uſe in the operation. It is alſo applied to any fraction or part of a fraction which is thrown away.

3. The *Antiſurdal* point placed over a figure (thus $\ddot{5}$) denotes that figure to be read one larger than its nominal value. It is placed over the right hand quotient figure, to force a ſtop in diviſion, where the remainder is ſuch as would continue the diviſion forever, without bringing out the fraction with perfect exactneſs.

It is alſo uſed in reducing decimals, for the ſame purpoſe as the Dexter point, where its right hand figure is as large as 5, or larger.

Q. *May not the ſame number, ſum, or quantity, be both an Integer and a Fraction?*

A. Yes. This is ever the caſe with the middle denominations in mixed quantities. For inſtance a dime is a fraction of a dollar, and an integer of a cent and a mill. The higheſt denomination is never a fraction, and is called the *ultimate integer*: The loweſt denomination is never an integer, and called the *ultimate fraction*. The intermediate denominations, are in relation to each other, integers or fractions, and, as ſuch, may be called *meſne* integers, and *meſne* fractions.

LESSON V.

ADDITION of Decimals.

Q. HOW *is the Addition of Decimals performed?*

A. 1. Place the ſiniſter points in a perpendicular line, and the firſt left hand figure of each fraction in the next column, and ſo on.

2. Add the ſeveral numbers together, and ſet down their ſum total juſt as in ſimple Addition of whole numbers.

3. Place the ſiniſter point in the ſum total, directly under thoſe in the ſtatement, and the left hand figure, or figures, will be integers; thoſe upon the right, decimals.

Q. *How is the Addition of Integers and Fractions performed?*

A. Place the fractions as before, the integers upon the left hand of the point; then add all together as whole numbers, and place the ſiniſter point in the ſum total as before.

EXAMPLES *in Fractions.*

·4	·37	·375	·4592	·56843	·348659
·5	·25	·625	·2954	·73846	·648341
·9	·62	1...	·7546	1·30689	·997...

·4	·54	·573	·2954	·34865	·986431
·7	·06	·052	·0008	·68437	·34128
·8	·3	·001	·0095	·92303	·5934
·2	·025	·06	·0524	·04395	·19

EXAMPLES *of Integers and Fractions.*

£	[illegible]	*yds.*
245·073	22·52 6	542·378
542·065	33·26 5	245·56
479·5	44·69 5	974·5

Bushels.	*lb. oz. dw. gr.*	*Mwt. c. lb. oz. dr.*
67·125	3 · 4 5 6	4 · 6 37 5 8
66·25	2 · 8 3 7	7 · 8 25 4 2
38·375	3 · 7 0 7	· 4 37 3 6

NOTE. *Where, as in the foregoing examples, the right hand figure, or figures in the sum total are cyphers, it is needless to express them.*

LESSON VI.

SUBTRACTION of Decimal Fractions.

Q. HOW *is this Subtraction performed?*

A. RULE. Set down the numbers as in Addition, placing the Substratum, or that fraction whose left figure is the larger, uppermost; then perform the subtraction as in whole numbers, and place the finister point in the remainder, directly under that in the Subtrahend. When the Substratum and Subtrahend conſiſt of unequal numbers of figures, you may repreſent right hand cyphers, by as many dots.

EXAMPLES.

.735	.6....	.4562843	.004..
.224	.57892	.36.....	.00032
.511	.02108		

Of Integers and Fractions.

532.45	235 43	857.6542	35.1.
421.34	159 54	47.3456	27.09

Of the Federal Tables.

	lb. oz. dw. gr.	*Buſhels.*	*Mwt. c. lb. oz. dr.*
$33.26 5	3. 7 0 7	13.25	7. 8 25 4 2
22.52 6	2. 8 3 7	9.75	4. 63 75 8

NOTE. *For exvmples in the other Federal tables, ſee Part I, Leſſon XVI.*

LESSON VII.

MULTIPLICATION of Decimals.

Q. HOW *do you multiply Decimal Fractions?*

A. RULE. Multiply the factors together in the common method, whether they are pure or mixed fractions, as if they were whole numbers, or, which will be much ſhorter, by Croſs Multiplication as in Part I, Leſſon XX, and then place the ſiniſter point in the product, as many figures from the right hand, as there were decimal figures in both the factors ; and if there are not so many figures in the product, supply their deficiency by prefixing cyphers.

In multiplying together two mixed quantities, whether of the same, or of different tables, observe the following directions, viz.

1. In the thing bought or sold, make that denomination the integer, upon which the price is predicated.

2. Take that factor for the Multiplier which has the fewer figures.

3. If, in either factor, any or all the middle denominations are vacant, as in 3 dollars and 5 cents, or 4 pounds and 6 grains, then fill each vacant denomination with as many cyphers, as it will admit significant figures.

4. After you have fixed the sinister point in the product, count off from that towards the right hand, the lower denominations in their order, to the lowest denomination ; there, (in case there are figures still further towards the right) apply the dexter point ; but if the next figure be as large, or larger than 5. set the antisurdal point, and the remaining figures in either case are thrown away.

5. The product will belong to the same table with that of the price.

Q. *What do you observe that is still further distinguishing and curious in the multiplication of Fractions ?*

A. To multiply a fraction by a fraction, diminishes its value and makes the product less than either factor ; and to multiply an integer by a fraction invariably makes the product less than the multiplicand.

Q. *What is the reason of this ?*

A. It is because a fraction in its nature and operation is an exact contrast to an integer, having single unity for the middle term. Thus to multiply by 1, neither adds nor diminishes, but to multiply by any number more than 1 increases, therefore to multiply by any part, or parts less than unity or 1, of course diminishes; so that to multiply one half by one half, is the same thing as dividing it by 2, or halving it into a quarter.

EXAMPLES *in pure Fractions.*

1.	2.	3.	4.
·75	·537	·7354	·73512
×·5	×·92	×.867	×·0007
·375	·49404	.6375918	.000514794

In Integers & Fractions.

5.	6.	7.	8.
35·57	47·65	53·008	864.453
×·72	×·003	×·32	×468.354
25·6104			

In the Federal Tables.

9.	10.	11.
$ // /	*lb.oz.dw.gr.*	*Mwt. c. lb. oz.*
25·47 3	19·7 5 6	35·3 64 3
×·365	×48	×7·009
9 29 7645:		

12. What cost 17 *lb.* 6 ℥ 5 ʒ 4 ℈ of medicine, at //33 ⅌ *oz.*?

℥176.54 ×·33 = $58.25 8 *Ans.*

13. I contract with Ned Sawyer for 48968 feet of pine boards, at $4.45 ⅌ thousand feet: what must I pay him for the whole?

Td. 48.968 × 4·45 = $217.90 7 *Ans.*

14. A merchant purchased 217.55 yards of Holland, at //75 ⅌ *yd.* what is the amount of the whole?

217·55 × ·75 = $163.16 5 *Ans.*

15. I took Sampson Whiskey's note for 644 gallons of cider *(federal measure)* at ꝑ 5.50 ꝑ hogshead: what was the sum of the note?

Hhd. 6.64×5.5=ꝑ38.52 *Ans.*

16. What is the worth of 65.625 bushels of flax-seed, at //83 3 ꝑ bushel?

Bush. 65.625×.833=ꝑ54.66̈5 *Ans.*

17. The farmer purchased of the bloomer 5*cwt.* 3*c.* 25*lb.* of iron, and paid him in wheat, at the rate of 6.625 bushels ꝑ *cwt.* what was the number of bushels paid?

Cwt. 53.25×6.625=ꝑ353.03 1 *Ans.*

NOTE. *The foregoing Examples in Decimal Multiplication, the author conceives, present a method of calculation more compendious in practice, and less puzzling in theory to the learner, than that of dividing by the aliquot parts of the given price, and by parts of a part, &c. with a different ratio for every different price, according to the method prescribed in the old complicated rule denominated* Practice; *and also to supersede the use of making several multipliers to bring out the total product of a composite number, in the rule commonly called* Compound Multiplication.

LESSON VII.

DIVISION of Decimals.

Q. HOW *do you place the parts in Decimal Division?*

A. Just in the same order as in the Division of whole numbers?

Q. *What is to be done with the last remainder?*

A. Annex a cypher to it and continue the division, until you have exhausted the dividend, and completed the fraction in the quotient.

Q. *Where the dividend may be exactly measured by the divisor, what is the fraction called, arising from that division?*

A. A *terminate* decimal.

Q. *Is it not sometimes the case, that the last remainder is such a number as will not give the quotient fraction with perfect exactness; altho' you annex cyphers, and continue the division ever so long?*

A. Yes; and such decimals, in contradistinction to the former, are called *infinite* or *circulating* decimals, and sometimes *repeatin* decimals, because one or more figures always repeat, *ad infinitum;* as .666, .32573257, &c.

Q. *How is such a decimal to be terminated?*

A. It is unnecessary to protract the quotient to any greater number of figures, than what will contain the ultimate fraction sought; then force a stop by applying the surdal point to the last remainder, denoting it thrown away; and if the number in the last remainder equals, or exceeds the one half of that expressed in the divisor, set the antisurdal point over the last figure in the quotient.

This method reduces the circulating, into a terminate decimal; and, tho' it does not ascertain the fraction with perfect exactness, yet the variation is so very inconsiderable, that what is wanting in exactness, is abundantly compensated in practical convenience.

Q. *What do you further remark as particular in the nature of Decimal Division?*

A. That it is just the reverse of Whole Numbers, in that, dividing an integer by a fraction, or a fraction by a fraction, instead of diminishing, increases its value, or the quotient will ever be greater than the dividend.

Q. *What is the method of dividing Decimal fractions*?*

---

* *Division of decimals is the most complex of any of the fundamental rules in decimal Arithmetic, and, indeed, the*

A. The general rule is to divide as in Whole Numbers, enlarging the number of the dividend, if necessary, by annexing one or more cyphers; then, in the question, count off as many decimal places, as the dividend has more than the divisor; and if there are not so many places in the quotient, supply the defect with left hand cyphers. For the greater ease, and clearer apprehension of the learner, this General Rule may be distributed into the several following Cases, in which all the various modifications of decimal numbers are pointed out, with a particular Rule directly applied to each.

---

only one which is not perfectly simple and easy. The great difficulty is, to know, with precision, in what place to set the sinister point in the quotient. The General Rule is, indeed, just and extensive, and, to the man of figures well versed in the art, sufficiently clear and explicit. It is the young learner, *however, who has that practical knowledge still to acquire, who needs the benefit of a written rule; and yet is benefited by it no further, and no faster, than he understands it, and becomes able to apply it. But, in the case before us, so diversified are the examples in decimal Division, by the different relations of the operating parts, the different modifications of the decimal numbers, and their different effects upon the value of the quotient, that it must be very difficult, if not impracticable, to state any one general rule, sufficiently definite to be at once clearly comprehended and easily applied by the young student. To remedy this inconvenience, the author is induced to vary from the common method, by analysing the General Rule, and classing the different cases which arise, under as many* particular *rules: these, being more simple, may be more easily applied; as the student, in any proposed example, will readily see under which Case it falls, and there find a familiar rule, explicitly in point.*

CASE 1.

Decimals divided by Decimals.

Rule. If the Divisor and Dividend are both decimals only, and the Dividend have the smaller number of decimal places, make them equal, by annexing one or more right hand cyphers. Then,

If the divisor be a smaller fraction than the dividend, or just equal to it, the quotient will be integers, until all the figures in the dividend are brought down; but, after you annex a cypher to the last remainder, all the subsequent quotient figures will be decimals. But,

If the divisor be the larger fraction, annex one or more cyphers to the dividend, until the number will contain the divisor, and the quotient will be only fractions.

Examples.

1.	2.	3.
Divide .75 by .3	.8÷.648 ..	.648÷.8
.30).75(2.5	.648).800(1.234	.8).648(
150	1520	.81
(0)	2240	
	2960	
	368:	

CASE 2.

Integers divided by larger Integers.

Rule. When the divisor and dividend are both integers, and the dividend the smaller, annex a cypher or cyphers to the dividend, until it be large enough to divide, and prefix as many cyphers, save one, to the quotient.

EXAMPLES.

4. Divide 225 by 250

250)225.0(.9

(0)

5. Divide 5 by 379

379)5.00(.0131

121.0

73.0

351:

CASE 3.

Decimals divided by Integers.

RULE. When the Divisor is an Integer, and the dividend a Decimal, expressed by a smaller number, annex one or more cyphers to the dividend, and prefix as many left hand cyphers to the quotient, and if there were any left hand cyphers in the dividend, prefix as many more to the quotient; which will be a fraction, as much smaller than the dividend, as the divisor was larger.

EXAMPLES.

6. Divide .7 by 8

8).70(.0875

60

40

(0)

7. .66÷96

96).0600(.000625

240

480

(0)

8. .17÷680

680).1700(.0025

3400

(0)

CASE 4.

Decimals divided by Integers.

RULE. If the Divisor be an Integer, and the dividend a Decimal, expressing a larger number than the divisor; place the first significant figure, in the quotient, as far from the sinister point, as the right hand figure of the first dividual is from its point.

EXAMPLES.

9.	10.	11.
Divide .16 by 4	.175÷90	.4÷1234..
4).16(.04	90).175(.00194	1234).4000(.000324
	850	2980
	400	5120
	40:	1184:

CASE 5.

Integers divided by Decimals.

RULE. If the divisor be Decimals and the dividend Integers, annex, decimally, to the dividend, as many cyphers as there are figures in the divisor; and the quotient will be Integers, until all the dividend-figures are brought down.

EXAMPLES.

12.	13.	14.
Divide 75 by .015	659÷.7	5÷.375
.015)75.000(5000	.7)659.0(	375)5.000(13.333
	941.428	1250
		1250:

CASE 6.

Integers and Decimals divided by Decimals.

RULE. If the divisor be Decimals only, and the dividend Integers and Decimals, then annex to the integers, by the *dexter* point, as many of the decimal figures as there are figures in the divisor, (thus, 72.34'5) and if there be not so many decimal places in the dividend, supply them with cyphers, (thus, 72.300') and the quotient, arising from all the figures upon the left of the dexter point, will be Integers.

EXAMPLES.

15.
Divide 168.81 by .3
.3) 68.8·1(
562.7

16.
72.0003÷.08
.08)72.00 03(
900.00375

17.
9.68÷.053.
.053)9 680 (182,6
438
140
340
22:

CASE 7.

Decimals divided by Integers and Decimals.

RULE. If the divisor be Integers and Decimals, and the dividend Decimals only, and expressing a larger number than the divisor, divide as in whole numbers, and the quotient will be decimals. But,

If the dividend be the smaller nunber, annex cyphers until you can divide, prefixing to the quotient as many cyphers, save one, as you annexed to the dividend.

EXAMPLES.

18.
Divide .6125 by 4.5
4.5).6125(.136
162
275
5:

19.
Divide .45 by 63.95.
63.95).45000(.007036
23500
43150
4780:

CASE 8.

Integers and Decimals divided by Integers.

RULE. If the divisor be integers only, and the dividend Integers and Decimals; the quotient of the dividend integers will be integers, and those of the decimals, decimals. But,

If the Dividend Integers will not contain the divisor, annex a sufficient number of the decimal figures by the dexter point, prefixing to the quotient as many cyphers, save one, as there are figures between the dexter and sinister point in the dividend.

EXAMPLES.

20. Div. 9.6 by 3

```
3)9.6(3.2
```

21. 6 5÷75..

```
75)6.50(.0866
   ----
    500
    ---
     50:
     ---
```

22. 1474.227÷54

```
54)1474.227(27.3005
   ----
    394
    ---
     162
     ---
     ...270
        ---
          0
         ---
```

CASE 9.

Integers divided by Integers and Decimals.

RULE. If the divisor be Integers and Decimals, and the dividend Integers only, and greater in value than the divisor, then annex to the dividend as many decimal cyphers, as there are decimal figures in the divisor, and the quotient will be integers, until the last figure in the dividend is brought down. But,

If the dividend be smaller in value than the divisor, annex only so many cyphers as will make it larger and then the quotient will be decimals.

EXAMPLES.

23. Divide 810 by 32.4

```
32.4)810.0(25
     -----
     1620
     ----
      (o)
```

24. Divide 54 by 432.8

```
432.8)54.00(.1247
      ----
      10720
      -----
       20640 &c.
```

CASE 10.

Integers and Decimals, divided by Integers and Decimals.

RULE. If the divisor and dividend both consist of Integers and Decimals, make the number of decimal figures equal in each; place the dexter point to the dividend, and the quotient will be integers: But, if the dividend does not contain the divisor, then annex to it a right hand cypher, and the quotient will be decimals.

EXAMPLES.

25.
Divide 75.3 by 3.75
3.75)75.30.(20.08

3000

(0)

26.
Divide 75.6 by 151.2
151.2)75.6.0(.5

(0)

CASE 11.

The Divisor an Integer and Decimal Denominator.

RULE. When the divisor is an integer, and its number any Decimal Denominator, such as 10, 100, 1000, &c. whether the dividend be integers only, or integers and decimals, or decimals only, you have but to remove the sinister point as many figures towards the left hand as there are cyphers in the divisor.

EXAMPLES.

27.	28.	29.
Divide 10. by 100.	45 7 ÷ 10	.3 ÷ 1000
.1 *Ans.*	=4.5 7	=.0003

CASE 12.

The Divisor a Decimal formed by a single Unit.

RULE. If the divisor be a decimal made by a single unit, or an unit and any number of left hand cyphers, such as .1, .01, .001, &c. remove the sinister point in the dividend as many figures towards the right, as there are figures in the divisor; or annex as many cyphers, without the point, as the case may be.

Examples.

30.	31.	32.
Div. 10 by .1 = 100	4·557 ÷ .01 = 455·7	.00039 ÷ .001 = ·39

Promiscuous Examples.

	Dividend.		*Divisor.*		*Quotient.*
33)	13[illegible].62	÷	4	=	33·905
34)	74621	÷	·9	=	8291.2
35)	39·2[illegible]5	÷	367	=	.1069
36)	·7[illegible]94	÷	734	=	.00099
37)	4·98[illegible]69	÷	4·5	=	1.1077
38)	.09875	÷	·984	=	·10035
39)	5·83	÷	841.	=	.006932
40)	78	÷	·983	=	79·3489
41)	72.8745	÷	23	=	3·1684
42)	28	÷	.007563	=	3702.23
43)	56	÷	70	=	.8
44)	·932	÷	37·5	=	.024853
45)	·45	÷	55·7	=	.08969
46)	480	÷	27·3	=	17·58

LESSON VIII.

Commutation of Decimals.

Q. How *do you change a* vulgar *into a* decimal *fraction?*

Rule. Annex a cypher or cyphers to the numerator, and divide by the denominator; the quotient will be a decimal fraction of the same value.

Examples.

Change $\frac{3}{4}$	Change $\frac{5}{20}$	Change $\frac{3}{474}$
4)3·0(·75	20)5.0(.25	474)3·000(.00632
		1560
		1380
		432:

LESSON IX.

Of Mixed Quantities.

Q. WHAT *is the General Rule of changing* mefne *or ultimate fractions into the decimal parts of a* mefne *or ultimate integer, in all the tables of mixed quantities?*

RULE. The fame as that in the laft Leffon, after expreffing the given fum or quantity in the form of a vulgar fraction, as thus, 18*f* is $\frac{18}{20}$ of a pound; 6*d.* is $\frac{6}{240}$ of a pound, and $\frac{6}{12}$ of a fhilling; 3 farthings are $\frac{3}{4}$ of a penny, $\frac{3}{48}$ of a Shilling, and $\frac{3}{960}$ of a Pound.

1. *Of* MONEY.

EXAMPLES.

What are the decimal parts of a Pound in 18 Shillings. 18*f* = $\frac{18}{20}$ of a Pound. Therefore 18 ÷ 20

2|0)18|.0(.9£

What are the decimal parts of a Shilling and of a Pound in 6 Pence?

6*d.* = $\frac{6}{12}$ of a Shilling, and $\frac{6}{240}$ of a Pound.

f. £.

12)6.0(.5 24|0)6.0|0(.025

What are the decimal parts of a Penny, of a Shilling, and of a Pound, in 3 Farthings?

$\frac{3}{4}$ Penny $\frac{3}{48}$ Shilling $\frac{3}{960}$ Pound.

d. *f.* £.

4)3.0(.75 48)3.00(.0625 960)3.000(.003125

	120	1200
	240	2400
	(0)	4800
		(0)

Therefore,

Farthings.		*Pence.*		*Shillings.*		*Pounds.*
3	=	·75	=	.0625	=	.003125
		6.0.	=	.5...	=	.025...
				18.0...	=	.9.....
$6\frac{3}{4}$	=	6.75	=	.5625	=	.028125
$18/6\frac{3}{4}$	=======			18.5625	=	.928125
£$1,,18,,6\frac{3}{4}$	=============					1.928125

SECT. 2.

Another method of changing Shillings, Pence and Farthings into an equivalent decimal of a Pound.

Rule. 1. Write the given numbers perpendicularly under each other for dividends, inverting their order, or beginning with the ſmalleſt denomination.

2. Oppoſite to each dividend, in a left hand column, ſet the terminus of each for its diviſor, with the ſign of Diviſion between them.

3. Divide the higheſt dividend by its terminus, and annex the quotient as decimal parts to the next lower dividend; proceeding with all the remaining dividends in the ſame manner; and the laſt quotient will be the equivalent decimal of the given ſum.

Change 18*ſ.* 6*d.* $\frac{3}{4}$, into the decimal of a pound.

4) 3.00
12) 6.75
20) 18.5625
.928125 the decimal required.

Here, in dividing 3 by 4, I annex two cyphers, and the quotient is .75, which I annex to the 6*d.* This quotient, *viz.* 6.75, being pence and decimal parts of a penny, I divide by 12, and the quotient, .5625, I annex to the 18*ſ.* for decimal parts of a ſhilling. This quotient, divided by 20, gives the decimal ſought.

SECT. 3.

Federal Money.

In federal money, no other Commutation is required, but only to read together all the lower denominations, as one aggregate decimal of that denomination propofed for the integer; prefixing cyphers, as the cafe may require, and fetting the point accordingly. This will be fufficiently explained by the following

SCALE.

Confolidation.

			1	=	.1	=	.01	=	.001
					1.0	=	.1	=	.01
							1.0	=	.1
		1	1	=	1.1	=	.11	=	.011
	1	1	1	=	11.1	=	1.11	=	.111
1	1	1	1	- - - - - -				=	1.111
1	0	1	1	- - - - - -				=	1.011
1	0	0	1	- - - - - -				=	1.001

Reduction.

1.001	- - - - - -				=	1	0	0	1
1.011	- - - - - -				=	1	0	1	1
1.111	- - - - - -				=	1	1	1	1
.111	=	1.11	=	11.1	=		1	1	1
.011	=	0.11	=	1.1	=		0	1	1
.1	=	1.0	=	10.0	=		1	0	0
.01	- - -		=	1.0	=		0	1	0
.001	- - - - - -				=		0	0	1

L E S S O N X.

The fame.

Q. IS *there not a fhorter method of confolidating fhillings, pence and farthings, into decimals?*

A. Yes, by the following rules, *viz.*

RULE. 1. To change Shillings into decimals, halve them, and prefix the finifter point; thus, the decimal of 14*s.* is .7. If it be any odd number of fhillings, halve them with a fuppofed cypher annexed; thus, 19*s.* is 190÷2=.95. For 1 fhilling, prefix a cypher to the half, or, in other words, put the ſignificant decimal figure in the place of hundreds ; thus, 1ſ.=.05 : Or you may multiply any odd number of ſhillings by 5, for parts of a hundred.

2. To change Pence into decimals of a Pound, multiply them by 4, and the product will be thouſandths ; to which add 1 for every 24 it contains.

3. To change Farthings into decimals of a Pound, call every farthing .001 : This falls ſhort of perfect exactneſs, but immaterially.

EXAMPLE.

Conſolidate 18/6¾, into the decimal of a Pound.

$$
\begin{aligned}
18 \div 2 &= .9 \\
6 \times 4 + 1 &= .025 \\
3 \times .001 &= .003 \\
\hline
\end{aligned}
$$

£.928 *the decimal required.*

This formal addition of the decimals, is only to make the example the more plain; but is unneceſſary to the decimal practitioner; who may perform the additionin his mind only, and read the decimal merely by inſpection. Let him but obſerve to add the third of the pence-decimal to the place of Hundreds, in that of Shillings, and the farthing-decimal to the place of Thouſandths ; and the operation is performed almoſt at a glance : Thus, 18/6¾=.928. In this caſe, he has only to take the half of 18, or 9, and annex to it the product of 4 times 6, with the addition of 1 for the 24 and 3 for the farthings, or 28, making .928.

Q. *What is the ſhorter method of writing pence and farthings in the decimal of their* meſne *integers?*

RULE. 1. To expreſs pence in the decimal of a ſhilling, multiply them by 8, and add to the product 1 for every 3 in the given number, placing the finiſter point. This, in 3*d.* 6*d.* and 9*d.* will be perfectly exact ; in the others it will fall a trifle ſhort ; therefore it will be beſt to add 1 for 2*d.* 2 for 5*d.* 3 for 8*d.* and 4 for 11*d.*

2. To change Farthings into the decimal of a Shilling, multiply them by .021, and prefix a cypher: into the decimal of a Penny, by multiplying them into .25.

Change 9 pence into the deeimal of a ſhilling.

$9\times8+3=.75$ *Anſ.*

Change 3 farthings into the decimal of a ſhilling and of a Penny.

$3\times.021=.063$ *Shilling.*
$3\times.25=.75$ *Penny.*

LESSON XI.

How to change the lower Denominations of the ſeveral Tables of Weights & Meaſures into Decimal parts of their reſpective Integers.

Q. IS *there not another and ſhorter wethod of performing this operation, than by the* General Rule, *in* Leſſon IX?

A. Yes, by the medium of the following decimal Tables of weights and meaſures, conciſely expreſſing the decimal of each lower denomination, in relation to all its integers, or higher denominations.

Rule. Multiply the number of each denomination in the given quantity, into that number which expreſſes the decimal of 1 of the ſame denomination and integer in the table, and add their products together, for the whole Decimal.

1. Troy-Weight*.

gr.	dw.	oz.	lb.
1 =	.0417 =	.0021 =	.00018
	1. =	.05 =	.00416̈
		1. =	.083̈

Examples.

1. What are the decimal parts of a pound in 20 grains?

.00018 *the decimal of* 1 *grain.*
×20

.0036|0
Ans. .0036

2. Change 9*grs.* 13*grs.* and 18*grs.* into their respective decimals of a Penny-weight.

Ans. 9*gr.*=.37, 13*gr.*=.54, 18*gr.*=.75.

Change 13*dwt.* 7*gr.* into decimals of an ounce. *A.* .664

21 *grs.* - - - -	*ditto*	.0441
19 *grs.* - - -	*Penny weight,*	.7923
20 *grs.* - - -	*Pound,*	.0036
13 *dwts.* - - - -	*ditto.*	.054
17 *dw.* 3 *gr.* - - -	*ditto.*	.70944
11 *oz.* - - - - - -	*ditto.*	.924
23 *grs.* - - - -	*ditto.*	.00414

---

* Ounces *Troy, may be changed into decimals of a Pound in the same manner as Pence into decimals of a Shilling.* Penny-weights *into decimals of a Pound wt. as Pence into decimals of a Pound currency: and into decimals of an Ounce by halving them like Shillings.* Grains *into decimals of an Ounce by doubling them, and adding to the product* 1 *for every* 24 *it contains, which will be parts of a thousand; into decimals of a Penny wt. by multiplying them into* 4, *and adding to the product one for every* 24 *it contains.*

SECT. 2.

Avoirdupois-Weight.

oz.	lb.	qrs.	Cwt. *	Ton.
1	=.063	=.0023	=.0005	=.000025
	1.	=.036	=.008	=.0005
		1.	=.25	=.0125
			1.	=.05.

Note. *Drams are omitted as too minute to be of any special account in common practice.*

Examples.

		Answers.
Change 14 *Cwt.* into the decimals of a	Ton	=.7
ditto 2 *qrs.* - - -	*ditto*	=.025
ditto - - -	*Hund.*	=.5
25*lb* - - - -	Ton	=.0125
ditto - - -	Hund.	=.2
ditto - - -	Quarter	=.9
11*oz.* - - -	Ton	=.000275
ditto - - - -	*Cwt.*	=.0055
ditto - - -	Quarter	=.0253
ditto - - -	Pound	=.693
7*lb.* 3*oz.* - - -	Ton	=.003575
ditto - - -	*Cwt.*	=.0575
ditto - -	Quarter	=.2589
3*qrs.* 7*lb.* 8*oz.* -	Ton	=.0447
ditto - - -	*Cwt.*	=.89
16*Cwt.* 1*qr.* 27*lb.* 15*oz.*	Ton	=.814225

SECT. 3.

Apothecary-Weight.

gr.	℈	ʒ	℥	lb.
1	= .05	= .016	= .002	= .00018
	1.	= .33	= .041	= .0035
		1.	= .125	= .001
			1.	= .083

---

* *Hundreds may be decimalized in the same manner as Shillings.*

Examples.

			Pound.
Change	12 *grs.* =	into dec. of a	= .00216
	2 ℈ =		= .007
	7 ʒ. =		= .007
	2 ℥ =		= .168
	2 ℥. 7 ʒ. 2℈. 12 *gr.*		= .18716

SECT. 4.

Long-Measure.

A League is .05 of a Degree.

A Mile is .017 of a Degree, and 33 of a League.

A Furlong is .002 of a Degree, .041 of a League, and .125 of a Mile.

A Rod is .000052 of a Degree, .001 of a League, .003 of a Mile and .025 of a Furlong.

A Yard is .000015 of a Degree, .0003 of a League, .0009 of a Mile, .003125 of a Furlong, and .29 of a Rod.

A Foot is .0000125 of a Degree, .000025 of a League, .00018 of a Mile, .00151 of a Furlong, .06 of a Rod, and .33 of a Yard.

An Inch is .000000087 of a Degree, .0000052 of a League, .0000157 of a Mile, .000126 of a Furlong, .005 of a Rod, .028 of a Yard, and .084 of a Foot.

Examples.

		Answers.
Change 7 Inches into the dec. of a League		=.0000364
1 Foot and 7 Inches,	*ditto*	=.0000614
8 yards, 1 foot, 7 inches	*ditto*	=.0009614
32 Rods, 3 yds. 1 foot, 7 inches	*ditto*	=.0329614
Furlongs, 6,,32,,3,,1,,7 inches	*ditto*	=.3369614
Miles, 2,,6,,32,,3,,1,,7 inches	*ditto*	=.9549614

SECT. 5.

CLOTH-MEASURE.

Nail.	*Quarter.*	*Yard.*	*Fl. Ell.*	*Eng. Ell.*
1 =	.25 =	.0625 =	.084 =	.05
	1. =	.25 =	.34 =	.2
		1. =	1.25 =	.8
			1. =	.6

& .75 of a yard.

EXAMPLES.

Change 4 *yds.* 3 *qrs.* 2 *na.* into the dec. of an Eng. Ell.

4 ×.8=3 .2
3 ×.2= .6
2 ×.05= .1

Anſ. 3 .9 *Eng. Ells.*

SECT. 6.

LAND MEASURE.

Sq. foot.	*yd.*	*Pole.*	*Rood.*	*Acre.*
1 =	.11 =	.00037 =	.00001 =	.00000229
	1. =	.034 =	.0016 =	.00038
		1. =	.025 =	.0625
			1. =	.25

EXAMPLES.

Change 6 feet into the decimal of a *yard*, =.67
3 yds. 6 feet. - - - *Pole* =.10416
1 Pole, 27 yds, 8 feet - - *ditto* =.98896
1 Rood, 15 Poles, 12 yds. 7 feet, *Rood* =.39427
2 Roods, 25 Poles, 8 yds. 3 feet, *Acre* =.65929689

SECT. 7.

LIQUID MEASURE.

Pt.	*qt.*	*gall.*	*bar.*	*tierce.*	*hhd.*	*punch.*	*pipe.*	*tun.*
1=	.5=	.125=	.004=	.003=	.002=	.0015=	.001=	.0005
	1. =	.25=	.008=	.006=	.004=	.003=	.002=	.001
		1. =	.0318=	.024=	.016=	.012=	.008=	.004
			1. =	.75=	.5 =	.375=	.25=	.125
				1. =	.67=	.5 =	.334=	.167
					1. =	.75 =	.5 =	.25
						1. =	.667=	.334
							1. =	.5

EXAMPLES.

Change 19*gal.* 3*qts.* 2*pts.* into the dec. of a *Bar.*=.6352
1*bar.* 9*gal.* 3*qts.* 1*pt.* - - *Tierce.*=.987
1*tierce*, 1*bar.* 23*gal.* 3*qts.* - - *Hhd.*=1.55
1*hhd.* 2 *tierces*, 13*gall.* 2*qts.* - *Pun.*=1.412
1 *pun.* 1*hhd.* 1*tr.* 1*b.* 1*g.* 1*qt.* - *Pipe.*=1.764

SECT. 8.

DRY MEASURE.

Quart.	*gallon.*	*peck.*	*bush. U. S.*	*bush. Can.*
1 =	.25 =	.125 =	.03125 =	.025
	1. =	.5 =	.125 =	.1
		1. =	.25 =	.2
			.1 =	.8

EXAMPLES.

Change 3*pecks*, 1*gal.* 2*qts.* into the decimal of a *bush.* U. S. - - - - =.9375

Ditto, - - *bush. Can.* .75

SECT. 9.

Of TIME*.

Day.	*Week.*	*Month.*	*Year.*
1 =	.14 =	.034 =	.003
	1. =	.25 =	.02
		1. =	.083

EXAMPLE.

What is the decimal of a year in 7 months, 3 weeks, and 3 days?

Months 7 × .083 = .581
Weeks 3 × .02 = .06
Days 3 × .003 = .009

Ans. .65. of a year.

---

* *The above decimal table of Time is not conformed to a mathematical exactness, but to the purpose of greater convenience in common practice, and particularly to the usual method of reckoning Time in the calculation of Interest, in which its utility principally consists. For this reason, also, it does not descend to hours, minutes and seconds. Those who wish to be more minute, may apply the general rule, or consult the decimal Table.*

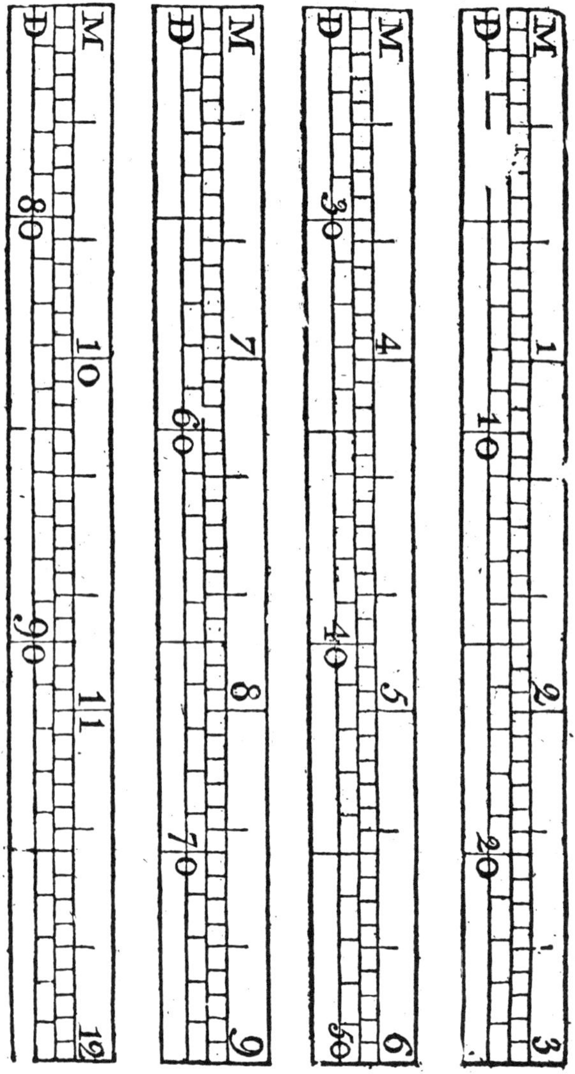

To facilitate the art of decimalizing *Time*, the foregoing Scale is propofed, defigned as an ufeful companion to the man of bufinefs, efpecially in the calculation of intereft; as it will enable him to find the decimal of any requifite part of a year, merely by infpection, and in a decimal of only two places of figures.

Explanation of the Scale.

The Scale reprefents the period of 1 year divided into 100 equal parts; each ftave contains one quarter or .25 of a year. The fpace M divides the year into the 12 months and numbers them; the narrow fpace next below it fubdivides the months into periods of two days; on the line D are marked the decimal parts of a year, having 100 for the integer or decimal denominator, and numbered at every ten. Therefore to find the decimal of any part of a year, find the given time upon the Scale, by the months and days; this being done take the mark ftanding directly, or the neareft under it, for the number of its decimal.

Apply the laft example for a fpecimen.

Look 7 months and 24 days upon the Scale, and the decimal directly under it is .65, the fame as before.

LESSON XII.

Reduction of Decimals.

Q. WHAT *is the common and general rule of operation in reducing decimals of all the tables of mixed quantities?*

Rule. Multiply the given decimal by the *terminus* of the denomination next lower than its integer; then point off from the product as many right hand figures as there were decimal figures in the multiplicand; the figures pointed off are fo many of that denomination, of which the multiplier was the terminus, and the figures pointed off are decimals of that denomination, and muft be multiplied by the next lower terminus, and fo on, as before.

EXAMPLES *in each Table.*

Reduce .928125 of a pound to its equivalent value in shillings, pence, &c.

```
     .928125
         ×20
     -------
S.  18.5625(00
         ×12
     -------
D.   6.75(00
         ×4
     -------
Q.   3.00   Ans. 18/6¼
```

2. Reduce .9877 of a pound Troy weight.

Ans. 11*oz.* 13*dw.* 1*gr.*

3 Reduce .913955 of a Ton.

Ans. 18*Cwt.* 1*qr.* 3*lb.* 4*oz.* 2*dr.*

4 Reduce .9549614 of a League.

M. fur. r. yds. f. in.

Ans. 2,,6,,36,,4,,0,,7.

5 Reduce .572 of an English Ell.

Ans. 2*qrs.* 3*nails.*

6. Reduce .23916 of a pound (Apothecary-weight.)

Ans. 2℥. 6ʒ. 2℈. 17*gr.*

7. Reduce .65929689 of an Acre.

Ans. 2 *Roods,* 25*P.* 14*yds.* 7*feet.*

8. Reduce .987 of a Tierce.

Ans. 1*bar.* 10*gal.* 1*pint.*

9. Reduce .9375 of a Bushel U. S.

Ans. 3*pecks.* 1*gal.* 2*qts.*

10. Reduce .735 of a year.

Ans. 8*mo.* 3*weeks,* 2*days.*

LESSON XIII.

Decimal Commutation of Money continued.

Q. WHAT *shorter method is there of reducing the decimals of this Table?*

RULE. If the integer be pounds, point off with the *dexter* point the three left hand figures, or with the antisurdal point, if the fourth be as large or larger than 5, then multiply them by 2, setting down the product of the left hand figure only, which is so many Shillings.

If this be an odd number, then subtract *five* from the second figure, and to the remainder annex the 3d figure, and after casting out 1 for every 25, divide by 4; the quotient will be pence and the remainder farthings. If the Shillings be an even number, then the *second* and *third* figures form a dividend as they stand. In this way the reduction may be performed merely by inspection.

EXAMPLES.

1. Reduce .928·125 of a pound.

Ans. 18/6¼ *See the reverse, in page* 205

2. Reduce .579 of a pound.

Ans. 11/7

Explanation.

Example 1. Take off the three left hand figures, 928, with the dexter point, the rest are thrown away: then say, twice 8 is 16—twice 2 is 4, and 1 is 5; then twice 9 is 18, which last product only I set down for shillings; that being an even number, I take the 2d and 3d figures as they stand, subtracting only 1 for the 25 which they contain, which leaves 27 for a dividend; this divided by 4, gives quotient 6 for pence, and remainder 3 for farthings.

Example 2. $2\times9=18$; $2\times7=14+1=15$; $2\times5=10+1=11$; which I set down for shillings: this being an odd number, subtract 5 from the second figure 7, which leaves 2—the 9 annexed makes 29: 1 subtracted for the 25, leaves 28; this divided by 4, quotients 7 pence.

NOTE. *If there be only two decimal figures, annex a right hand cypher; if there be but one, double it, and you have it in shillings.*

LESSON XIV.

A concise Decimal method of exchanging the several Currencies of Federal Money, and Pounds, Shillings and Pence.

Q. HOW *do you apply the following Table, for the exchange of currencies?*

RULE. After changing the parts of a Pound, if any, into decimals, look for the *currency* of the given sum at the left hand, and for *that* of the sum required, at the top: tracing from them, mark the decimal where their rows meet; then multiply by that tabular number, and the product will be the answer sought.

	Sterl.	*S. C.*	*Irish.*	*Hal.*	*N. E.*	*N. J.*	*N. Y.*	*Fed.*
Federal.	.225	.233	.244	.25	.3	.375	.4	
N. York.	.5625	.584	.609	.625	.75	.9375		2.5
N. J.&c.	.6	.622	.65	.667	.8		1.007	2.667
N. E.&c.	.75	.778	.8125	.834		1.25	1.334	3.334
Halifax.	.9	.934	.975		1.2	1.5	1.6	4
Irish.	.923	.957		1.003	1.23	1.538	1.641	4.003
S. Car.	.964		1.0446	1.007	1.286	1.607	1.714	4.286
Sterling.		1.004	1.084	1.112	1.334	1.667	1.778	4.447

EXAMPLES.

Consolidate £133,,12, N. Jersey, &c. currency, into S. Carolina and Georgia currency.

133.6
Tabular number, × .622

Ans. 83.099·2=£83,,01,,11¼.

Reduce £34,,7,,6 Halifax, into the currency of N.E.

34·375
Tabular number, × 1.2

Ans. 41.2500=£41,,5.

Consolidate $315.75, into the currency of N.Y, &c.
Tabular number, ×.4

£126.300=£126,,6 *Anſ.*

For further examples, under this rule, the learner may turn back to Leſſons V, IX and X, of the Second Part.

LESSON XV.

Exchange between various foreign Monies of account, and Federal Money.

RULE. Look the federal money value of the money unit of the given foreign currency in Leſſon XIX, Second Part; then, if the operation be Conſolidation, multiply, if Reduction, divide by that decimal number, and the product or quotient is the anſwer required.

EXAMPLES.

Change 5379 livres Tournois into federal money.
×.19

$680.01 *Anſ.*

NOTE. *To reverſe the exchange in this and all the following Examples, you have only to reverſe the operation by the ſame decimal.*

Change 574 mill rees of Portugal into federal money.
×1.24

$711.76 *Anſ.*

Change 1000 guilders into federal money.
×.39

$390.00 *Anſ.*

Change 1235 marcs banco of Hamburgh.

3)1235(

$411.66 7 *Ans.*

Change 440 Chinese tales into federal money.

×1.48

$651.20 *Ans.*

Change 749 rupees of Bengal into federal money.

×.555

$415.695 *Ans.*

Change 683 pagodas of India into federal money.

×1.94

$1325.02 *Ans.*

LESSON XVI.

PROPORTION.

Q. WHAT *is the nature and effect of this rule?*

There are ever three numbers, or terms given, by which to find a fourth. These numbers are either simple and expressed, or complex and involved in two or more factors, and bear relation to each other in a comparative proportion, as hereafter explained. Of these four terms, the first and second form an *Hypothesis* or Supposition, stating a certain *cause* as producing a certain *effect*—the third and fourth terms form a *Consequence* deduced from the second and third, inferring, as an answer to the question, a certain other cause or effect, corresponding in kind with that given in the Hypothesis.

Q. *What are the general and common divisions of this Rule?*

A. 1. *Direct* Proportion, or Sngle Rule of Three.
2. *Indirct* Proportion or Rule of Three inverse.
3. *Compound* Proportion or Double Rule of Three.
Give a concise explanation of each.

A. Direct proportion, is where the answer sought is the *effect* of a certain given cause in the Consequence, and is of the same kind with the 2d. term, or the effect stated in the Hypothesis; and bears the same proportion to it, as the cause in the Consequence does to the cause in the Hypothesis—or, the fourth term bears the same relation to the second, as the third does to the first. This is arguing from cause to effect, as, if 4 men eat 1 Bushel of wheat in a week, *then* 16 men will eat 4 Bushels in the same time. Which numbers may be thus divided and classed.

Hipothesis.		*Consequence.*	
cause.	*effect.*	*cause.*	*effect.*
4 men.	1 Bushel.	16 men.	4 Bushels.

2. *Indirect* Proportion, is when the answer required is the *cause* of the effect stated in the Consequence, and bears the same proportion to the second term, or the effect in the Hypothesis, as the first term, or cause in the Hypothesis, does to the third given term, or the effect in the Consequence. This is the reverse of the former, or reasoning from the effect to its cause; that is, if such a given effect be produced by such a particular cause, what cause is necessary to produce another certain given effect. *Example.* If ℔ 100 in 12 months gain 6 *pr. cent.* interest, ℔ 150 will gain the same sum in 8 months.

Hypothesis.		*Consequence.*	
cause.	*effect.*	*cause.*	*effect.*
℔ 100 in 12*m.*	6	℔ 100 in 8*m.*	6 interest

3. *Compound* Proportion, may be either direct or indirect and commonly consists of five numbers. It is where two of the given terms are complex and lie involved in the square of two or more given numbers, connecting with the cause or effect, some certain cir-

cumſtance or quality, material to the queſtion, and inſeperable in its operation; ſuch as, *the* diſtance *of goods carried—the* number, quantity, weight &c. *of any commodity bought or ſold—the* time *of money lent, or advanced as ſtock in trade* &c &c. Example. If ℳ 100 at intereſt 10 months gain 5. what ſum will 150 gain in 5 months? Here the cauſe in the Hypotheſis is a complex term, conſiſting of 2 numbers, 100 and 10 months; and ſo alſo in the Conſequence 150 and 5 months.

Q. *How are the given numbers to be prepared for the work, in every kind of Proportion?*

A. 1. Expreſs the correſponding parts in numbers of the ſame name or denomination, and the fractional numbers, if any, in decimals.

2. Take that or thoſe numbers which expreſs the cauſe in the Hypotheſis, and write them down in one line; then its effect, at a convenient diſtance towards the right hand, and draw a line from one to the other.

3. Place the terms of the Conſequence in the ſame manner, each under its coreſponding term, or number of the ſame name in the Hyphotheſis; ſupplying the vacant term or number with the letter Q, and then draw a tranſverſe line from the effect in the Hypotheſis to the cauſe in the Conſequence, connecting the horizontal lines in the form of the letter Z.

Q. *What is the general Rule of operation in all kinds of Proportion?*

A. After ſtating the terms as above, then obſerve the following Rule, viz.

Rule. If the queſtion or Q falls under the *effect*, it is Direct Proportion, if under *cauſe* it is Indirect Proportion—in the *firſt* caſe, multiply the number or numbers, if any, conſtituting the cauſe in the line of Conſequence, with the number or numbers expreſſing the effect in the line of Hypotheſis, at the other end of the croſs line, for a *Dividend*; and all the other numbers together for a Diviſor. In the *ſecond* caſe, multiply the firſt mentioned terms together for a diviſor, and all the numbers ſtanding at the other two corners for a Dividend; and the quotient, in either caſe, is the anſwer, or fourth term; and of the ſame name or denomination with the number ſtanding above Q. See the illuſtration of the Rule in the following

EXAMPLES.

1. If $4\frac{1}{2}$ yards of Broadcloath coſt 18 Dallars what muſt I pay for 90 yards?

Statement.		*Cauſe.*		*Effect.*
	Hypotheſis,	4.5*yds*	Z	18
	Conſequence,	90		Q.

Operation $Q.=90\times18\div4.5=\$360$.

Here the Q falling under *effect*, the proportion is *direct*.

2. If 360 dollars purchaſe 90 yards of broadcloth, what is the price of 4.5 yards?

	Cauſe.		*Effect.*
Hyp.	\$360	Z	90 *yds.*
Con.	Q.		4.5

$Q.=360\times4.5\div90=\$18$. *Anſ.*

Here the Q, falling under *cauſe*, denotes *Indirect* Proportion, and the number oppoſite it, (90) is, of courſe, the diviſor. Theſe two examples mutually prove each other; they may alſo be proved in another method, by this rule, *viz.* that the ſquare of the two *extremes*, if the operation be true, will ever be equal to the ſquare of the *meſnes*—that is, the product of the 1ſt and 4th terms, in the order they are ſtated, will be the ſame number as that of the 2d and 3d.

Proof. $\begin{cases} 4.5\times360=18\times90=1620 \\ 360\times4.5=90\times18=1620 \end{cases}$

3. If \$100, at intereſt 10 months, gain 5, what will 150 gain in 5 months?

	Cause.		Effect.
Statement.	Hyp. 100 for 10 months,	Z	5 int.
	Con. 150 5		Q.

Operation. 150×5×5÷100×10=$3.75 *Anf.*

Here the first and third term, being complex, the example is in Compound Proportion, while the place of the question denotes it to be *direct.*

Proof. 100×10×3 75=150×5×5=3750.

4. If $150 gain 3.75, in 5 months; what principal will gain $5 intereft in 10 months?

	Cause.		Effect.
Statement.	Hyp. 150, 5 months,	Z	3.75
	Con. Q. 10		5

Operation. 150×5×5÷10×3.75=$100. *Anf.*

Proof. 150×5×5=100×10×3.75=3750.

Here the Q falling under *caufe*, the rule of Indirect Proportion applies, and the 2d and 3d terms involve the divifor.

5. If 64 Canada bufhels are equal to 80 bufhels of the United States meafure, and each of the former contains 40 quarts; how many quarts does the U. S. bufhel contain?

	Cause.		Effect.
Statement.	Hyp. 64 C.b. 40 qts.	Z	equal the whole*.
	Con. 80 Q.		equal the fame.

Operation. 64×40÷80=32qts. *Anf.*

6. If 8*lb.* of Hyfon tea coft £3,,2, what will be the expence of 39*lb.*?

Cause.		Effect.
Hyp. 8*lb.* caufes the expence of	Z	£3.1
Con. 39*lb.*		Q. (how much?)

Anf. £15.1125=15,,2,,3.

---

* *Where the* effects *in both parts are the fame, neither of them can be the object of inquiry, nor need to be expreffed.*

7. If £100, in 12 months, gain £6 intereſt; what principal will gain the ſame ſum in 8 months?

Cauſe. *Effect.*
Hyp. £100, in 12 months, Z a ſum of intereſt.
Con. Q. 8 the ſame ſum.

Anſ. £150.

8. If I pay my landlord \$2.25 for 1 week's board, what will be his bill for 30 weeks?

Anſ. \$67.50.

9. If a footman performs a journey in 3 days, when the days are 16 hours long; how many days of 12 hours length, will it require for him to perform the ſame journey? *Anſ.* 4 days.

10. If 27 grains of American gold be equal to 1 dollar, what is the worth of 1*lb.* 9*oz.* 8*dw.* 6*gr.*?

Anſ. \$380.66 6.

11. If 3*lb.* of ſtandard gold be worth £256 of the currency of N.York; what is the weight of £1000?

Anſ. 11*lb.* 8*oz.* 11*d.* 21*gr.*

12. How many yards of carpeting that is 1.5 yard wide, will cover a floor that is 18 feet wide and 30 feet long? *Anſ.* 60.

13. If 1 ton can be tranſported 40 miles for 5 dollars, how many *cwt.* may be carried 100 miles for 8 dollars?

Anſ. 12*cwt.* 3*qrs.* 5*lb.* $9\frac{3}{5}$*oz.*

14. If 72 gallons of Brandy coſt 111. dol.//60, what would 97.5 *gall.* coſt? *Anſ.* \$ 151.12 5

15. How long muſt I lend my friend \$ 123.45 to requite his kindneſs in lending me \$ 54.36, for 327 days. *Anſ.* 144 days.

16. If 82 buſhels of the United States are equal to 19 ſetiers of Paris, how many ſetiers are contained in 410 buſhels? *Anſ.* 95 ſetiers.

17. If 44 canes of Rome be equal to 100 yards of America; how many yards are contained in 57 canes?

Anſ. 129.54 yards.

18. If 37 dollars equal 25 Chinese tales, what is the federal money value of 212.5 tales?

Ans. $314.5.

19. How many shingles will it require to cover the roof of a house 40 feet in length, and of 18 feet rafters, allowing each shingle to cover 24 square inches?

Ans. 17280.

20. What number of Bricks will it require to build an house, 40 feet long and 30 feet wide, with a wall of 17 feet to the eaves, and 1 foot thick, allowing 27 inches to 1 cubic foot, and a deduction of 1 quarter for the space of doors and windows?

Ans. 26808 Bricks.

21. If $67\frac{1}{2}$ acres be plowed by 6 men in 15 days; how many acres can 18 men plow in 60 days?

Ans. 8100 acres.

22. If 9 tailors can make 36 suits of clothes in 6 days; how many tailors, in 36 days, can clothe an army of 2520 men? *Ans.* 17.5 tailors.

23. How many yards of shalloon, 5 quarters wide, will line 15 coats, each containing $3\frac{1}{2}$ yards of cloth, of 3 quarters wide? *Ans.* 31.5 yards.

24. A. put 257 dollars to interest for 8 months, and then received, for principal and interest, 267 dollars, 28 cents: I demand at what rate *per cent. per annum* he received interest?

Ans. 6 *per cent. per ann.*

25. At the rate of 6 *per cent. per ann.* what principal will amount to 100 dollars in 12 months?

Ans. $94.34, *almost.*

26. If a stick of timber 56 feet long, 9 inches broad, and 13 inches thick, cost £11,,18; what is the worth of 6 sticks, 37 feet long, 10 inches broad, and 7 inches thick? *Ans.* £28.224.

27. If 40 men in 15 days can perform a certain piece of work, how many men will accomplish another 3 times as great, in a fifth part of the time?

Ans. 600 men.

28. How much Sugar at 9 pence *pr.* ℔ *lb.* must be given in barter for 127*lb.* of Tea at 3/6 *pr.* ℔ *lb.* ?

Anſ. 27*lb.* 3 *oz.*

29. A farmer ſold wheat to his merchant, to the amount of 342 dollars, 75 //; at the rate of 75 cents *pr.* Buſhel—what was the number of Buſhels ſold?

Anſ. 457.

30. But the merchant failing before payment, was able to remit but 64 // upon the dollar—how much did the farmer loſe ? and what were his avails ?

Anſ. Avails $ 219.36
Loſs 123.39

31. The farmer, contriving how to regain his property in the uſual method of ſpeculation, veſted the avails of his wheat in weſtern wild lands, at the price of 62 // *pr.* acre, and afterwards ſold the ſame for $ 1.75 *pr.* acre—What gain *pr. cent.* did he make ? and what was his whole profit.

Anſ. $ 182.258 *pr. cent.*
399.80 whole profit.

32. The farmer now reſolved to commence the more elegant life of a merchant—accordingly repairs to New-York, lays out the whole avails of his lands in goods, and takes up as much more on 6 months credit —he retails them chiefly upon truſt, at the advance of 25 *per cent.* upon the firſt coſt, in addition to the expence of tranſportation. At the end of 6 months, he found his buſineſs in the ſituation following, *viz.* His wife and daughters had taken up, in articles of dreſs, furniture, ſugars, ſpices, &c. &c. to the amount of 500 dollars—his clerk embezzled 117 dollars, // 92—as much as 340 dollars worth of his goods were ſo illy choſen as to be perfectly unſaleable—all the reſt of his goods were retailed, and the money received in, 144 dollars, // 79. Six of his cuſtomers who owed him in all 191 dollars, // 69, abſconded—*Queſtion.* How much *per. cent.* excluſive of all contingent expences, did the farmer-merchant loſe ? what was the ſum

total of his loſs—and how much did he realize in the end?

Anſwer.

He loſt $ 74.41 3 *pr. cent.*
1149.61 in the whole.
And realized but 398.29.

LESSON XVII.

EQUATION OF PAYMENTS.

Q. WHAT *is the nature and uſe of this Rule?*

A. It is to find an equitable mean time for the payment of a debt, or ſeveral debts, due at different times.

Q. *What is the rule of operation?*

A. Take the debt, or the ſum total of the ſeveral debts, for a diviſor; and the ſum of the products, made by multiplying each payment with its reſpective time, for a dividend; and the quotient will be the equated time.

EXAMPLES.

1. S. owes T. £597,,15, of which £143 is to be paid in 5 months and 12 days; £287 in 8 months and 18 days, and £167,,15 in 14 months: but S. agreeing to diſcharge the whole debt in one payment, to how long a pay-day is he entitled?

143 × 5.54= 779.35
287 × 8.72=2402.64
167.75×14 =2348.50

597.75)5530.49(9.2522=9mo. 7 days.

NOTE. *Find the decimal parts of time in the above example, by the Scale in page 214.*

2. There is due to a merchant the ſum of 1148 dollars, from one man, in three ſeveral notes of hand; one for 135 dollars, //15, becoming due in 3 months; another for 684 dollars, in 6 months and ten days, and the reſt in a third note, in 12 months. The debtor takes up thoſe notes, and gives one note for the whole debt. What time of payment muſt the note expreſs?

Anſ. 7months and 20 days.

LESSON XVIII.

PARTNERSHIP.

Q. WHAT *is* Partnerſhip ?

A. It is where two or more merchants, or others, by voluntary agreement, form a company, and unite their property in a common ſtock, for their mutual advantage in buſineſs.

Q. *What is incidental to ſuch a partnerſhip ?*

A. 1. Each partner muſt ſhare in the eventual gain or loſs of the company, in proportion to his individual ſhare of ſtock in the common capital, unleſs otherwiſe ſtipulated in the agreement of the company.

2. The contracts of each partner are binding upon the whole company, and the reverſe ; and they are ſeverally liable for each other's debts contracted during the time of their partnerſhip.

Q. *How is a partnerſhip diſſolved ?*

A. By the mutual agreement of its members, and a public notification given of the ſame, according to the cuſtom of merchants, and the rules preſcribed by law.

Q. *How is Partnerſhip divided ?*

A. 1. Into Simple Partnerſhip, that is, when the ſtocks of each partner continue for an equal term of time. And,

2. Compound Partnerſhip, that is, when the ſtocks continue an unequal length of time.

SECT. I.

Simple Partnership.

Q. *To what other caſes in practice does this rule apply, beſides that of mercantile and other companies formed by voluntary aſſociation ?*

A. It applies to the diviſion of the eſtate of a bankrupt, or an inſolvent inteſtate, among his individual creditors, according to the ſum of their ſeveral claims—

Q

to the aſſeſſment of ſchool, town, county or ſtate taxes, where they are made up by a common ratio of pence upon the pound, or cents upon the dollar, &c. and indeed to all imaginable caſes, where, by the operation of law, or the principles of equity and common juſtice, a common loſs or gain, according to a certain proportion, is to be ſhared by a number of individuals.

Q. *What is the rule of operation?*

Rule. As the ſum of the ſeveral ſtocks is to the total gain or loſs; ſo is each man's ſhare in ſtock, to his ſhare of the gain or loſs.

By this rule of ſtating, make as many ſeveral operations in Direct Proportion, as there are partners in company, or perſons concerned in the gain or loſs.

Q. *How is the truth of the operation proved?*

A. By adding all the ſhares together, and finding their ſum equal to the whole loſs or gain: Or,

By inverting the operation, making the total gain or loſs, the firſt term; the ſum of the ſeveral ſtocks, the ſecond, and each man's ſhare of the gain or loſs, the third.

Examples.

1. A. and B. purchaſed goods in company. A. paid 12 dollars, and B. 27: their gain in the ſale of the goods was 9 *doll.* 75 *cts.* What was each man's ſhare?

A. — 12+27=39 Z 9.75 — 12 Z *Q.*=$3 *Anſ.*

B. — 39 Z 9.75 — 27 Z *Q.*=6.75. *Anſ.*

2. George Selby, merchant, broke for 25000 *doll.* The whole amount of his property was but 9875 *doll.* How much upon the dollar could he average to his creditors? and what was their reſpective loſſes, who ſeverally claimed as follows, *viz.* J. S. 7239*doll.* 75*cts.* A. W. 3257*doll.* 75*cts.* R. N. 5486*doll.* 55*cts.* and G. L. 9016*doll.* 45*cts.*? *Anſ.* .39 5 *upon the doll.*

J. S. loſt	$4380.10 7	R. N. loſt	3319.36 3
A. W.	1970.63 6	G. L.	5454.98 4

3. A town-tax is to be made up, of 3 cents upon the dollar, affeffed upon a number of men, according to the amount of their rateable property in their feveral lifts, annexed to their names, as follow, *viz.* James Grimftead 2745*doll.* 25*cts.* Charles Tucker 1263*doll.* 84*cts.* Jonathan Hooke 857*doll.* 43*cts.* Elcazer Carey 420*doll.* 67*cts.* Ifaiah Warner 89*doll.* 85*cts.* and Nicholas Heifter 3568*doll.* 72*cts.* What was each man's tax?

Anfwer.

J. G.	82.35 3
C. T.	37.90
J. H.	25.72
E. C.	12.62
I. W.	2.69 6
N. H.	107.06 2

NOTE. *In this laft Example, and in all others of the fame kind, you need only to multiply each man's ftock or lift, by the rate of the tax, or the number of cents expreffed in decimals of a dollar, as* .03, *and the product will be the anfwer fought.*

Take James Grimftead's lift for an example, and it will fufficiently explain the rule to the learner.

2745.25
Multiplied by .03

J. G.'s tax, 82.3575

SECT. 2.

COMPOUND PARTNERSHIP.

Q. *What is Compound Partnerfhip?*

A. It is where the ftocks continue an unequal term of time, and each partner is to fhare in the whole gain or lofs, in proportion to the *compound* ratio of his particular ftock and time taken together: Wherefore it is called *Compound Partnerfhip.*

Q. *What is the rule of ftating?*

RULE. Multiply each man's ftock into its time, and add the feveral products together, for a firft term in

Direct Proportion. Take the whole gain or loss for the second term; and each particular product, or the square of each man's stock and time for the third term.

Q. *How is this rule proved?*

A. As in Simple Partnership.

EXAMPLES.

1. A. and B. were joint tenants of a mill, in the building of which A. laid out 150 dollars, and B. 270. At the end of 7 months, A. sold his share to B. and at the end of the first year B. sold the mill. They then made a settlement; and, the year's profit of the mill being ascertained at 350 dollars; what was each man's share?

150× 7=1050
270×12=3240

A.
4290 Z 260
1050 Z Q.

B.
4290 Z 260
3240 Z Q.

Ans. A. $63.63 6 B. 196.36 4

2. Three merchants traded together: A. put in 400 dollars, for 9 months; B. 333*doll.* 33*cts.* for 16 months, and C. 366*doll.* 67*cts.* for 14 months. They gained 350 dollars. What was coming to each?

Ans. To A. 89.57
B. 132.70
C. 127.73

3. Jacob M'Ewen, Giles Jackson, John Hastings, and Anthony Minot, were joint tenants of a certain toll bridge, which they held for the term of 14 years, by charter. Their whole expence in building the bridge was 25745*doll.* 50*cts.* of which M'Ewen paid 4896.67, Jackson 1675, Hastings 12392.37, and Minot 6780.96. At the end of 2½ years, M'Ewen sold out to Peter Thomson; at the end of 5 years, Jackson sold out to Jeremiah Apthorp; at the end of 10 years, Hastings sold his share to James Hawkins; at the ex-

piration of the fourteen years, the whole tollage amounted to $30000 : What was each man's ſhare?

	Anſwers.
M'Ewen,	$1018.90 3
Jackſon,	697.07
Haſtings,	10314.87 1
Minot,	7901.52 8
Thomſon,	4686.95 3
Apthorp,	1254.72 7
Hawkins,	4125.94 8

LESSON XIX.

SIMPLE INTEREST.

Q. WHAT *is* Simple Intereſt?

A. It is the profit ariſing from a ſum of money lent, or for the forbearance of any debt due. Upon the ſame principle, and by the ſame rule of operation, it alſo extends to the premiums given for *factorage, brokerage, ſtorage, inſurance, buying and ſelling of ſtocks, &c. &c.*

Q. *What are the technical parts of this Rule?*

A. 1. The PRINCIPAL, or the ſum lent, or due.

2. The RATIO, or Rate *pr. cent.* which is a certain ſum, payable for every 100 pounds or dollars principal; and in the ſame proportion for any ſum greater or ſmaller.

3. The TIME, or length of forbearance for which intereſt is to be computed.

4. The INTEREST, or premium due for forbearance, according to the given Ratio and Time.

5. The AMOUNT, or principal and intereſt added together.

LESSON XX.

How to reckon Intereſt upon any Sum, at any Rate *pr. cent.* for 1 Year; the ſame Rule equally applying to *Factorage, Brokerage, Storage, Impoſt, Inſurance, buying* and *ſelling* of *Stocks*, &c.

Q. WHAT is *the Rule in this Caſe?*

A. 1. Expreſs the principal decimally, if there be parts of a pound, or of a dollar, in the given ſum.

2. Multiply the principal by the Ratio, decimally expreſſed, and the product is the intereſt ſought, in pounds and decimals, or in dollars and cents.

SECT. I.

The PRINCIPAL, in *Pounds, Shillings, &c.*

EXAMPLES.

1. What is the intereſt of £35,,10,,6, for 1 year, at 6 *pr. cent?*

Prinс. 35·525
Ratio, ×·06

Intereſt, 2.13150 = £2,,2,,7½.

NOTE. *If the* Ratio *be* 5 *per cent. you have only to read the pounds and decimals, principal, as ſhillings and decimals, intereſt.*

2. What is the intereſt of £175,,3,,6, at 5 *pr. cent?*
Anſ. ſ. 175·175=£8,,15,,2.

3. What is the intereſt of £987,,17,,9 at ½ *pr. cent.*
Anſ. £4,,18,,9½

	Anſwers.
4. Of £325,,17,,11, at 1 *pr. cent.**?	£3,,5,,2
5. Of 231,,5,,9, at 2 *pr. cent.*?	4,,12,,6

* *In this ratio you have only to remove the decimal point two figures towards the left hand.*

	£.	Answers.
6.	263,,7,,4½, at 3 *pr. cent.*?	£7,,10
7.	823,,5,,5, at 4 *pr. cent.*?	32,,18,,7¼
8.	5721,,15,,8 at 5 *pr. cent.*?	286,,1,,9
9.	89,,12,,6, at 6 *pr. cent.*?	5,,7,,6½
10.	6520,,4,,5, at 7 *pr. cent.*?	456,,8,,3¼
11.	375,,13,,4, at 8 *pr. cent.*?	30,,1
12.	257,,16, at 9 *pr. cent.*?	23,,4
13.	345,,6,,8, at 10* *pr. cent.*?	34,,10,,8
14.	192,,1,,1, at 11 *pr. cent.*?	21,,2,,6
15.	3752,,17,,1, at 12 *pr. cent.*?	450,,6,,7¼

SECT. 2.

FEDERAL MONEY.

1. What is the interest of $118.40, for 1 year, at 6 *pr. cent. pr. ann.*?

118.40.
×.06
$7.1040 *Ans.*

2. What is the interest of $583.92, at 5 *pr. cent.* for 1 year?

NOTE. *At 5 pr. cent. interest on Federal money, nothing more is necessary, but to remove the point one figure towards the left hand and then halve the sum as follows:*

2) 58.392
$29.186 *Answ.*

Again, remove the decimal point in the principal as before: and, if the ratio be 9 *pr. cent.* subtract the principal from itself; but, if 11 *pr. cent.* add it; observing, in either case, to set the first left hand figure of the lowermost number, under the second in the upper number. See the next examples.

3. What is the interest of $385.29, for 1 year, at 9 *pr. cent.*?

---

* *At* 10 per cent *ratio, only remove the decimal point in the principal one figure towards the left hand, and the interest is found.*

38.529
−3.8529

\$34.6761 *Ans.*

4. What is the intereſt of \$67.45, at 11 *pr. cent.* for one year?

6.745
×.6745

\$7.4195 *Ans.*

5. What is the intereſt of \$3292.80, at ½ *per cent.*?

Anſ. \$16.46 4

	Anſwers.
6. \$1086, at 1 *per cent.*?	\$10 86
7. 769, at 2 *per cent.*?	15.38 9
8. 887.89, at 3 *per cent.*?	26.33 7
9. 2744.23, at 4 *per cent.*?	10.77
10. 19072.62, at 5 *per cent.*?	953.63
11. 278.75, at 6 *per cent.*?	16.72 5
12. 853.34, at 7 *per cent.*?	59.73
13. 252.20, at 8 *per cent.*?	20.20
14. 119.50, at 9 *per cent.*?	10.755
15. 1151.12, at 10 *per cent.*?	115.112
16. 640.35, at 11 *per cent.*?	70.43 8
17. 622.77, at 12 *per cent.*?	75.73

LESSON XXI.

How to compute intereſt at 6 *per cent. per ann.* for any length of time.

Q. WHAT *conciſe Rule have you of caſting intereſt at* 6 per cent. *for any length of time?*

A. Rule. Multiply the principal by one half the given time, reckoning in months and decimals, and point off for decimals in the product ,two figures more than the number of decimal figures in both the factors.

EXAMPLES.

1. What is the interest of £38,,10 for 8 months and a half at 6 *per cent, per ann.* ?

38.5
×4.25

1.63625=£1,,12,,8¾ *Anf.*

	Principal.	*Ratio.*	*Time.* yr. mo. d.	*Interest.*
2.	£127,,15,,6	6 *per cent.*	1 3,, 7	£8,,13,,4½
3.	87,, 9,,2	*do.*	11,, 8	5,, 0,,9
4.	1000	*do.*	1	3,,5
5.	1,, 1,,1	*do.*	7,, 5,,24	9,,5¾
6.	63,,17,,4	*do.*	8,,19	2,,15,,2¾
7.	529,,19,,9	*do.*	5,, 7,, 6	178,, 1,,6
8.	137,,13,,9	*do.*	16,, 8	137,,13,,9

SECT. 2.

FEDERAL MONEY.

1. What is the interest of $128.34, for 8½ months?

×4.25

Anf. 5.454'450

	Principal.	*Ratio.*	*Time.* yr. mo. d.	*Interest.*
2.	$425.91	6 *per cent.*	1,, 1,, 7	$28.74 8
3.	291.53	*do.*	11,, 8	16.76
4.	212.89	*do.*	8,,19	9.16
5.	1766.63	*do.*	5,,7,, 6	595.54

LESSON XXII.

Where the Principal is in the Currency of N. England, or N. York, &c. to find its Interest or Amount in Federal Money.

1. *Interest for 1 Year, at 6 per cent.*

RULE. Multiply the principal, if N. E. money,

by .2; if N. Y. &c. currency, by .15, and if at 7 *per cent.* by .175

EXAMPLES.

1. Interest required in federal money, on £127,,3, N. E.

127.15
×.2

$25.530 *Ans.*

2. Interest required, at 6 and at 7 *per cent.* on £235,,8, N. Y.

235.4 ×.15 — $35.310 *Ans.* at 6 ℔ *ct.*

235.4 ×.175 — 41.1950 *Ans.* at 7 ℔ *cent.*

2. *The Amount, from 1 to 7 per cent. and from 1 to 12 years, by the following Tables.*

RULE. Multiply by that tabular number standing where the given time and ratio meet.

1. NEW-ENGLAND *Money.*

yr	rat. 1	2	3	4	5	6	7
1	3.367	3.4	3.734	3.47	3.5	3.534	3.567
2	3.4	3.467	3.534	3.6	3.334	3.734	4.8
3	3.434	3.534	3.667	4.734	3.834	3.934	4.334
4	3.467	4.6	3.734	3.867	4.	4.134	4.267
5	3.5	3.667	3.834	4.	4.167	4.334	4.5
6	3.534	3.634	3.934	4.134	4.34	4.534	4.734
7	3.567	3.8	4.034	4.267	4.5	4.734	4.967
8	3.6	3.867	4.134	4.4	4.667	4.934	5.2
9	3.634	3.934	4.234	4.534	4.834	5.134	5.434
10	3.667	4.	4.334	4.667	5.	5.334	5.667
11	3.7	4.667	4.333	4.8	5.167	5.534	5.9
12	3.734	4.134	4.534	4.934	5.34	5.734	6.134

2. New-York, &c. Currency.

yr.	rat. 1	2	3	4	5	6	7
1	2.525	2.55	2.575	2.6	2.625	2.65	2.67
2	2.55	2.6	2.65	2.7	2.75	2.8	2.85
3	2.575	2.65	2.725	2.8	2.875	2.95	3.025
4	2.6	2.7	2.8	2.9	3.	3.1	3.2
5	2.625	2.625	2.875	3.	3.125	3.25	3.375
6	2.65	2.8	2.95	3.1	3.25	3.4	3.55
7	2.675	2.85	3.025	3.2	3.375	3.55	3.725
8	2.7	2.9	3.1	3.3	3.5	3.7	3.9
9	2.725	2.95	3.175	3.4	3.625	3.85	4.075
10	2.75	3.	3.25	3.5	3.75	4.	4.25
11	2.775	3.05	3.325	3.6	3.825	4.15	4.275
12	2.8	3.1	3.4	3.7	4.	4.3	4.6

Examples.

1. Required the amount in federal money, of £287, N. E. on intereſt 7 years, at 5 *per cent.*

287
Tabular number, 4.5

$1291.5 *Anſ.*

2. The amount of £37.9: N. Y. in 4 years, at 7 *per cent.* *Tab. number,* 3.2

$121.28 *Anſ.*

LESSON XXIII.

How to compute Intereſt for any Principal, Ratio, or Time.

Rule. Find the decimal parts of a year, if any, by the Scale, page 214, and multiply the principal by the product of the ratio and time.

Examples.

1. Required the intereſt of £113,,4,,9, for 2 months and 23 days, at 2 *per cent. per annum.*

2*mo.* 2*d.*=.17×.02=.0034   113.2375
×.0034

.38500750=7/8½ *Ans.*

2. Intereſt on $187.62, at 3 *per cent.* for 1 year, 9 months and 3 days.

187.62

1*yr.* 9*mo.* 3*d.*=1.76×.03 = .0528

9.806336=$9.80 6 *A.*

	Principal.	*Ratio.*	*Time.*	*Intereſt.*
3	£85,,7,,7	4 *per cent.*	*mo.*4,,2	£1,,3,,7¼
4	$331.58	5	*yr.*1,,6,,6	$8.62 1
5	£27,,10,,5	6	*mo.*6,,19	£0,,18,,2
6	$1728.72	7	*mo.*7,,18	$76.23 6
7	£77,,15,,3	8	*yr.*1,,3,,9	£7,,10,,7¼
8	$222.70	9	*mo.*9,,16	$15.93 4
9	£0,,18,,1	10	*mo.*10,,15	£0,,1,,7

LESSON XXIV.

How to reckon Intereſt, by Days, on any Principal, and on ſeveral Principals, for different Times—Accounts-current, Inſtalments, &c.

RULE. Multiply each principal by its reſpective number of days, and divide the product, or the ſum of the products (when more than one) after removing the decimal point two figures towards the left, if

At 5 *per cent.* by 73.
At 6 *do.* by 56.
At 7 *do.* by 51. And the quotient will be the anſwer.

EXAMPLES.

1. What is the intereſt of 36*doll.* for 125 days, at 5 *pr. cent pr. ann.*?

36×125÷7300=0.61 6 *Anſ.*

2. What is the interest of 360 dollars, for 87 days, 118 for 125 days, and 400 for 158 days, at 6 *per cent. per annum?*

Principal.		*Time.*
360	×	87=31720
118	×	125=20750
400	×	158=63200

56)1156.70($20.66, *nearly.*

3. The purchaser of my estate is to pay me 1700 dollars in 4 yearly instalments of 425 dollars each, with interest on each, from the time of contracting, at 7 *per cent. per annum.* What is the whole interest arising upon the several instalments?

Ans. $297.40

LESSON XXV.

Interest on Bonds and Obligations, having partial Payments endorsed.

RULE 1. Conpute the interest upon the whole principal, for the whole time; then separately upon each indorsement for its respective time, and subtract the whole amount of the one from that of the other.

RULE 2. (*Established by the Superior Court of the State of Connecticut,* A. D. 1784.) "Compute the interest to the time of the first payment; if that be one* year or more from the time the interest commenced; add it to the principal, and deduct the payment from the sum total. If there be after payments made, compute the interest on the balance due to the next payment, and then deduct the payment as above; and in like manner from one pay-

* *By comparing this with the Introduction, the second paragraph of page 38, the reader will observe a small mistake of the author, in the construction of this rule.*

"ment to another, till all the payments are absorbed; "provided the time between one payment and ano- "ther be one year, or more. But if any payment be "made before one year's interest hath accrued, then "compute the interest on the principal sum due on "the obligation for 1 year, add it the principal, and "compute the interest on the sum paid, from the time "it was paid, up to the end of the year; add it to "the sum paid, and deduct that sum from the princi- "pal and interest, added as above.

"If any payments be made of a less sum than the "interest arisen at the time of such payment, no in- "terest is to be computed but only on the principal "sum, for any period."

Take the following note of hand, by both rules, for an

EXAMPLE.

Value received, I promise to pay to George Appleton, the sum of one hundred and twenty dollars, with lawful interest. [6 *per cent. per annum.*] Witness my hand. PETER FRISBIE.

January 1, 1795.

Endorsed thus:

June 1, 1795. Rec'd on the within note 50*doll.*
Oct. 1, 1795. Rec'd - - - 40*doll.*

The last payment was made January 1, 1796.

By Rule 1.

120*doll.* Principal, or sum of the note.
7.20 Interest for the whole time.

127.20 Amount.

50 First payment.
1.75 Interest.

51.75 Amount.

40 Second payment.
.60 Intereſt.

40.60 Amount.

51.75 } Several amounts of payments.
40.60 }

92.35 Total amount—ſubtract it from amt. of debt.

$34.85 Remains due on the note.

By Rule 2.

120*doll.* Note.
7.20 Intereſt for one year.

127.20 Amount.
51.75 Firſt payment, deducted.

75.45 Due June 1, 1795.
4.52 Intereſt for 1 year.

79.97 Amount.
41.60 Second payment, deducted.

38.37 Due October 1, 1795.
.57 Intereſt to January 1, 1796.

$38.94 Amount, or ſum due, by Rule 2.
34.85 Ditto, by Rule 1.

4.09 Difference.

Contraction of Rule 1.

Rule. Point off the right hand figure of each principal for a decimal; multiply each by its particular time, and add the products. If the principal were pounds, &c. the ſum total will be ſhillings and decimals; but if federal money, halve it for dimes, intereſt, which, added to the laſt principal, gives the ſum due.

Reſume the former Example.

		Time.
1ſt Principal,	$12.0 × 5*mo.*	=60
2d *do.* - -	7.0 × 4	=28
3d *do.* - - -	3.0 × 3	= 9
		2)97
		4.85 Intereſt.
		30 Laſt principal.
		$34.85 Amount due.

NOTE. *To find either the Principal, Time, or Ratio, when the other terms are expreſſed in the queſtion, apply the* Rule of Three, *according to the ſpecimens in the 7th, 15th, 24th and 25th Examples, in* Leſſon XVI.

LESSON XXVI.

COMPOUND INTEREST.

Q. WHAT *is* Compound Intereſt?

A. It is Intereſt upon Intereſt, or taking the amount of principal and intereſt for the firſt year, as a new principal for the ſecond year, and the amount of the ſecond, for that of the third, and ſo on.

Q. *Is there not a ſhorter proceſs of reckoning Compound Intereſt?*

A. Yes. Take a different *time*, which bears the ſame proportion to the given time, as Compound does to Simple Intereſt; then reckon Simple Intereſt on the given principal for that *aſſumed* time, which will be its Compound Intereſt for the given time: and if there be any fractional part of a year, make a ſecond operation at Simple Intereſt for that.

By the following Table, containing the given time in the left hand column, and the assumed time written against it at the right hand, from 4 to 10 *per cent.* Compound interest may be reckoned upon any principal, for any number of complete years, from 2 to 20, by operation of the Rule in Lesson XXIII.

NOTE. *The table is not calculated to give the Compound Interest with perfect exactness; yet the variation is so very small, that it will conveniently answer every practical purpose.*

Given Time. Years.	4 ꝑ ct.	5 ꝑ ct.	6 ꝑ ct.	7 ꝑ ct.	8 ꝑ ct.	9 ꝑ ct.	10 ꝑ ct.
2	2.04	2.05	2.06	2.07	2.08	2.09	2.1
3	3.12	3.15	3.18	3.21	3.24	3.28	3.31
4	4.25	4.3	4.37	4.43	4.05	4.57	4.64
5	5.42	5.52	5.63	5.74	5.86	5.98	6.1
6	6.64	6.8	6.97	7.14	7.33	7.52	7.71
7	7.93	8.14	8.39	8.64	8.92	9.2	9.48
8	9.24	9.55	9.89	10.24	10.63	11.03	11.43
9	10.61	11.	11.48	11.96	12.48	13.12	13.57
10	12.04	12.57	13.17	13.8	14.	15.29	15.83
11	13.54	14.2	14.96	15.86	16.15	17.66	18.42
12	15.09	15.93	16.86	18.07	16.49	20.24	21.27
13	16.69	17.72	18.87	20.43	21.02	23.05	24.41
14	18.33	19.6	21.	22.96	23.75	26.11	27.86
15	20.09	21.58	23.26	25.67	26.69	29.45	31.66
16	21.9	23.65	25.8	28.57	29.88	33.09	35.84
17	23.5	25.83	28.49	31.67	33.32	37.06	40.43
18	25.44	28.02	31.34	35.09	37.04	41.39	45.48
19	27.58	30.32	34.36	38.64	41.05	46.11	51.04
20	29.84	32.74	37.56	42.44	45.38	51.25	57.16

RULE. Multiply the principal by the product of the *assumed* time and given ratio, and that product will be the Compound Interest for the given time.

EXAMPLES.

What is the compound intereſt of $235.75, for 7 years, at 4 *per cent. per annum*?

Aſſumed time is	7.93	235.75
Ratio,	×.04	.3172
	.3172	$74.779900 *Anſ.*

	Principal.	*Time.*	*Ratio.*	*Comp. Intereſt.*
2.	$623.16	8 *years.*	5 *per cent.*?	$297.56
3.	75.50	9 *do.*	6 *do.*	52.
4.	326.61	3 *do.*	7 *do.*	73.39
5.	350.	7 *do.*	8 *do.*	249.76
6.	115.55	6 *do.*	9 *do.*	78.20 5
7.	327.45	5 *do.*	10 *do.*	199.74 4
8.	121.21	$6\frac{1}{2}$ *do.*	5 *do.*	45.27 2
9.	144.	18 *do.*	6 *do.*	270.77 7

LESSON XXVII.

DISCOUNT.

Q. WHAT *is* Diſcount?

A. It is the reverſe of Intereſt, being a ſum allowed to the debtor for the payment of a debt before it becomes payable; or, it is the payment of ſo much preſent money, as, being put out to intereſt, would amount to the given ſum, due in future payment.

Q. *How is the diſcount, and preſent worth of any ſum of money, found?*

A. By the Rule of Proportion, in Leſſon XVI, and ſtated as follows, *viz.*

RULE 1. To find the *Diſcount*, take the amount of 100 dollars, or pounds, for the given time and ratio, for the firſt term; the given ratio, for the ſecond, and the principal for the third.

RULE 2. To find the *preſent worth*, take 100 for the ſecond term, and the given principal for the third.

RULE 3. Subtract either the discount, or present worth when found, from the principal, and the remainder will be the other sum.

EXAMPLES.

1. What is the discount of 100 dollars, for 1 year, at 6 *per cent.*?

106 Z 6
100 Q. = \$5.66 *Ans.*

2. What is the present worth of 100 dollars, payable in 1 year, discounting at 6 *per cent. per annum*?

106 Z 100
100 Q. = \$94.34 *Ans.*

Note. *These examples mutually prove each other, as either answer, being subtracted from* 100 *dollars, leaves the other.*

3. What is the discount of \$175.55, for 2.5 years, at 5 *per cent. per annum*? *Ans.* \$19.50 4

4. What is the present worth of 350 dollars, payable in 4 years, at 7 *per cent. per ann.* discount?

Ans. \$273.4375

SECT. 2.

Discount, at Compound Interest.

RULE. Take the *assumed* time for the given time, by the Table, and calculate the discount at Simple Interest upon that.

1. What is the present worth of 350 dollars, payable in 4 years, at 7 *per cent. per annum*, compound interest discount?

Assumed time 4.3 × *ratio* 7 = 131.01 Z 100
350 Q = \$267.15 5

2. What is the compound interest discount on 500 dollars, for 8 years, at 6 *per cent. per annum*?

Ans. \$186.20 6

3. What is the present worth of 1000 dollars, payable in 12 years, discounting in compound interest, at 10 *per cent. per annum*? *Ans.* \$319.79.5

A COMPENDIOUS TREATISE ON

BOOK KEEPING;

OR,

ACCOMPTANTSHIP REDUCED TO PRACTICE.

THE importance of Accomptantship is so generally known, and its utility so universally acknowledged, that any commendation will be unnecessary, further than to observe, that a thorough knowledge of the art is essential to the character of a Man of Business. The *Italian* method of Book-Keeping is so perfect a system of its kind, that the mercantile world have generally adopted it in the management of accompts. Its principles are founded in reason, since it is evident, that no transaction can be made, that is not accountable to another. It is my object, therefore, to give a concise specimen of Book-Keeping, in the method of double-entry.

Of BOOKS *of* ACCOMPT.

Three books are indispensably necessary for every man in mercantile business, *viz.* the WASTE-BOOK, JOURNAL, and LEDGER; besides a number of subsidiary books, according to the variety and extent of his business.

1. *The* WASTE-BOOK.

The *Waste-Book* contains the subject matter from which the two other books are formed. It opens with an Inventory of the several articles composing a merchant's stock, together with the debts incumbering it; after which follow the daily occurrences of trade, such as buying, selling, &c. In this book, every transaction relating to a merchant's business, ought to be explicitly entered, without paying that particular attention to method and style which ought to be observed in the Journal, where the several Debits and Credits are clearly ascertained.

2. *The* Journal.

The *Journal* is a book preparatory to the Ledger, into which every entry from the Waſte-Book, ought to be fairly tranſcribed in a legible hand, and in that kind of laconic ſtyle peculiar to merchants. This book is conſidered by men of mercantile buſineſs as eſſentially neceſſary, and indeed its utility is obvious—the hurry in which entries are frequently made in the Waſte-Book—the inaccuracy and negligence of young clerks who are allowed to write in that book—the difficulty of poſting from it into the Ledger, together with the miſtakes that would probably ariſe from that practice, are good and ſubſtantial reaſons with merchants for uſing this intermediate book, *The Journal.*

The principle upon which this method of Book-Keeping is founded, precludes the neceſſity of writing the word *Credit*, at all in the Journal ; for, as before obſerved, no tranſactionc an be made that is not accountable to another ; that is, no charge can in reaſon be made, that does not anſwer to ſome correſponding credit. Hence ariſes the neceſſity of raiſing fictitious accompts, as *Profit and Loſs*, &c.—The Journal ſhould be written in a fair hand, with great attention to neatneſs and accuracy.

3. *The* Ledger.

The *Ledger* is the grand book of accompt, made up from the Journal, wherein the ſeveral articles compoſing the different accompts, are ſo arranged under their proper heads, as to exhibit at one view, a true ſtatement of a merchant's affairs, which is the ſole end and deſign of Accomptantſhip.

Every accompt in the Ledger ought to be opened in a fair text hand; and great care ſhould be taken that no blots or eraſements happen in this book.

Of Subsidiary Books,

I nave not room to ſay much. The Invoice and Letter Books are uſed by moſt men in buſineſs. The others, ſuch as Bill-Book, Book of Commiſſions, Book of Accompts current, &c. are of ſuch a nature, that they muſt be left to the ingenuity and diſcretion of merchants, to uſe, as the variety and extent of their buſineſs may require.

General Rules *for Journalizing, and for poſting into the Ledger.*

In Journalizing, or tranſcribing from the Waſte-Book into the Journal, it is neceſſary to keep, in idea, this fundamental principle, that, when any accompt, whether real, perſonal, or fictitious, is charged, ſome other accompt muſt be diſcharged to the ſame amount. Hence the neceſſity of clearly expreſſing the correſponding Credit, to every Debit in the Journal. The term, *Profit and Loſs*, was invented to ſupply the defect of a debtor or creditor, when no other accompt could in reaſon be debited or credited, for any things received in, or paid out. So likewiſe the term, *Stock*, has been ſubſtituted for the Merchant's own name.

In poſting from the Journal into the Ledger, the date of the tranſactions muſt be inſerted in a column allotted for that purpoſe; after which, the accompt, Debited, or Credited, muſt be expreſſed, noting, in the column immediately preceding the money-columns, its reference to the folio in the Ledger, where its correſponding accompt is opened: and if any error be diſcovered in either the Debit or Credit ſide of the Ledger, make no eraſement or interlineation to rectify it, but balance the error by a correſponding entry on the oppoſite page of the folio.

To the Ledger, an *Index* is neceſſary, wherein the names, and titles of every accompt, are arranged in alphabetical order, quoting the folio where ſuch accompt ſtands.

Of Balancing.

Merchants are induced, once in every year, or oftener, to balance their books; as well to ſhew the true ſtate of their affairs, as to determine whether their accompts have been kept with accuracy. To accomplish this, purſue the following

DIRECTION.

Begin with the firſt accompt in your Ledger, omitting, however, the accompts of Stock, and of Profit and Loſs; perſonal accompts uncloſed, muſt be evened by balance—the balance being in your favor, carry it to the debit ſide of Balance-accompt; if againſt you, carry it to the credit ſide. In accompt of goods, if any remain unſold, (which will appear by adding up each ſide of the inner columns, ruled for that purpoſe) carry the difference of quantity, at the original coſt, to the debit ſide of Balance-accompt—then balance the money column, by Profit and Loſs: If gained by this article, Profit and Loſs muſt be credited; if loſt, that accompt muſt be debited for the difference. In this way, proceed thro' the Ledger; after which, balance Profit and Loſs accompt, and carry the difference to Stock-accompt. *Laſtly*, balance Stock-accompt; and if the difference between the debit and credit ſide of this accompt, will even Balance-accompt, your books are, moſt aſſuredly, kept accurately; if not, there is, as certainly, ſome error—for the diſcovery of which, your books muſt be pricked over, and the whole foregoing proceſs gone thro' a ſecond time.

GENERAL OBSERVATIONS.

After all, it will be extremely difficult for a *retailer* ſtrictly to adhere to the formality of this method of Book-Keeping. The great variety of articles in which he deals, the ſmall quantities in which they are dealt out, together with the hurry and confuſion in which buſineſs is frequently tranſacted in a retail-ſhop, render it almoſt impracticable to keep an accurate Sales-accompt of the quantity of commodities ſold. To obviate this difficulty, men acquainted with buſineſs in the retail line, have adopted the practice of opening a general accompt, termed *Merchandize General*, to which all purchaſes and ſales of merchandize have reference. The foregoing rules for balancing are equally applicable to this method, only it will be neceſſary in this caſe, at the time of balancing, to take an Inventory of all goods remaining on hand, which come under the common denomination of *Merchandize general*.

In a book of this kind, it is impoſſible to comment with minuteneſs upon each particular branch of ſo extenſive a ſyſtem, as the Italian method of Book-keeping: The general rules and fundamental principles, only, can be compriſed in this imperfect compendium. It is hoped, however, that the foregoing rules and obſervations, exemplified and illuſtrated by the following practical Specimen, will convey a general knowledge of the art to the ſtudent, and thus anſwer the important purpoſe for which they are introduced.

WASTE-BOOK. (1)

Lansingburgh, September 1st, 1796.

		Dolls.	Cts.
Inventory of the money, effects and debts, belonging to, and owing by me, PETER LOVETRADE.			
I have in Cash	Dolls. 1500		
5 Puncheons Rum, 600 *gall.* which I value at 1.25 per *gall.*	750		
100 Rolls Plug Tobacco 1400*wt.* .14	196		
200 Sides Sole Leather, 3225*wt.* at .18	580.50		
1500 Bush. Salt, at .75	1125		
4 qr. Casks Sherry Wine, 130*gall.* at 1.12 per *gall.*	145.60		
4 Hhd. Molasses, 440*gall.* at .60 per *gall.*	264.		
John Hamilton owes me, per note, on demand,	231.19		
William Jones, pr. acct.	97.71		
Benjamin Conner, pr. *do.*	110.		
		5000	
I owe as follows:			
To Henry Bell, per acct.	Dolls. 250.		
To John Farrow, per *do.*	75.		
To Joseph Redfield, per note, 15 days to run	375.		
		700	
— 6*th.* —			
Sold for Cash 47 sides Sole Leather, 630*wt.* at .21 pr. *lb.*		132	30
— 10*th.* —			
Rec. of J. Hamilton in full of his note		231	19

(2) *WASTE-BOOK.*

	$	cts
September 15th.		
Paid my note to Joſeph Redfield, in full	375	
20th.		
Sold Abram Cunningham 1 Punch. Rum, 123*gall.* 1.50 per *gall.* 184.50 350 Buſh. Salt, at 1.10 per *buſh.* 385. 1 Hhd. Molaſſes, 108 *gall.* at .75 81. To pay at 30 days.	650	50
24th.		
Paid Henry Bell in full	10	
26th.		
Paid Diſtrict Collector, for licence to retail Spiritous Liquors & Wines	10	
27th.		
Bought for Caſh $376\frac{20}{60}$ *buſh.* Wheat, at 1.50 per Buſhel	564	50
30th.		
Paid Charges this Month	34	15
October 3d.		
Sold James Carey 37 Sides Sole Leather, 592*lb.* at .22 per *lb.* and rec'd in money 76.24 His note at 30 days for remainder } 54.	130	24
5th.		
Paid John Farrow, in full,	75	
8th.		
Rec'd of William Jones, in full,	97	71
10th.		
Bought for Caſh $432\frac{40}{60}$ *buſh.* Wheat, at 1.50 per Buſhel	657	64
12th.		
Rec'd of Benjamin Conner, in full,	110	

WASTE-BOOK. (3)

	$	//
October 14th.		
Ship'd for New-York, on board the sloop Tryall, Capt. Hickok, 815*bush.* Wheat, at measure, consign'd to him for sales and return; and paid charges of boating, &c. till on board	24	45
17th.		
Sold for Cash one Puncheon Rum, containing 120*gall.* at 1.45	174	
20th.		
Sold Peter Olds 600*bush.* Salt, at 1.10, to pay at 20 days	660	
22d.		
Sold Joshua Johnson 2 Casks Sherry Wine, 67*gall.* at 1.50, for which rec'd his note, at 30 days, for	100	50
25th.		
Rec'd of Abram Cunningham 347*bush.* Wheat, on acct. at 1.55 — 537.85 10 Casks Flaxseed, cont'g 70*bush* at 1.60, and casks at $ 1 each — 122.	659	85
Paid Abram Cunningham the balance due him on acct. of his Wheat and Flaxseed	9	35
27th.		
Bought of Nicholas Grocer, New-York, 4 Chests Bohea Tea, weighing, nett, 1388*lb.* at .35 per *lb.* — 485.80 600*lb.* Lump Sugar, at .26 — 156. For which gave my note at 60 days.	641	80
29th.		
Capt. Hickok has returned from N. York, and I have settled with him on the sales of my Wheat: it weighed out $806\frac{40}{60}$ *bush.* Sold at 1.84 pr. *bush.* — 1484 $26\frac{1}{2}$ Deduct for Freight, &c. — 34 $26\frac{1}{2}$ Nett Proceeds rec'd in full.	1450	

(4) *WASTE-BOOK.*

		D	C
October 31st.			
Paid Charges this Month		51	23
November 1st.			
Barter'd 250 *bush.* Salt, at 1.12, for 20 Casks Flaxseed, cont'g 140*bush.* at 2.		280	
Paid Cash for the Casks, at 1. each		20	
3d.			
Rec'd of James Carey 20*bush.* Wheat, at 1.52	30 40		
Cash in full of his note	23.60		
		54	
Paid Freight and Charges on my Tea and Sugar, this day rec'd from N. York		5	
5th.			
Bought 639$\frac{45}{60}$*bush.* Wheat of Joseph Farmer, at 1.76 per Bushel; for which paid as follows:			
Salt 250*bush.* at 1.12	280.		
Bohea Tea, 1 Chest, nett 349*lb.* at .42 per *lb.*	146 58		
50 Sides Sole Leather, 750*lb.* at .21	175 50		
200*lb.* Lump Sugar, at .29	58.		
1 Puncheon Rum, 120*gall.* at 1.48	189.44		
1 *qr.* Cask Sherry Wine, 33*gall.* at 1.50	49.50		
Cash in full	244.94		
		1125	96
10th.			
Bought for Cash 450*bush.* Wheat, at 1.76 per Bushel		792	
12th.			
Sold for Cash 2*hhd.* Molasses, 218*gall.* at .72 per Gallon		156	96
Rec'd of Peter Olds, in full		660	

WASTE-BOOK.

(5)

		Dolls.	Cts.
	November 16th.		
	Sold Abram Perkins 1 Puncheon Rum, 120 *gall.* on account of which I have received 56*bush.* Wheat, at 1.75 per Bushel 98.		
	And his draught on Wm. Johnstone, for remainder 82.	180	
	19th.		
	Lent Peter Punctual, to be paid on demand,	100	
	23d.		
	Ship'd for New-York, on board sloop Hare, Capt. Johnson, 1473*bush.* Wheat, at measure, with orders to sell for Cash, and purchase for me 4 Puncheons Rum; paid charges till on board	47	10
	28th.		
	Rec'd of Joshua Johnson, in full of his note	100	50
	30th.		
	Paid Charges this Month	39	25
	December 1st.		
	Ship'd my 30 Casks of Flaxseed on board the Ranger, Capt. Green, consigned to Henry Stewart, New-York, to sell for my account: Paid Charges till on board	4	50
	7th.		
1	Settled with Capt. Johnson on the sale of my Wheat: weigh'd in New-York $1455\frac{1}{2}$*bush.* at 2.25 per Bushel, and receiv'd as follows, in full:		
	4 *hhd.* Rum, 488*gall.* at 1.25 610.		
	Charges on *do.* 5.		
	Do. on Wheat 59.28		
	Cash in full 2600.59	3274	87

(6) *WASTE-BOOK.*

		Dolls	Cts
December 12th.			
Sold Jonathan Brewster, at 60 days,			
1 Puncheon Rum, 117*gall.* at 1,50	175.50		
1 Chest Tea, 347*lb.* at .40	138.20		
100*lb.* Lump Sugar, .30	30.		
		343	70
15th.			
Rec'd advice from Henry Stewart, that my 30 Casks of Flaxseed had arrived safe. Amount, with Charges,		455	10
17th.			
Paid Capt. Green the Freight and Charges on my Flaxseed		28	60
20th.			
Rec'd of Peter Punctual in full of borrowed money		100	
26th			
Rec'd in full of Abram Perkins, a draught on William Johnstone		82	
28th			
Taken up my note to Nicholas Grocer, of 641.80, as follows:			
Paid in money	423.		
in a draught on Henry Stewart at sight	218 80	641	80
31st.			
Paid charges this month		47	
January 2d, 1797.			
Sold Robert Dunston at 45 days			
37 Rolls Tobacco, 518*lb* at .17	88.06		
23 sides Sole Leather 299*lb.* .21	62.79		
12 Lumps Sugar 146*lb.* .29	43.34		
		194	19
12th			
Rec'd of Jonathan Brewster 120 *bush.* Wheat, at 1,25 per Bushel, in part		150	

WASTE-BOOK. (7)

		$	100
January 18th.			
Sold George Gordon 1 Hhd. Rum 126 gallons at 1.45 per gall.	182.70		
13 Rolls Tobacco 195*lb.* at .17 per *lb.*	33.15		
to pay at 30 days		215	85
25th			
Rec'd advice from Henry Stewart, New-York that he hath sold my Flaxseed—Nett proceeds pr. account of sales transmitted me, amounting to 541.13, for which received a post bill on Albany bank in full		322	33
31st		32	57
Paid charges this month.			
February 2d.			
Sold Andrew King 1 Hhd. Rum 119 gallons at 1.50. per gallon	178.50		
10 sides Sole Leather 130*lb.* at .21	27.30		
for which rec'd his note at 90 days		205	80
6th			
Bartered with Derick Hough of Vermont as follows: viz.			
1 chest Tea 353*lb.* at .42 pr. *lb.*	182.26		
350 *lb.* Tobacco at .18 pr. *lb.*	63.		
Delivered.		245	26
For 1300 *lb.* Cloverseed at .12 pr. *lb.*	156		
600 Bushels Rye at .90 per Bush.	540		
Received.		696	
10th			
Bought 750 Bushels Wheat of Thomas Taylor at 1.25 pr. Bushel, for which paid as follows:			
Cash	337.50		
My note at 3 months	600.		
		937	50

(8) *WASTE-BOOK.*

		$	¢
February 13*th.*			
Rec'd of Jonathan Brewster in part		100	
16*th*			
Rec'd of George Gordon 130 Bushels Rye at .90 per Bushel in part		117	
20*th*			
Sold Joel Kent			
1 Puncheon Rum 128 *gall.* at 1.50 per *gall.*	192		
32 sides Sole Leather 454 *lb.* at .21 per *lb.*	95.34		
10 Rolls Tobacco 120*lb.* at 18 pr. *lb.*	21.60		
		308	94
Rec'd as follows in part			
Cash	115.50		
Rye 70 Bushels at .90 per Bush.	63		
		178	50
25*th*			
Sold Derick Hough of Vermont pr. his order 1 *qr.* cask Sherry Wine, 30 gallons, at 1.50 per gallon.		45	
28*th*			
Paid charges this month, including store-house rent 6 months		137	96

JOURNAL. (1)

Lanſingburgh, 1ſt September, 1797.

			$	//
	Sundries Dr. to Stock			
1	Caſh for ready money	1500.		
2	Rum 5 Puncheons 600 gallons at 1.25 per gallon	750.		
2	Tobacco 100 Rolls 1400 *lb.* at .14	196.		
3	Sole Leather 200 ſides *wt.* 3225 *lb.* at .18 per *lb.*	580.50		
3	Salt 1500 Buſhels at .75	1125.		
2	Sherry wine 4 caſks 130 gallons at 1.12 per gallon	145.60		
3	Molaſſes 4 Hhds. 440 gallons at .60	264.		
4	Bills receivable for John Hamilton's note on demand	231.19		
4	William Jones per acct.	97.71		
4	Benjamin Conner per do.	110.		
5			5000	
5	Stock Dr. to Sundries			
5	To Henry Bell per acct.	250.		
5	To John Farrow per do.	75.		
6	To bills payable for my note to Joſeph Redfield 15 days to run	375.		
			700	
	6th			
1	Caſh Dr. to Sole Leather 132.30			
3	Rec'd for 45 ſides *wt.* 630 *lb.* at .21 pr. *lb.*		132	30
	10th			
1	Caſh Dr. to Bill's receivable 231.19			
4	Rec'd in full of John Hamilton's note		231	19
	15th			
5	Bills payable Dr. to Caſh 375.			
1	Paid my note to Joſeph Redfield		375	

(2) *JOURNAL.*

		Dolls.	Cts.
	September 20th.		
6/2	Abm. Cunningham Dr. to sundries 650.50 To Rum for 1 Puncheon 123 *gal.* at 1.50 — 184 50		
3	To Salt for 350 Bushels 1.10 — 385.		
3	To Molasses 1 Hhd. 108 *gal.* at .75 — 81. to pay at 30 days	650	50
	24th		
5/1	Henry Bell Dr. to Cash 250. Paid him in full	250	
	26th		
6/1	Profit and Loss Dr. to Cash 10. Paid district Collector for Licence to sell Spirituous Liquors and Wines	10	
	27th		
6/1	Wheat Dr. to Cash 564.50 Paid for 376 20/60 Bushels at 1.50 pr. bush.	564	50
	30th.		
6/1	Profit and Loss Dr. to Cash Paid charges this month	34	15
	October 3d		
	Sundries Dr. to Sole Leather 130.24		
1	Cash — 76.24		
4/3	Bills receivable for James Carey's note at 30 days for the balance of 37 sides 592 *lb.* at .22 per. *lb.* — 54.	130	24
	5th		
5/1	John Farrow Dr. to Cash 75. Paid him in full	75	
	8th		
1/4	Cash Dr. to William Jones 97.71 Rec'd in full	97	71
	10th		
6/1	Wheat Dr. to Cash 657.64 Paid for 432 40/60 Bushels at 1.50 pr. bush.	657	64
	12th		
1/4	Cash Dr. to Benjamin Conner 110. Rec'd in full.	100	

JOURNAL. (3)

	October 14th.	$	⁄⁄
6/1	Wheat Dr. to Cash 4 45 Paid charges of shipping 815 Bushels at measure, pr. the Tryall, Capt. Hickok, consigned to him for sales and returns.	24	45
	17th		
1/2	Cash to Rum 174. Rec'd for 1 Puncheon 120 *gal.* at 1.45 per gallon.	174	
	20th.		
2/3	Peter Olds Dr. to Salt 660. For 600 Bushels at 1.10 per Bushel to pay at 20 days.	660	
	22d.		
4/2	Bills received Dr. to Sherry wine 100.50 for 2 casks 67 gallons at 1.50 per *gall.* sold Joshua Johnston per note at 30 days.	100	50
	25th.		
	Sund. Dr. to Abm. Cunningham 659.85		
6	Wheat 347 Bushels at 1.55 537.85		
4/6	Flaxseed 10 casks containing 70 *bush.* at 1.60 and 1. each for the casks 122.	659	85
6/1	Abram Cunningham Dr. to Cash 9.35 Paid the balance due him.	9	35
	27th.		
	Sundries Dr. to Bills payable 641.80		
7	Bohea Tea for 4 chests, nett *wt.* 1388 *lb.* at .35 per *lb.* 435.80		
7/5	Lump Sugar 600 *lb.* at .26 per *lb.* 156 Bought of Nicholas Grocer, New-York, per my note at 60 days	641	80
	29th		
1/6	Cash Dr. to Wheat 1150 Rec'd of Capt. Hickok in full of net proceeds on the sales of 806 $\frac{40}{60}$ bush.	450	

(4) *JOURNAL.*

Folio	Entry	Amount	Dollars	Cents
	October 31st.			
6/1	Profit and Loss Dr. to Cash 51.23			
	Paid charges this month		51	23
	November 1st.			
4	Flaxseed Dr. to Sundries 300.			
3	To Salt 250 Bushels at 1.12 per Bushel. Bartered for 20 casks seed 140 Bushels at 2. per Bushel	280.		
1	To Cash paid for the casks at 1. each	20.		
			300	
	3d.			
	Sundries Dr. to Bills receivable 54.			
6	Wheat 20 Bushels at 1.52 per Bushel	30.40		
1/4	Cash received of James Carey in full of his note	23.60		
			54	
6/1	Profit and Loss Dr. to Cash 5.			
	Paid charges on my Tea and Sugar this day rec'd from New-York		5	
	5th.			
6/3	Wheat Dr. to Sundries 1125.96			
	To Salt for 250 Bushels at 1.12 per Bushel	280.		
7	To BoheaTea 1 chest, nett 349 *lb.* at .42 per *lb.*	146.58		
3	To Sole Leather 50 sides 750 *lb.* at .21 per *lb.*	157.50		
7	To Lump Sugar 200 *lb.* at .29 pr. *lb.*	58.		
2	To Rum 1 Puncheon 120 gallons at 1.48 per gallon	189.44		
2	To Sherry Wine 33 gallons at 1.50	49.50		
1	To Cash paid Joseph Farmer in full for $639\frac{45}{60}$ Bushels.	244.94		
			1125	96

JOURNAL. (5)

		$	¢
	November 10th.		
6/1	Wheat, Dr. to Cash 792. Paid for 450 *bush.* at 1 76 per *bush.*	792	
	12th.		
1	Cash, Dr. to Sundries 816.96		
3	To Molasses, Rec'd for 2 Hhd, 218 *galls.* at .72 per *gall.* 156.96		
2	To Peter Olds, Rec'd in full, 660.		
		816	96
	16th.		
	Sundry accounts Dr. to Rum, 180.		
1	Cash in payment of 1 Puncheon, 120 *galls.* at 1.50 per *gall.* 98.		
4/2	Bills Rec'd. for Abram Perkins draught on Wm. Johnston, 82.		
		180	
	19th.		
7/1	Peter Punctual, Dr. to Cash 100. lent him to be repaid on demand.	100	
	23d.		
6/1	Wheat, Dr. to Cash, 47.10 Paid Shipping charges on 1473 *bush.* at measure per the Hare, Capt. Johnston, consigned to him for sales and return.	47	10
	28th.		
1/4	Cash Dr. to Bills receivable 100.50. Rec'd in full of Joshua Johnston's note.	100	50
	30th.		
6/1	Profit and Loss, Dr. to Cash, 39.25 Paid charges this month.	39	25

(5) *JOURNAL.*

	December 1st.		$	//
4	Flaxseed, Dr. to Cash, 4.50.			
	Paid charges till on board the Ranger, Capt. Greene.		4	50
1	Consigned to Henry Stewart, New-York.			
	7th.			
	Sundries Dr. to Wheat,			
2	Rum, 4 Hhds. 488 *galls.* at 1.25 per *gall.* and charges. on do. from New-York	615.		
1	Cash Rec'd of Capt. Johnston,			
6	in full of nett proceeds on the sales of 1455½ *bush.*	2600.59½	3215	59
	12th.			
7	Jonathan Brewster, Dr. to Sundries,	343.70		
2	To Rum for 1 Puncheon 117 *galls.* at 1.50	175.50		
7	Tea, 1 Chest, 347*lb.* at .40	138.20		
7	Lump Sugar, 100*lb.* at .30	30.		
	to pay at 60 days.		343	70
	15th.			
7	Henry Stewart, my acct. of Flaxseed, Dr. to Flaxseed .455.10			
4	Consigned to him 30 Casks to sell for my account.		455	10
	17th.			
4	Flaxseed, Dr. to Cash, 28.60			
1	Paid Capt Greene for freight and charges.		28	60
	20th.			
1	Cash, Dr. to Peter Punctual, 100.			
7	Rec'd in full.		100	

JOURNAL. (7)

Fol.	Entry		Dolls.	Cts.
	December 26th.			
1	Caſh, Dr. to Bills receivable, 82.			
4	Rec'd Perkins on Johnſton, in full.		82	
	28th.			
5	Bills payable, Dr. to Sundries 641.80			
1	To Caſh,	423.		
8	To Henry Stewart, my account current for my draughts	218.80		
	Taken up my account to Nicholas Grocer.		641	80
	31ſt.			
6	Profit and Loſs, Dr. to Caſh, 47.			
1	Paid charges this month.		47	
	January 2d, 1797.			
8	Robert Dunſton, Dr, to Sund. 194.19			
2	To Tobacco, 37 Rolls, 518*lb.* at .17 per *lb.*	88.06		
3	To Sole Leather, 299*lb.* at .21	62.79		
7	To Lump Sugar, 146*lb.* at .29	43.34		
	to pay at 45 days.		194	19
	12th.			
6	Wheat, Dr. to Jonathan Brewſter, 150.			
7	Rec'd. 120 *buſh.* at 1.25 per *buſh.* in part.		150	
	18th.			
8	George Gordon, Dr. to Sund. 215.85			
2	To Rum, for 1 Hhd. 126 *galls.* at 1.45 per *gall.*	182.70		
2	To Tobacco, 13 Rolls, 195*lb.* at .17 per *lb.* payable in 30 days.	33.15	215	85

(8)

JOURNAL.

Fol.	Entry	Ds.	Cts.
	January 25th.		
8	Henry Stewart, my acct. cur.		
7	Dr. to do. my acct. of Flax-feed, 541.13		
	For nett proceeds of 30 Casks per account of sales transmitted me.	541	13
1	Cash, Dr. to Henry Stewart,		
8	my account current.		
	Rec'd a post bill in full.	322	33
	31st.		
6/1	Profit and Loss, Dr. to Cash, 32.57		
	Paid charges this month.	32	57
	February 2d.		
4	Bills receivable, Dr. to Sund. 205.80		
2	To Rum 1 Puncheon, 119 *galls.* at 1.50 per *gall.* 178.50		
3	To Sole Leather, 130 *lb.* at .21 per *lb.* 27.30		
	Sold Andrew King, and rec'd his note at 90 days.	205	80
	6th.		
8	Derick Hough, Dr. to Sund. 245.26		
7	To Bohea Tea for 1 Chest 353 *lb* at .42 per *lb.* 182.26		
2	To Tobacco, 350 *lb.* at .18 63.		
	delivered in Barter.	245	26
	Sundries, Dr. to Derick Hough, 696.		
8	Cloverseed for 1300 *lb.* at .12 per *lb.* 156.		
9/8	Rye for 600 *bush.* at .90 per *bush.* rec'd in Barter. 540.		
		696	

JOURNAL. (9)

			$	//
	February 10*th.*			
6/1	Wheat, Dr. to Sundries, 937.50			
	To Caſh,	337.50		
5	To Bills payable for my note to Thomas Taylor, at three months in full of 750 *buſh.* Wheat, bought of him.	600.		
			937	50
	13*th.*			
1/7	Caſh, Dr. to Jonathan Brewſter, 100. Rec'd in part.		100	
	16*th.*			
9/8	Rye, Dr. to George Gordon, 117. Rec'd 130 *buſh.* at .90 per *buſh.* in part.		117	
	20*th.*			
9/2	Joel Kent, Dr. to Sundries 308.94			
	To Rum, 1 Puncheon, 128 *gall.* at 1.50	192.		
3	To Sole Leather, 454 *lb.* at .21	95.34		
2	To Tobacco, 120 *lb.* at .18	21.60		
			308	94
	Sundries, Dr. to Joel Kent, 178,50			
1	Caſh,	115.50		
9/9	Rye, for 70 *buſh.* at .90 pr. *buſh.*	63.	178	50
	25*th.*			
8/2	Derick Hough, of Vermont, Dr. to Sherry Wine, 45. for 1 Qr. Caſk, 30 *galls.* at 1.50 per *gall.* per order.		45	
	28*th.*			
6/1	Profit and Loſs, Dr. to Caſh, 137,96 Paid charges this month, including Store-Houſe rent 6 mo.		137	96

ALPHABET.

A.	B.	C.
	Bills Rec'able 4 Bell Henry 5 Bills Payable 5 Brewster Jona. 7	Cash 1 Conner Benj. 4 Cuningham A. 6 Clover Seed 8
D.	**E.**	**F.**
Dunston Robt. 8		Farrow John 5 Flaxseed 4
G.	**H.**	**I.**
GordonGeorg. 8	Hough Derick 8	Jones William 4
K.	**L.**	**M.**
Kent Joel 9	Leather Sole 3	Molasses 3
N.	**O.**	**P.**
	Olds Peter 2	Profit and Loss 6 Punctual Peter 7
Q.	**R.**	**S.**
	Rum 2 Rye 9	Salt 3 Stock 5 Sugar (Lump) 7 StewartHenry &c. 7 Do. do. my account cur. 8
T.	**U.**	**V.**
Tobacco 2 Tea (Bohea) 7		
W.	**Y.**	**Z.**
Wine (Sherry) 2 Wheat 6		

(1) *LEDGER.*

1796.		Dr. CASH.		$	///
Sept.	1	To Stock,	5	1500	
	6	To Sole Leather,	3	132	30
	10	To Bills Receivable,	4	231	19
Oct.	3	To Sole Leather,	3	76	24
	8	To William Jones, in full,	4	97	71
	12	To Benjamin Connor, do.	4	110	
	17	To Rum, for 1 Puncheon, 120 *galls.*	2	174	
	29	To Wheat, per Capt. Hickok, on sales,	6	1450	
Nov.	3	To Bills receivable, in full of Carey's,	4	23	60
	12	To Sundries per Journal,		816	96
	16	To Rum, in part payment of 1 Puncheon,		98	
	28	To Bills receivable in full of Johnston's,	4	100	50
Dec.	7	To Wheat on sales, per Capt Johnston,	6	2600	59
	20	To Peter Punctual,	7	100	
	26	To Bills receivable, Perkins on Johnston in full	4	82	
1797. Jan.	25	To Henry Stewart, my acct. current in full,	8	322	33
Feb.	13	To Jonathan Brewster, in part,	7	100	
	20	To Joel Kent,	9	115	50
				8130	92

(1) *LEDGER.*

1796.		Contra Cr.		$	//
Sept.	15	By Bills payable Joseph Redfield,	5	375	
	24	By H. Bell paid him in full	5	250	
	26	By Profit and Loss,	6	10	
	27	By Wheat,	6	564	50
	30	By Profit and Loss,	6	34	15
Oct.	5	By John Farrow in full,	5	75	
	10	By Wheat,	6	657	64
	14	By do. paid shipping charg.	6	24	45
	15	By Abram Cunningham,	6	9	35
	31	By Profit and Loss, paid charges this month,	6	51	23
Nov.	1	By Flaxseed,	4	20	
	3	By Profit and Loss, paid charges on Tea & Sugar	6	5	
	5	By Wheat paid Joseph Farmer in full,	6	244	94
	10	By do. paid for 450 *bush.* at 1.76 per *bush.*	6	792	
	19	By Peter Punctual to be paid on demand,	7.	100	
	23	By Wheat paid charges of Shipping,	6	47	10
	30	By Profit and Loss paid charges this month,	6	39	25
Dec.	1	By Flaxseed paid charges,	4	4	50
	7	By do. paid do.	4	28	60
	28	By Bills payable,	5	432	
1797.	31	By Profit and Loss,	6	47	
Jan.	31	By do.	6	32	57
Feb.	10	By Wheat,	6	337	50
	28	By Profit and Loss,	6	137	96
March	1	By Balance remaining,		3820	18
				8130	92

(2) *LEDGER.*

1796.		Dr. RUM.	*galls.*		Ds	//
Sept.	1	To Stock for	600	5	750	
Dec.	7	To Wheat for	488	6	615	
1797. March	1	To Profit and Loſs gained		6	235	39
			1088		1600	39
		Dr. TOBACCO.	*lbs.*			
Sept.	1	To Stock,	1400	5	196	
1797. March	1	To Profit & Loſs gained		6	40	1
			1400		236	19
		Dr. SHERRY WINE.	*galls.*			
Sept.	1	To Stocks,	130	5	145	60
1707. March	1	To Profit and Loſs gained		6	49	40
			130		195	
		Dr. PETER OLDS.				
Oct.	20	To Salt, at 20 days,		3	660	

LEDGER. (2)

		Contra Cr.	*galls*		$	//
1796.						
Sept.	20	By Abram Cunningham,	129	5	184	50
Oct.	7	By Cash at 1.45 per *gall.* for	120	1	174	
Nov.	5	By Wheat at 1.48 per *do.*	120	6	189	44
	16	By Sundries,	120		180	
Dec.	12	By Jonathan Brewster at 60 days for	117	7	175	50
1797.						
Jan.	18	By George Gordon,	126	8	182	70
Feb.	2	By Bills receivable,	110	[illegible]	178	50
	20	By Joel Kent,	128	[illegible]	192	
March	1	By Balance remaining at prime cost,	115		143	75
			1088		1600	39

		Contra Cr.	*lbs.*			
1797.						
Jan.	2	By Robert Dunston for	518	8	88	16
	18	By George Gordon,	195	8	33	15
Feb.	6	By Derick Hough,	350	8	63	
	20	By Joel Kent,	120	9	21	60
March	1	By Balance at prime cost	217	9	30	38
			1400		236	19

		Contra Cr.	*galls.*			
Oct.	22	By Bills receivable for	67	4	100	50
Nov.	5	By Wheat,	33	6	49	50
'97 Feb.	25	By Derick Hough,	30	8	45	
			130		195	

		Contra Cr.				
Nov.	12	By Cash in full,		1	660	

(3) *LEDGER.*

1796.		Dr. SOLE LEATHER.	*lbs.*		$	//
Sept.	1	To Stock,	3225	5	580	50
1797.						
March	1	To Profit and Loss gained		6	91	57
			3225		672	07
		Dr. MOLASSES.	*galls.*			
Sept.	1	To Stock,	440	5	264	
1797.						
March	1	To Profit and Loss gained		6	42	36
			440		306	36
		Dr. SALT.	*bush.*			
Sept.	1	To Stock,	1500	5	1125	
1797.						
March	1	To Profit and Loss gained		6	517	50
			1500		1642	50

(3) *LEDGER.*

		Contra Cr.	*lbs.*		$	//
1796.						
Sept.	6	By Cash,	630	1	132	30
Oct.	3	By Sundries,	592		130	24
Nov.	5	By Wheat,	750	6	157	50
1797.						
Jan.	2	By Robert Dunston,	299	8	62	79
Feb.	2	By Bills receivable,	130	4	27	30
	20	By Joel Kent,	454	9	95	34
March	1	By Balance remaining at prime cost,	370	9	66	60
			3225		672	07

		Contra Cr.	*galls.*			
Sept.	20	By Abram Cunningham,	108	6	81	
Nov.	12	By Cash,	218	1	156	96
1797.						
March	1	By Balance remaining,	114	9	68	40
			440		306	36

		Contra Cr.	*bush.*			
Sept.	20	By Abram Cunningham,	350	6	385	
Oct.	20	By Peter Olds at 1.10 per *bush.* for	600	2	660	
Nov.	1	By Flaxseed,	250	4	280	
	5	By Wheat,	250	6	280	
1797.						
March	1	By Balance on hand at prime cost,	50	9	37	50
			1500		1642	50

(4) *LEDGER.*

						$	//
'96.		Dr. Bills Rec. *when payable.*					
Sept.	1	To Stock for J. Hamilton's on demand			5	231	19
Oct.	3	To Sole Leather, J. Carey's	Nov.	3	3	54	
	22	To Sherry Wine, Joshua Johnston's,		22	2	100	50
Nov.	16	To Rum, A. Perkins on Wm. Johnston,			2	82	
'97. Feb.	2	To Sundries, And'w King's note.	May	3		205	80
						673	49

		Dr. William Jones.			
Sept.	1	To Stock,	5	97	71

		Dr. Benj. Conner.			
Sept.	1	To Stock,	5	110	

			casks.	bush.			
		Dr. Flaxseed.					
Oct.	25	To Abram Cunningham, for	10	70	6	122	
Nov.	1	To Sundries,	20	140		300	
Dec.	1	To Cash paid charges,			1	4	50
	17	To do. paid do.			1	28	60
			30	210		455	10

LEDGER. (4)

		Contra Cr.			Dolls.	Cts.
'96. Sept.	10	By Cash John Hamilton's in full,		1	231	19
Nov.	3	By Sundries in full of James Carey's,			54	
	28	By Cash in full of Joshua Johnston's,		1	100	59
Dec.	26	By do. Perkins on Johnston,		1	82	
'97. Mar.	1	By Balance for Andrew King's note,		9	205	80
					673	49

		Contra Cr.				
Oct.	8	By Cash in full,		1	97	71

		Contra Cr.				
Oct.	12	By Cash in full,		1	110	

		Contra Cr.	ca.	bu.			
Dec.	15	By Henry Stewart, my acct. of Flax-seed,	30	210	7	455	10
			30	210		455	10

(5) *LEDGER.*

				$	¢
1796.		Dr. STOCK.			
Sept.	1	To Sundries per Journal,		700	
1797.					
March	1	To Balance the nett of my estate.	9	6006	24
				6706	24
		Dr. HENRY BELL.			
Sept.	24	To Cash in full,	1	250	
		Dr. JOHN FARROW.			
Oct.	5	To Cash in full,	1	75	
		Dr. BILLS PAYABLE.			
Sept.	15	To Cash paid my note, Joseph Redfield,	1	375	
Dec.	28	To Sundries paid do. to Nicholas Grocer,		641	80
1797.					
March	1	To Balance for my note to Taylor,	9	600	
				1616	80

		Contra Cr.			£	s
1796. Sept.	1	By Sundries per Journal,			5000	
1797. March	1	By Profit and Loss, nett gain last 6 months,		6	1706	24
					6706	24

		Contra Cr.			
Sept.	1	By Stock per account,		5	250

		Contra Cr.			
Sept.	1	By Stock per account,		5	75

		Contra Cr.	*when pa.*			
Sept.	1	By Stock to Joseph Redfield,	Sept. 16	5	375	
Oct.	27	By Sundries to N. Grocer,	Dec. 27		641	80
1797. Feb.	10	By Wheat to T. Taylor,	May 10	6	600	
					1616	80

(6) *LEDGER.*

Date	Day	Particulars	bu.	lb.	Fol.	$	cts.
1796.		Dr. A. CUNNINGHAM.					
Sept.	20	To Sundries at 30 days,				650	50
Oct.	25	To Cash,			1	9	35
						659	85
		Dr. PROFIT & LOSS.					
Sept.	26	To Cash paid for license to retail Liquors, &c.			1	10	
	30	To do. paid char. this month				34	15
Oct.	31	To do. paid do. do.				51	23
Nov.	3	To do. paid do. on my Tea and Sugar,				5	
	30	To do. paid char. this month				39	25
Dec.	31	To do. paid do. do.				47	
'97 Jan.	31	To do. paid do. do.				32	57
Feb.	28	To do. do.				137	96
March	1	To Wheat for short meas.			6	6	30
		To Stock for neat gain since 1st Sept. last,			5	1706	24
						2069	70
		Dr. WHEAT.	bu.	lb.			
Sept.	7	To Cash,	376	20	1	564	50
Oct.	0	To do.	432	40	1	657	64
	4	To do. paid charges of Shipping,			1	24	45
	25	To A. Cuningham for	347		6	537	85
Nov.	3	To Bills rec. for	20		4	30	40
	5	To Sundries for	639	45		1125	96
	0	To Cash for	450		1	792	
	23	To do. paid charges of Shipping,			1	47	10
'97 Jan.	12	To J. Brewster,	120		7	150	
Feb.	10	To Sundries for	750			937	50
March	1	To Profit and Loss gained,			6	891	99
			3135	45		5759	39

LEDGER. (6)

1796.		Contra Cr.			$	//
Oct.	25	By Sundries per Journal,			659	85
					659	85

1797.		Contra Cr.				
March	1	By Rum gained,		2	235	39
		By Tobacco do.		2	40	19
		By Sherry Wine do.		2	49	40
		By Sole Leather do.		3	91	57
		By Molasses do.		3	42	36
		By Salt do.		3	517	50
		By Wheat do.		6	891	99
		By Bohea Tea gained,		7	99	89
		By Lump Sugar do.		7	15	38
		By Henry Stewart, my account of Flaxseed,		7	86	03
					2069	70

1796.		Contra Cr.	bush. lbs.			
Oct.	29	By Cash paid Capt. Hickok on sales,	806 40	1	1450	
Dec.	7	By Sundries per Journal,	455 30		3215	59
1797. March	1	By Balance on hand,	870	9	1087	50
		By Profit and Loss for short measure,	3 35	6	6	30
			3135 45		5759	39

(7) *LEDGER.*

Date			Account	chests	lbs.	Fol.	$	//
1796.			Dr. BOHEA TEA.	*chests.*	*lbs.*		$	//
Oct.		27	To Bills payable,	4	1388	5	485	80
'97. Ma.		1	To Profit and Loss gained,			6	99	89
				4	1388		585	69
			Dr. LUMP SUGAR.		*lbs.*			
Oct.		27	To Bills payable,		600	5	156	
'97. Ma.		1	To Profit and Loss gained,				15	38
					600		171	38
			Dr. PETER PUNCTUAL.					
Nov.		19	To Cash lent to be repaid on demand,			1	100	
			Dr. JONA. BREWSTER.					
Dec.		12	To Sundries per Journal,				343	70
							343	70
			Dr. HENRY STEWART.					
Dec.		15	To Flaxseed to sell for my acct. 30 Casks,				455	10
'97 Ma.		1	To Profit and Loss,				86	03
							541	13

		Contra Cr.	chests	lbs.		$	//
Nov.	5	By Wheat, for	1	349	6	146	58
Dec.	12	By Jonathan Brewster for,	1	347	7	138	20
'97 Feb.	6	By Derick Hough,	1	353	8	182	26
March.	1	By Balance remaining,	1	339	9	118	65
			4	1388		585	69

		Contra Cr.	lbs.			
Nov.	5	By Wheat,	200	6	58	
Dec.	12	By Jonathan Brewster,	100	7	30	
'97 Jan.	2	By Robert Dunston,	146	8	43	34
March.	1	By Balance remaining,	154	9	40	04
			600		171	38

		Contra Cr.			
Dec.	20	By Cash in full,	1	100	

		Contra Cr.			
1797.					
Jan.	12	By Wheat in part,	6	150	
Feb.	13	By Cash do.	1	100	
March.	1	By Balance,	9	93	70
				343	70

		Contra Cr.			
1797.					
Jan.	25	By do. my acct. current,	8	541	13
				541	13

(8) *LEDGER.*

				℔	//
		Dr. HENRY STEWART. (my acct. current.)			
1797. Jan.	2	To do. my account of Flaxseed,	7	54	3
		Dr. ROBERT DUNSTON			
Jan.	2	To Sundries per Journal,		194	9
		Dr GEORGE GORDON.			
Jan.	18	To Sundries per Journal,		215	8
		Dr. DERICK HOUGH.			
Feb.	6	To Sundries,		245	26
	25	To Sherry Wine per order,	2	45	
March	1	To Balance due him,	9	405	74
				696	
		Dr. CLOVER SEED.			
Feb.	6	To Derick Hough, 1300	8	156	

LEDGER. (8)

				$	//
1796.		Contra Cr.			
Dec.	28	By Bills payable for my draught,	5	218	80
1797.					
Jan.	25	By Cash rec'd. in full,	1	322	33
				541	13
		Contra Cr.			
March	1	By Balance,	9	194	19
		Contra Cr.			
Feb.	16	By Rye in part,	9	117	
March	1	By Balance,	9	98	85
				215	85
		Contra Cr.			
Feb.	6	By Sundries per Journal,		696	
		Contra Cr.			
March		By Balance, 1300	9	1[illegible]6	

(9) *LEDGER.*

					$	c
1797.		Dr. RYE.	*bush.*			
Feb.	6	To Derick Hough,	600	8	540	
	16	To George Gordon,	130	8	117	
	20	To Joel Kent,	70	9	63	
			800		720	
		Dr. JOEL KENT.				
Feb.	20	To Sundries per Journal,			308	94
		Dr. BALANCE.				
March.	1	To Cash remaining,		1	382[illegible]	18
		To Rum 1 Puncheon 115 *galls.* at 1.25 per *gall.*		2	14[illegible]	75
		To Tobacco, 217*lb.* at .14		2	[illegible]	[illegible]8
		To Sole Leather 370*lb.* at .18 per *lb.*		3	66	60
		To Molasses 1 Hhd. 114 *galls.* at .60 per *gall.*		3	68	40
		To Salt 50 *bush.* at .75		3	37	[illegible]0
		To Bills receivable for Andrew King's note,		4	20	80
		To Wheat 870*bush.* at 1.25		6	108	[illegible]0
		To Bohea Tea 1 Chest 339*lb.* at .35 per *lb.*		7	118	65
		To Lump Sugar 154*lb.* at .26		7	4[illegible]	[illegible]4
		To Robert Dunston,		8	19[illegible]	19
		To George Gordon,		8	9[illegible]	85
		To Clo. Seed 1300*lb.* at .12		8	15[illegible]	
		To Rye 800 *bush.* at .90		9	2[illegible]	
		To Jonathan Brewster,		7	9[illegible]	[illegible]0
		To Joel Kent,			13[illegible]	14
					[illegible]01[illegible]	98

LEDGER. (9)

				Ⓓ	″
		Contra Cr. *bush.*			
March	1	By Balance on hand, 800		720	
1797.		Contra Cr.			
Feb.	20	By Sundries per Journal,		178	50
March	1	By Balance,	9	130	44
				308	94
		Contra Cr.			
March	1	By Bills payable to Thomas Taylor,	5	600	
		By Derick Hough, due him,	8	405	74
		By Stock, the nett of my estate,	5	6006	24
				7011	98

X

THE following method of BOOK-KEEPING, by single entry, will be found convenient and useful to Farmers, Mechanics, many Country merchants, and indeed to all whose business and connections are not very extensive.

RULE. Commence the Ledger (which is the only book of account to be used) with a blank alphabetical Index, indented and lettered in the usual form, to be filled with names, and paginal references, as occasion requires. *Nextly*. Open every man's accompt with his name, written in a fair text hand; then enter the specific articles of debt, and those of

1795.	TIMOTHY FAIRDEAL Dr.	$	//
Jan. 15.	To 45 bushels of Wheat, at 1.50, to be paid in 60 days,	72	50
Mar. 18	To 3 days' work, myself, waggon and team, at 2.50 per day, to transport a load of Salt,	6	75
	To my expences in the aforesaid journey,	4	
May 7.	To 6 days' plowing, 1 man at .50, 1 boy at .30, and 2 yoke of oxen at .50 per day,	7	80
June 10	To 1 barrel of Vinegar, at // 12.5 per gallon,	4	
July 17	To 3 *cwt*. Bar Iron, at 5.	15	
Aug. 1.	To 2½ days' work, reaping, at .75,	1	87
Sept. 21	To the use of my Cider-mill 4½ days, at .66,	2	97
		114	89

correſponding credit upon the oppoſite pages of the folio, inſerting the dates of the ſeveral entries in the left hand column, and the prices carried out in the right hand, in two ruled columns, for Dollars and Cents; alloting the whole, or but a part of a folio, to each man's accompt. *Laſtly*. Balance the book, by comparing the ſum total of the debit, with that of the credit ſide, and carrying the difference, whether in favor of debtor or creditor, to its proper page, in a new accompt, unleſs it ſhould be previouſly diſcharged by payment, note of hand, or ſettlement on book. See the following Specimen.

1795.	Contra Cr.	Dolls.	Cts.
Mar. 16	By Caſh for 45 buſhels Wheat,	72	50
April 3.	By do. in part pay for tranſporting a load of Salt from Albany,	5	56
May 1.	By 10½ yards check'd Linen, at .42,	4	41
27.	By the ſettlement of my note to Peter Dun,	13	37
Oct. 5.	By Caſh for the balance due, *or*		
Oct. 5.	By your note for the balance due,	19	05
	Or,		
Oct. 5.	Reckoned and ſettled all accounts, and find due to Jonathan Homeſpun, to balance, Dolls. 19.05. *Timothy Fairdeal*, *Jonathan Homeſpun*.		
		114	89

A FEW FORMS IN CLERKSHIP.

An OBLIGATORY BOND.

KNOW all men, by these presents, that I, R. W. of in the county of am held and firmly bound to N. H. of in the penal sum of to be paid to the said N. H. his certain attorney, executors or administrators; to which payment, well and truly to be made and done, I bind myself, my heirs, executors and administrators, firmly, by these presents. Signed with my hand, and sealed with my seal. Dated at this day of A. D. 1797.

The Condition of this obligation is such, That if the above bounden R. W. &c. *(Here insert the condition.)* Then this obligation to be void, and of none effect; otherwise to remain in full force and virtue.

Signed, sealed and delivered,
in the presence of }

A GENERAL DISCHARGE.

RECEIVED of L. T. of twenty dollars, in full of all debts, dues and demands. Witness my hand, this day of 1797.

A BILL *of* SALE.

KNOW all men, by these presents, that I, A. B. of for and in consideration of to me in hand paid by C. D. of the receipt whereof I hereby acknowledge, have bargained, sold and delivered, and, by these presents, do bargain, sell and deliver, unto the ſaid C. D. *(Here ſpecify the property ſold.)* To HAVE and to HOLD the aforeſaid bargained premiſes, unto the ſaid C. D. his executors, adminiſtrators and aſſigns, forever. And I, the ſaid A. B. for myſelf, my executors and adminiſtrators, ſhall and will warrant and defend the ſame againſt all perſons, unto the ſaid C. D. his executors, adminiſtrators and aſſigns, by theſe preſents. In witneſs whereof, I have hereunto ſet my hand and ſeal, this day of 1797.

In preſence of

A BILL *of* DEBT.

KNOW all men, by theſe preſents, that I, F. G. of do owe and am indebted unto J. K. of the ſum of which ſaid ſum I promiſe to pay unto the ſaid F. G. his executors, adminiſtrators or aſſigns, on the day of next enſuing.—Witneſs my hand and ſeal, this day of A. D. 1797.

A GENERAL LETTER *of* ATTORNEY.

KNOW all men, by theſe preſents, the I, A. B. of have made, ordained, conſtituted and appointed, and, by theſe preſents, do make, ordain, conſtitute and appoint C. D. of my true and lawful attorney, for me, and in my name, and for my uſe, to aſk, demand, ſue for, recover and receive, of and from all perſon and perſons whatſoever, all ſum and ſums of money, debts, dues, claims and demands whatever, now due, owing or accruing to me, and to give good and ſufficieut diſcharges for the ſame, and to adjuſt, ſettle or compound all debts or demands due to me, and to accept ſuch ſecurity or ſatisfaction for the ſame as he ſhall think fit. And I do hereby give and grant to my ſaid attorney, my full and whole power in and concerning the premiſes, and will ratify and confirm whatever he ſhall lawfully act or do therein. *In witneſs whereof*, I have hereunto ſet my hand and ſeal, the day of A. D. 1797.

Signed, ſealed and delivered,
in preſence of

A LETTER *of* CREDIT.

SIR,

THE bearer, Mr. H. T. being on his travels, may have occaſion for money: Pleaſe to furniſh him, as occaſions may require, taking his receipts; and your draughts for the value ſhall receive due honor, from,

Sir, your humble ſervant,

C. A.

To Mr. S. J. Merchant,
London.

A LEASE *of a* HOUSE.

KNOW all men, by theſe preſents, that I, J. C. of in county, for and in conſideration of the ſum of received to my full ſatisfaction of P. T. of this day of in the year of our Lord, 1797, have demiſed and to farm let, and do, by theſe preſents, demiſe and to farm let, unto the ſaid P. T. his heirs, executors, adminiſtrators and aſſigns, one certain piece of land, lying and being ſituated in ſaid bounded, &c. *(Here deſcribe the boundaries)* with a dwelling houſe thereon ſtanding, for the term of 1 year from this date. To HAVE and to HOLD, to him the ſaid P. T. his heirs, executors, adminiſtrators and aſſigns for ſaid term, for him the ſaid P. T. to uſe and occupy, as to him ſhall ſeem meet and proper. And the ſaid J. C. doth *further covenant*, with the ſaid P. that he hath good right to let and demiſe, the ſaid letten and demiſed premiſes in manner aforeſaid, and that he the ſaid J. during ſaid time will ſuffer the ſaid P. quietly to HAVE and to HOLD, uſe, occupy and enjoy ſaid demiſed premiſes, and that ſaid P. ſhall have, hold, uſe, occupy, poſſeſs, and enjoy the ſame, free and clear of all incumberances, claims, rights and titles whatſoever. In witneſs whereof, I the ſaid J. C. have hereunto ſet my hand and ſeal this day of 1797.

J. C.

Signed, ſealed and delivered, in preſence of

An INLAND BILL *of* EXCHANGE.

$ 83.34 B. Auguſt 17, 1796.

TWENTY days after date, pleaſe to pay to Mr. S. B. or order, eighty-three dollars, and thirty-four cents, and place it to my account, as per advice from your humble ſervant,

E. P.

To Mr. T. W. Merchant,
New-York.

A PROTEST *on an* INLAND BILL *of* EXCHANGE.

KNOW all men, that I, S. B. on this day of 1796, at the uſual place of abode of

Mr. T. W. have demanded payment of the Bill (of which the above is a copy) which the said T. W. did not pay; wherefore I the said S. B. do hereby protest the said Bill. Dated at New-York, this day of 1796.

A DEED *of* BARGAIN *and* SALE.

To all People to whom these Presents shall come, Greeting.

KNOW ye, that I, N. O. of in the county of for the consideration of two hundred dollars, received to my full satisfaction of J. L. of said do give, grant, bargain, sell and confirm unto the said J. L. his heirs and assigns forever, a certain piece or parcel of Land, situated and lying in said containing acres, and bounded, &c. TO HAVE and to HOLD the above granted, and bargained premises, with the appurtenances thereof, unto him the said J. L. his heirs and assigns forever, to his and their own proper use and behoof. And also, I the said N. do for myself, my heirs, executors and administrators, covenant with the said J. L. his heirs and assigns, that at and until the ensealing of these presents, I am well seized of the premises as a good indefeasible estate in *fee-simple*, and have good right to bargain and sell the same, in manner and form as is above written, and that the same is free of all incumberances whatsoever. *And furthermore,* I, the said N. O. do by these presents, bind myself, and my heirs forever to warrant and defend the above granted and bargained premises to him the said J. L. his heirs and assigns, against all claims and demands whatsoever. In witness whereof, I have hereunto set my hand and seal this first day of January, A. D. 1797. N. O. (L.S.)

Signed, sealed and delivered, in presence of

NOTE. *The foregoing Inſtrument becomes a* MORTGAGE DEED, *by annexing a conditional clauſe like the following :* viz.

Provided nevertheleſs, if the ſaid N. O. his heirs, executors and adminiſtrators, ſhall well and truly pay to the ſaid J. L. his heirs, executors or adminiſtrators, a certain note of hand, by him the ſaid N. O. well executed, bearing date the day of A. D. 1796, for the ſum of according to the tenor thereof, then this deed is to be void.

A DEED *of* QUIT-CLAIM.

TO all perſons to whom theſe preſents ſhall come, Greeting. *Know ye*, that I, R. S. of for the conſideration of ſeventy dollars, received to my full ſatisfaction of B. G. of have remiſed, releaſed, and forever quit-claimed unto the ſaid B. G. all right and title which I the ſaid R. have in and to a certain piece or parcel of land, ſituated in ſaid containing acres, and bounded, &c. To HAVE and to HOLD all my right and title in and to ſaid remiſed, releaſed and quit-claimed premiſes, with the appurtenances thereof, to him the ſaid B. his heirs and aſſigns forever, to his and their own proper uſe and behoof. *And furthermore*, I the ſaid R. do for myſelf, my heirs, my executors and adminiſtrators, covenant with the ſaid B. his heirs and aſſigns, that from and after the enſealing of theſe preſents, I the ſaid R. will have and claim no right, in or to the above remiſed, releaſed, and quit-claimed premiſes. In teſtimony whereof, I have hereunto ſet my hand and ſeal, this day of A. D. 1796.

APPENDIX.

A Table, shewing the value of Shillings, Pence, &c. from a Farthing to a Pound, in Federal Money.

fa.	SC. &c.		NE&c.		NJ&c		NY&c	
	$ //	/	$ //	/	$ //	/	$ //	/
1	0.00	4	0.00	3	0.00	2	0.00	25
2	0.00	9	0.00	7	0.00	5	0.00	5
3	0.01	3	0.01		0.00	8	0.00	8
d.1	0.01	8	0.01	4	0.01	1	0.01	
2	0.03	5	0.02	8	0.02	2	0.02	
3	0.05	3	0.04	2	0.03	3	0.03	1
4	0.07	1	0.05	6	0.04	5	0.04	2
5	0.08	9	0.07		0.04	6	0.05	2
6	0.10	7	0.08	3	0.06	8	0.06	2
7	0.12	5	0.09	7	0.07	9	0.07	3
8	0.14	3	0.11	1	0.09		0.08	3
9	0.16	1	0.12	5	0.10	1	0.09	4
10	0.17	9	0.13	9	0.11	2	0.10	4
11	0.19	6	0.15	3	0.12	3	0.11	4
s.1	0.21	4	0.16	7	0.13	4	0.12	5
2	0.42	9	0.33	3	0.26	8	0.25	
3	0.64	4	0.50		0.40	3	.37	6
4	0.85	8	0.66	7	0.53	8	.50	2
5	1.07	2	0.83	3	0.67	2	.62	5
6	1.28	7	1.		0.80	7	.75	
7	1.50	1	1.16	7	0.94	1	.87	5
8	1.71	5	1.33	3	1.07	6	1.	
9	1.92	9	1.50		1.21		1.12	5
10	2.14	4	1.66	7	1.34	4	1.25	
11	2.35	8	1.83	3	1.47	9	1.37	5
12	2.57	2	2.		1.61	3	1.50	
13	2.78	7	2.16	7	1.74	8	1.62	5
14	3.00	0	2.33	3	1.88	2	1.75	
15	3.21	4	2.50		2.		1.87	5
16	3.43		2.66	7	2.13	4	2.	
17	3.04	4	2.83	3	2.26	8	2.12	5
18	3.85	8	3.		2.40	3	2.25	
19	4.07	2	3.16	7	2.53	8	2.37	5
£1	4.28	7	3.33	3	2.67	2	2.50	

APPENDIX.

A Table, ſhewing the value of Foreign and Federal Gold Coins, by weight, from a Grain to a Penny-weight.

	American, British & Portug. Gold.				French & Spaniſh Gold.			
	S. C.	N. E.	N. J.	N. Y.	S. C.	N. E.	N. J.	N. Y.
gr.	ſ. d. q.	ſ. d. q.	ſ. d. q.	ſ. d. q.	ſ. d. q.	ſ. d. q.	ſ. d. q.	ſ. d. q.
1	0 2	0 2 3	0 3 1	0 3 2	0 2	0 2 2	3	0 3 2
2	0 4	0 5 1	0 6 3	0 7	4	0 5 1	6	0 7
3	0 6 1	0 8	0 10	0 10 3	6	7 3	9 3	0 10 2
4	0 8 1	0 10 3	1 1 1	1 2 1	8 1	10 2	1 1	1 2
5	0 10 1	1 1	1 4 3	1 5 3	10 1	1 1	1 4 2	1 5 2
6	1 0 2	1 4	1 8	1 9 1	1 0 1	1 3 3	1 7 3	1 9
7	1 2 2	1 6 3	1 11 1	2 0 3	1 2 1	1 6 2	1 11	2 0 2
8	1 4 2	1 9 1	2 2 3	2 4 1	1 4 1	1 9	2 2 1	2 4
9	1 6 3	2	2 6	2 8	1 6 2	1 11 2	2 5 2	2 7 2
10	1 8 3	2 2 3	2 9 1	2 11 2	1 8 2	2 2 1	2 8 3	2 11
11	1 10 3	2 5 1	3 0 3	3 3	1 10 2	2 4 3	3	3 2 2
12	2 1	2 8	3 4	3 6 2	2 0 2	2 7 2	3 3 2	3 6
13	2 3	2 10 3	3 7 1	3 10	2 2 2	2 10 1	3 6 3	3 9 2
14	2 5	3 1 2	3 10 3	4 1 3	2 4 2	3 0 3	3 10	4 1
15	2 7	3 4	4 2	4 5 1	2 6 2	3 3 2	4 1 1	4 4 2
16	2 9 1	3 6 2	4 5 1	4 8 3	2 8 3	3 6	4 4 2	4 8
17	2 11 1	3 9 1	4 8 3	5 0 1	2 10 3	3 8 3	4 7 3	4 11 2
18	3 1 1	4	5	5 4	3 0 3	3 11 1	4 11 1	5 3
19	3 3 2	4 2 3	5 3 1	5 7 2	3 2 3	4 2	5 2 3	5 6 2
20	3 5 2	4 5 1	5 6 3	5 11	3 4 3	4 4 2	5 5	5 10
21	3 7 2	4 8	5 10	6 2 2	3 6 3	4 7 1	5 9	6 1 2
22	3 9 3	4 10 3	6 1 1	6 6 1	3 8 3	4 9 3	6 0 1	6 5
23	3 11 3	5 1 1	6 4 3	6 9 3	3 10 3	5 0 2	6 3 2	6 8 2
24	4 1 3	6 4	6 8	7 1 1	4 1	5 2 1	6 6 3	7

E R R A T A.

In some of the Copies the following Errors are noticed, and corrected in the following manner.

In the Introduction, page xxiii, line 7th, for 93, read 98.

In page 55, line 7th from the bottom, for 4.98 7, read 4.28 6; and in line 9th, for 4.81 4, read 4.10 3.

Correct the running title, from page 82 to page 90; for Subtraction, read *Addition*.

In page 93, 11th line above Lesson XXI, for *To 75 do.* read *To 57 do.*

Read the answer to Question 28th, page 227th, 592*lb.* 10*oz.*

In Lesson V of the Second Part, there are a few Examples, under Section 3d and 4th, erroneously wrought; particularly the 5th, 6th and 8th of Sect. 3d, and the 9th and 10th Examples of Sect. 4, which are not so easily corrected in an *Errata*. The man of figures, however; it is hoped, will candidly correct them, and any others which he may find, when he considers the extreme difficulty of publishing the first edition of such a work perfectly correct.

THE END.

A Liſt of the Names of Subſcribers for the AMERICAN ACCOMPTANT.

☞ *Official titles, and honorary additions, are inſerted in the following liſt, as far as they are known to the editor.*

VERMONT.

JOHN ADAMS
Calvin Adams
Heber Allen
Heman Allen
Samuel Allen
Abel Allis
Charles Ames
Robert Anderſon
Robert Anderſon
Ambroſe Atwater, jun.
Joſeph Atwill
Joſeph Auſtin
Capt. Robert Averil
Silas Babcock
Amos Bacon
Daniel Bacon
Simon Backus
Edward Baker
Abſalom Baker
Eraſtus Ball
Thomas Barney, Eſq.
William Barney
Truman Barney
John Barry
Joſhua Baſcom
Joſeph Baſsford
Eliſha Bartlet
Samuel Bartlet, Eſq.
Elihu Bartlet
Samuel Beach
Joſeph Beeman, 6 copies
Peter B. Beers
Jonathan Bell, Eſq. Sher. Rut. county.
Peter Benedict, Eſq.
Daniel Benedict
James Bellows
Joel Bigelow
Joel Bixby
Phinehas Bidwell
Reuben Beebe
Jonathan Bixby
Bradbury Blake
Obadiah Blake
Timothy Bliſs, Eſq.
Rev. Caleb Blood
William Bradley
Eliſha Bradley
Lemuel Bradley
Gilbert Bradley, Eſq.
Timothy Bradley
John T. Bradley
Julius Bradley
Sardius Blodget

John Bridgman
John Booth
Aaron Brownwell, 6 cop.
Timothy Brownſon, Eſq.
Timothy Brownſon, jun.
Amos Brownſon, jr. Eſq.
John Brownſon
Joel Brownſon, Eſq.
Oliver Bowman
Edward Brigham
Breck Brigham
Abram Brimſmaid
Elijah Bruſh
Nathaniel Bruſh, jun.
Abner Bruſh
Eli Bernard
Jonathan Brooks
Gardner Bullard
Thomas Butterfield
Miner Butler
Samuel Brown
Ebenezer Brownſon
Charles Bulkley, Eſq.
Amos Burnham
Ezekiel Buel
John Burdick
Thomas Chittenden, Eſq. Governor,
Hon. N. Chipman, Chief Juſtice,
John Calkins
Abel Caſtle
Luke Camp
Joſhua Chamberlain
Joſeph Carter
Elias Cittell
Noah Church, jun.
Nathaniel Collins
Stephen Cook
Ebenezer Child
Nathan Caſtle
Iſaac Chamberlain
Daniel Chipman, Eſq.
Amos Chipman, Eſq.
Joſiah Claſon
Levi Comſtock
William Cooper
Arzah Crane
Frederick Carter
Guy Clerk
Dr. Seth Cole
Dr. Matthew Cole
Amos Cutter
James Colben
Ichabod Chapin
John Cowee
William Coit, Eſq.
John Collard, 6 copies
Paul Champlain
Anthony Collamer
Samuel Collamore
Amos Callender
Iſaac Caſtle
Amaziah Church
Jaſon Comſtock
Peter Comſtock
Selah Canfield
Aaron C. Collins 12 cop.
Timothy Cobourn
Rev. Ruſſel Catlin
Cyrus A. Cady
John Cook, Eſq.
James Dockham
John Deming 6 copies
Francis Davis
William Douglaſs

Nathaniel Dickinſon
Peleg Douglaſs
William Dinſmore
Aſa Day, Eſq.
Abel Davis
Samuel Drury
Robert Donnely
John Davis
Juſtin Day
David Day
William S. Dickinſon
Col. J. Davis 6
Parley Davis
Moſes Doty
Barnabas Evans
Solomon Evarts
John Evarts
John Elmore, Eſq.
Stephen England
David Erwin
James Evarts, Eſq. 2
Capt. Reuben Evarts
Jeremiah Evarts
Samuel Eaton
Charles Everts
Dudley Everts
Jonathan Eddy
Jeremiah French
Shubael Fuller
Amos Friſbie
Joſhua Finch
Cephas Fordham
Aſa Foſter
Iſaac Freeman
Jonathan Fullerton
Polly French
Jonathan Fiſk
James Follet

Benjamin Follet
Jonathan Fullonton
David Fiſh
Dr. Thomas Fletcher
Simeon Graves
Abraham Gilbert
Jeſſe Gove
William Goſs
Nathan Graves
James Gilmore 6
Daniel Goodwin
Ezra Goodrich
Seth Griffith
Seth Gleaſon
Capt. Edmund Graves
Auguſtus Graves
Elijah Galuſha
Hon. Lot Hall, Eſq. Judge of the Superior Court,
Wm. C. Harrington, Eſq.
Dr. Aaron Haſtings
Hiram Houghton
Jonathan Hoit, Eſq.
Levi Hicks
Ithamar Hebard
William Hubbard jun.
Simeon Hooker
Sawtell Hart
Jacob Hobart
Ezra Hoyt
James Hall
John Heaton 6
Silas Hathaway, Eſq.
Benjamin Hart
Rufus Hall
Wm. Hicks
Rufus Hawley

Jacob Houghton 6
Ziba Hamilton
Ira Hill
Frederick Hill, Eſq.
Samuel Harriſon
Joſhua Hyde, jun.
Hira Hill
Benjamin Holmes
Gerſhom Holmes
Jedediah Hide
Abijah Hall
Samuel Hickok
Joſeph Hatch
Capt. Abm. Holenbeck
William Hickok 12
James Hill
Col. Daniel Hurlbut
Simeon Hine, Eſq.
Col. Udne Hay
Aſher Huggins 6
Gideon Hoxſie
Anthony Haſwell 18
Norman Hinſdill
Talme Hendrick
Peter Honey
John Howel
Zadoc Hard 2
Samuel Hoit
Joſeph Hoit
Henry Hyde, jun.
Richard How
Joſeph Hutchins
Joſhua Hathaway 6
Jacob Johnſon
Francis Joyner
Samuel Joſſelyn
Amaſa Joſſelyn
John Jackſon
Dorman Johnſon
Joſeph Iſham
Stephen Jackſon
George S. Kindall
Elijah Kirkum
Stephen Kinſley
Capt. Gideon King
David Knowles
James Kimball
Gideon King, jun.
Benjamin Kinney
John King
Abel Knap
Paul Knap
Rev. Daniel Kent
Iſaac Kellog
Miles Leet
Lemuel Laſſel
Gabriel Lakin
David Langly
Noah Lawrence
Horace Loomis
Jedediah Lane, jun.
Thomas Lowrey
Capt. John Lyman
Elon Lee
John Law, Eſq. 6
Samuel Lane, Eſq.
Capt. Samuel Leavitt 6
Phineas Lyman
Phineas Loomis
Jeſſe Loomis
Dr. Micah J. Lyman
Benjamin Lathrop
Larned Lamb
Thaddeus Munſon
Cornelius M'Eviney
Joſeph Mozier

Jonas Martin
Andrew Mills
Foreſt Micar
Peter M'Arthur
Samuel Montague, jun.
Theodore Melvin
Calvin Munger
Ezra Mead
John Megraw
Martin D. Mallit
Skiff Morgan
Eliſha Morehouſe
Solomon Miller, Eſq.
William Morrill
Samuel Mix
John Martin
William Meachan 6
David Munn
Joſeph M'Nall
Squire Morehouſe
William Munſon
George Morgan
Daniel Morgan, jnn.
John Meſſenger
Arad Munn
Iſaac Mattiſon
Jedediah Merrill 6
Archibald M'Mullen
Elnathan Merwin
John Mattocks, Eſq.
James Malery
Luther Moſely
Iſaiah Matteſon
Joſhua Nichols 6
Levi Naſh 6
Obadiah Noble, jun.
Philena Noble
Solomon Noble
Charles Nairn 6
Morgan Noble
Caleb Olin
Elijah Oſborn
Thomas Pentler
William Pariſh
John Place
Capt. Matthew Phelps
Reuben Parſon
Simon Powers
Stephen Pearl, Eſq. Sher. Chit. County
Joſeph Parker
Ambroſe Porter
Benjamin Parker
Edmund Parker
Hachaliah Purdy
Martin Powel, Eſq.
Ebenezer Peters
Martin Powel, jun.
Dr. John Pomeroy
John Polley
John Patric
Dr. Jabez Penniman 2
Alexander Phelps
Seth Pommeroy
Abiram Peet
Eliakim D. Perſon
Joſeph Palmer
Ichabod Peck
John Phelps
Benjamin Palmer
Robert Pierpont 6
William Rich
Reuben Rockwell
William Rounds

Thomas Richards
Dr. Wells Richardſon
Abner Rice
John Rowlſon
Iſaac D. Rowland
James Richardſon
Reuben Redfield
Jeſſe Rice
Dr. James B. Root
Thaddeus Rice, Eſq.
Joſeph Raner
David Robbins
Col. C. Roberts
Ephraim Scovill
John P. Smith
Henry Slater
Ella Smith
Jonathan Smith, Eſq.
Samuel Siblie
Samuel Smith
Abel Skinner
Nathan Spafford
Broadſtreet Spafford, jun.
Ezra Smith
William Smith
David Safford
Lemuel Scot
John Safford
Horace G. Spafford
John Swan
Samuel Stone 6
Abijah Stone
Joſhua Stanton, Eſq. 2
Capt. David Stanton
Joſhua Stanton jr. Eſq. 6
Solomon Stanton
Capt. Abraham Stevens
Samuel Stone

Nathaniel W. Seaver
Dudley Stone
John Sinclear
Ezra Slater
John Seely, Eſq.
Hannah Seely
John Storey
Caleb Smith, Eſq.
David Sheldon, Eſq. 6
Aſa Strong
Filer Sacket
Samuel Strong
Obadiah Seely
Stephen B. Seely
Joab Silveſter
Abijah Scovill
John Stevens
Samuel Sproat
Barnabas Spear
Barzillai Spear
Peter B. Smith
Aſahel Strong
Andrew Selden 6
Jacob Sherwin
John Stanley 6
Daniel Strong
Hinkley Stevens
Clark Stevens
Dr. Robert Spelman
Gen. Iſaac Tichenor, Senator in Congreſs
Samuel Tomſon
Robert Torrans
Nathan M. Torrey
Jacob Truman
Thomas Todd
Amos Thomſon 6
John Taplin

David Talman
Reuben E. Tayler
Samuel Ufford
Paul Varaly
Enoch Woodbridge, Efq. Judge of Superior Court,
Dr. Solomon Wyman
Dr. Lemuel Wheeler
Gen. Benjamin Wait 6
James O. Walker
Lewis Wilkinfon
Jonah Wood
Thomas Waid
Martin Winchel
Ebenezer Wells
Jofeph Wheeler, jun.
Bernard Ward
Nathaniel Warden
Jofeph Wickwire
Juftus Warner
Thomfon Woodworth
Nathan Woodworth
Amafa Woodworth III.
Amafa Woodworth
Morey Woodworth
Charles Woodworth
Hiel Williams
Shubael Woodruff
John Wilfon
Nathan White
Dr. Lemuel Winflow
Abel Waters, Efq.
John Winflow
Obadiah Winters
Daniel Wadfworth
Alvin White
Ifaac Webb
Lewis Warner
Francis Willard
Chauncey Whitney
Eben. Walbridge, Efq. 6
Ichabod Wood
Gideon Wellman
Reuben Webb
Thomas Williams
David Wing, jun. Efq.
Thomas Whittridge
Jerameel B. Wheeler
Ziba Woodworth
Thomas Weft, jun.
Rufus Wakefield
William Young
Elifha Yeomans

NEW-YORK.

JOHN AVERY
Jofeph Alexander
Jofeph Allen 2
Hon. Abraham Arnott
Hon. Leonard Bronk
Walter Broughton
Job Bemus
Rev. David S. Bogart
Samuel Auguftus Barker
John Bird, Efq.
Matthew Brown, jun.
Jofhua H. Brett
James Bill
Seth C. Baldwin
Jehu Burr
Jacob Bockee
Benjamin Beecher
John Buchannan 12
Robert Bix

Profper Brown
Dr. Abiel Bugbey
William Bell, Efq.
Ifaac Bloom, Efq.
Hon. Ebenezer Clark
Hon. D. Coe
Hon. John Cantine
Lemuel Chipman, Efq.
Jonathan Cooley
Samuel Clark
Rev. Jonas Coe
Levi Callender
F. Chandonet
Jonathan Choate
Hon. S. De Witt
Paul Dennis
Sylvefter Day
Cornelius Davis 6
John D. Dickenfon, Efq.
L. Dorfet
Hon. Johannes Dietz
Dr. Benjamin Delavirge
Zephaniah Edwards
Samuel Elward 2
Ebenezer Foot
Daniel Fellows, jun.
John Freeman
Bela Fofgate
Taylor Fordham
Hon. John Frey
Hugh Fegan 6
Hon. Leonard Ganfevoort
Hon. Thomas R. Gold
Reuben Guild
George Gardner
Gilbert Gardner 6
William Gilliland, Efq. Sher. Renffelaer County,
William Gillet 6
Allen Hill
Jacob Hochftraffer
Col. James Holcomb
Mordecai Hale
John C. Hogeboom
Luther Holly 6
William Holifter 6
David Henry
Theophilus Hyde
Jonathan Hoag, Efq.
Jonathan Hoag
Nicholas Harris
Stephen Hall
William Hufton
Hon. Richard Hatfield
Hon. Sam. Haight
Matthew Harrifon
John Jay, Efq. Gov. of the State of New-York, 2
Lemuel Johnfon
Elijah Janes
Samuel E. Jones
Judfon & Bontecou
Hon. James Kent
William Kennedy
Major John Keating
John Lovett, Efq.
Jonathan Little
Timothy Leonard
Samuel Lewis
Rofwell Leavens
Samuel Lathrop
Hezekiah Leavens
Thomas Loring
Benjamin Lyon
Aaron Lane
Jeremiah Landon

Bille Lawrence
Henry M'Neil
Jacob Morton
George Metcalſe
Sheſter Milich
Robert Moffitt & Co. 12
Rev. Jonathan Moſher
Theodore May, jun.
David Melich
Hercules Marriner
Robert M'Cheſney 4
Nathaniel M'Clellan
Hon. Jacob Morris
Hon. Michael Myer
Hon. Vincent Mathews
Hon. Thomas Morris
Wm. M'Connell
Jonas Morgan 6
Hon. Francis Nicoll 2
Simeon Newcomb
Ebenezer Niles
Zebulon Neal
Oliver Nexton 6
Nathaniel Ogden
James Oliver
Aaron Oſtrander
Hon. Andrew Onderdonk
John Prince
Charles Platt
William Pearce
William Poole
Luther Pratt
Andrew Proudfit
Annanias Platt 6
Stephen Paine
Hon. Ebenezer Ruſſell
Hon. John Richardſon
Calvin Read

Samuel Rodgers
William Rollo
Abner Reed
Iſaac Reed
William Root
William Radclift, jun. Eſq. Sh. Dut. Coun.
Hon. Ambroſe Spencer 2
Hon. Robert Sands
Hon. Jedediah Sanger
Hon. James Savage
Hon. Abraham Schenck
Hon. P. Sylveſter
Hon. Philip Schuyler, Senator of the U. S. from the State of N.Y.
Clement Sadlier
Edward Savage
Jacob Smith
Alexander Spencer
Warren Smith
Philip Smith
Adonijah Skinner
Jonathan Simpſon
Sanford Smith
Aaron Scott
John Stearns
Capt. Nath'l S. Skinner
John Strong
Iſaac Sacket
Calvin Stevens
Peter Sim
N. Schuyler, Eſq.
Hon. Chriſtopher Tappen
Hon. William Thomſon
Hon. Anthony Ten Eyck
Dirck Ten Broeck, Eſq.
Jeſſe Thomſon

Alexander Turner
Alexander Thomſon, jun.
C. Trueſdel
Daniel Torrey
John Tryon, Eſq. 6
Hon. S. Van Renſſelaer Lt. Governor of the State of New-York 2
Capt. James Van Ingen
Wm. B. Verplank, Eſq.
Jacob L. Viele
Henry Van Allen 6
Hon. Jacobus Van Schoonhoven 2
Hon. Moſes Vail
Hon. Joſeph White
Hon. James Watſon
William Wheeler, Eſq. 2
J. H. Wendell
Silas Wood
Daniel Wells
Thomas G. Whitaker
John Wendell
Nathaniel Williams
James Wicks 6
Thomas L. Witbeek, Eſq.
Conſtant W. Wadſworth
Abijah Wheeler
Judſon Webb
Seth Waſhburn
Jonathan Yates
Thomas Yates
Daniel Young

CONNECTICUT.

JOSIAH ARNOLD
James Benton
Ariel Bradley, jun.
Ebenezer Burr
Enſign Buſhnel
Iſaac Beebe
Edward Brownell
Jacob Balcom
Abiel Babit
Joſeph Canfield, Eſq.
Timothy Chittenden, jun.
Elijah S. Cuting
Jared Canfield
Heman Chapin
Iſaac Chamberlain
John C. Coffing
Jeremiah Dauchy
William Douglaſs
Obadiah Dickenſon 6
Rufus Eddy
John Enſign
Rev. Daniel Farrand
Peter Farnham
Ezra Graves
Nathan Hale, Eſq.
Elizabeth Hale
Lydia Hale
Frederic Harriſon
Amos Hunt
John Handy
Jacob Holt
James Holmes II.
Capt. Simon Jacqua
Daniel Johnſton
Ezekiel L. Judd
Capt. Lemuel Kingſbury
Phinehas Kingſbury
George Kingſbury
Nelſon Keith
Samuel Lee, Eſq. 4

Capt. Mylo Lee 2
Robert W. Lee
Charles Loveland
Rufus Landon
Daniel Moore 6
Samuel Moore
Julius Meigs
William Moore
Capt. Lott Norton 6
Daniel Nicholls
Amos Armſby
Auguſtus Porter
James Pumpily
Joſhua Parker
Samuel Robbins
Ammi R. Robbins
Salomi Robbins
Eſther Robbins
Stephen Reed
Daniel Reed
Major Luther Stoddard
Adin Stevens
Major Elijah Stanton 6
Abel Stark
Solomon Tyler
Daniel Talbot
Elizur Wright
Thomas Wilcox
Capt. David Waterman 6
John Whittleſey, Eſq.

MASSACHUSETTS.

WM. BRATTLE
Doctor William Buel
James Bardin, jun.
Joſhua Beals, Eſq.
Jepthah Baker
Ebenezer Centre
Rev. Timothy M. Cooley
Hezekiah Clarke
Samuel Powles
Moſes . Curtiſs
Rev. Jacob Catlin
Noah Church, jun.
John Dodge 6
Henry Durham
Capt. Paul Dewey 6
Ithamer H. Day 6
Daniel Day, jun.
Joſhua Danforth, Eſq.
Rev. Gordon Dorrance
Ebenezer Deane, jun.
Nathan F. Dixon
William Enſign
Rev. Eben. Fitch, D. D. President Wm. Coll.
Joſeph Faries
Jaſon Goodrich
Jacob Gallup
Charles Goodrich, Eſq.
Thomas Gold, Eſq.
John W. Hulbert
Wyllys Howe
Aſher Hickok
Abner Higby
Hackley & Fitch
Nathan Hall
John Harmon
Rev. Ephraim udſon
Daniel Kingſbury 6
Eliſha Lee, Eſq. 4
Walker Lincoln
Jonathan Lawrence
Dr. Jonathan Lee
Uriah Lathrop

Caleb Mead
Daniel Merriman, jun.
Nathaniel Morey
Seth Moore
Stephen Morſe
Stephen Neal
Pomeroy Noble
Elias Newbury
Benjamin C. Perkins
Azariah Root
Abner Root
Joſhua Smith
Joſeph Shearer
Loring Simons
Nathaniel Satterlie
Aſa Sheldon, jun.
Samuel Thomſon
Rev. James Thomſon
Barent Van Vleck
S. H. Wheeler
Paul Whitney 6
Samuel Whipple
Dr. Aſahel Wright
Henry Whitlock
William H. Williams

NEW-HAMPSHIRE.

MARY G. Goddard
Ob. Lang

C A N A D A.

JOHN BADGER
Gilber Hyatt 2
Joſeph Hull
Capt. Henry Hardie
David Jewett 6
Joel H. Ives
John M'Carty 6
Ebenezer Pleace